'A work of scholarship and erudition, and an engrossing investigation into three extraordinary minds. Stephenson has unearthed a trove of fascinating documents, but it is their treatment that enthralls the reader: the mysteries they reveal, the personalities they unveil, and their vindication of Victoria Ocampo – feminist, South American, cultural icon – as a woman for our times.'

Juan Gabriel Vásquez, author of *The Sound of Things Falling*

'Victoria Ocampo comes alive in these pages. A long-overdue recognition of Ocampo's immense influence on the literary culture of Argentina and the rest of the world. What Craig Stephenson has accomplished in this remarkable and deeply researched book is nothing less than an act of restoration. It is also a celebration of a brilliant South American writer, editor, and critic pushing back against a society still unprepared for her.'

Maaza Mengiste, author of *The Shadow King*, shortlisted for the 2020 Booker Prize

'Craig Stephenson has the rare knack of taking a singular, often forgotten moment in history and mining it for unexpected riches. In this early 20th century "whodunit", Stephenson shows himself to be a master psychological detective in his use of primary sources to uncover the unconscious dynamics of a fateful encounter between the animus of a wealthy, South American heiress and the anima of a powerful, cultured, European aristocrat. Although the story unfolds almost one hundred years ago and is filled with dated ways of communicating (they actually write letters to one another) and the luxuries only afforded the most wealthy, it has strangely contemporary resonances that are all the more poignant in their stylized setting of the era between two world wars.'

Tom Singer, co-author/editor of *The Cultural Complex, Psyche and the City*, and *Ancient Greece, Modern Psyche*

The Correspondence of Victoria Ocampo, Count Keyserling and C. G. Jung

The Correspondence of Victoria Ocampo, Count Keyserling and C. G. Jung centres on two pivotal meetings: Victoria Ocampo and Hermann von Keyserling's in 1929, and Ocampo and Carl Gustav Jung's in 1934. The first section of the book chronicles these encounters, which proved to be key moments in the lives of the players and had repercussions both private and public. The later sections consist of the correspondence and other writings that preceded and followed these meetings, translated from French, German, and Spanish, much of it for the first time.

Jung framed Keyserling's account of the encounter with Ocampo as "one of the most beautiful animus-anima stories I have ever heard." But that story, told here from the three points of view of the pioneering Argentine intellectual, the Baltic German philosopher, and the Swiss founder of analytical psychology, can also be read in the contexts of early-twentieth-century feminism and of gender and sexual politics, of the colonizing European gaze on the Americas, of Argentina and its cultural complexes, of typological impasses, and of Eros and the power of words.

The fraught relationships and power dynamics among three influential figures will be of interest to analytical psychologists, historians of psychological disciplines and of South America, as well as general readers.

Craig E. Stephenson is a Jungian analyst in private practice. His books include *Anteros: A Forgotten Myth, Jung and Moreno*, and *Possession: Jung's Comparative Anatomy of the Psyche*. He edited *On Psychological and Visionary Art: Notes from C. G. Jung's Lecture on Gérard de Nerval's Aurélia*.

The Correspondence of Victoria Ocampo, Count Keyserling and C. G. Jung

Writing to the Woman Who Was Everything

Craig E. Stephenson

Routledge
Taylor & Francis Group

LONDON AND NEW YORK

Cover image: Alejandro Magallanes

First published 2023
by Routledge
4 Park Square, Milton Park, Abingdon, Oxon OX14 4RN

and by Routledge
605 Third Avenue, New York, NY 10158

Routledge is an imprint of the Taylor & Francis Group, an informa business

British Library Cataloguing-in-Publication Data
A catalogue record for this book is available from the British Library

Library of Congress Cataloging-in-Publication Data
Names: Jung, C. G. (Carl Gustav), 1875–1961, correspondent. |
Stephenson, Craig E., 1955– editor. | Ocampo, Victoria, 1890–1979, correspondent. |
Keyserling, Hermann, Graf von, 1880–1946, correspondent.
Title: The correspondence of Victoria Ocampo, Count Keyserling and C.G. Jung : writing to the woman who was everything / [edited by] Craig E. Stephenson.
Description: Abingdon, Oxon ; New York, NY : Routledge, 2023. |
Includes bibliographical references. |
Identifiers: LCCN 2022025275 | ISBN 9781032209555 (hardback) |
ISBN 9781032207209 (paperback) | ISBN 9781003266099 (ebook)
Subjects: LCSH: Jung, C. G. (Carl Gustav), 1875–1961–Correspondence. |
Ocampo, Victoria, 1890–1979–Correspondence. |
Keyserling, Hermann, Graf von, 1880–1946–Correspondence. |
Psychiatrists–Switzerland–Correspondence. |
Authors, Argentine–20th century–Correspondence. |
Philosophers–Germany–Correspondence.
Classification: LCC BF173.J85 A4 2023 | DDC 150.19/5–dc23/eng/20220729
LC record available at https://lccn.loc.gov/2022025275

ISBN: 978-1-032-20955-5 (hbk)
ISBN: 978-1-032-20720-9 (pbk)
ISBN: 978-1-003-26609-9 (ebk)

DOI: 10.4324/9781003266099

Typeset in Times New Roman
by Newgen Publishing UK

This book is for Alberto.

Contents

Figures

Acknowledgments

The support of the Judith Harris Foundation made this book possible.

Thanks to Natalia Garnero for transcribing, and to Gottwalt Pankow, Achim Stanislawski, and Alberto Manguel for translating texts.

Thanks to Cristina Banegas, Edgardo Cozarinsky, and (stepping in at the last second for Edgardo) Alberto Manguel, who read these letters at a public event at Casa Victoria Ocampo, Buenos Aires, in August 2017. Thanks to Juan Gabriel Vásquez for recommending Carmenza Gómez and Carlos Manuel Vesga, who performed the letters at the IAAP Latin American Congress 2018, Bogotá. And thanks to Elena Gowland, Mariano Caligaris, and Fernando Marganet who read the letters at the IAAP International Congress 2022, Buenos Aires.

For inspiration, support, and friendship, thanks to John Beebe and Adam Fray, Alessandra Benedicty-Kokken, Annie Boland, Kristine Arnet Connidis, Denise Dickin, Deborah Egger and Axel Essbaum, Doreen Madden Elefthery, Ali Kazma, Arthur Kiron, Margaret Klenck, Patricia Llosa, Niall Martin, Maaza Mengiste, Susan Middleton and Chris Palin, Thierry Thieû Niang, Lucie Pabel, Hans-Joerg Renner, Audrey Rosa, Sonu Shamdasani, David Shimoni, John Smallbridge, Jillian Tomm, Jonathan Wood, and Beverley Zabriskie. Thanks to Marcus West, co-editor of the *Journal of Analytical Psychology*, for feedback.

Thanks to Alejandro Magallanes for the cover design.

Thanks to Alexis O'Brien at Routledge, Katie Randall at Taylor and Francis, and Suriya Rajasekar at Newgen for enthusiasm and patience. Thanks to Kathleen Kearns and Sara Marchington for copyediting.

In memoriam: Sierra Beverly, Robert Boudine, Graeme Gibson, Marion Woodman.

For permissions and much more, I thank Juan Javier Negri, President of the Consejo de Administración, Fundación Sur, and Thomas Fischer, former Director, and Carl Jung, Director, the Foundation of the Works of C. G. Jung. Thanks also to Annkathrin Wollert of the Paul and Peter

Fritz AG Literary Agency for assistance with the Jung permissions and to Gretel Unterstenhöfer, Team Historische Sammlungen, Universitäts- und Landesbibliothek Darmstadt for assistance with the Keyserling archives.

Text

Translations, 2022, Gottwalt Pankow, Achim Stanislawski, Alberto Manguel, Craig E Stephenson
2007 Foundation of the Works of C. G. Jung, Zürich
2022 Fundación Sur, Buenos Aires

Images

Fundación Sur; Bridgeman Images.

Part One

Introductory Essay

> I feel as if *I'm almost saying goodbye to you on this piece of paper, goodbye to the person you were to me* and who will stop being that person a few hours from now, in Versailles. How will I manage without that Keyserling of mine, made up by me?
>
> Victoria Ocampo to Hermann Keyserling,
> 3 January 1929, 7:00 p.m.

The pioneering Argentine intellectual Victoria Ocampo first encountered Hermann Keyserling in 1929 in the Hôtel des Réservoirs, Versailles, a moment both parties would struggle to understand for the rest of their lives. Keyserling, who was born in 1880, had acquired a following as an erudite aristocrat in exile. His Livonian estate had been lost to the Russian Revolution in 1918, and he lived in Germany with his wife, the granddaughter of the Iron Chancellor, Otto von Bismarck. Keyserling's best-known work, *The Travel Diary of a Philosopher*, describes his quasi-philosophical responses to the places and people he encountered on the road in Europe and Asia in 1911. In 1920, at the invitation of the Grand Duke Ernst Ludwig von Hessen, he opened a so-called School of Wisdom at Darmstadt, Germany, in which he advocated a kind of generalized renewal of "Spirit": "Its particular teachings … aim at nothing else than a regeneration of mankind on the new basis created by the War".[1] He invited thinkers such as Paul Tillich, Herman Hesse, Richard Wilhelm, and C. G. Jung to address contemporary European problems of Spirit by looking to wisdom traditions from other cultures.

Victoria Ocampo was a cultural icon both in her native Argentina and in Europe throughout the twentieth century. The magazine *Sur*, which she founded in 1931 on the advice of the American writer Waldo Frank and the Spanish philosopher José Ortega y Gasset, and the publishing company Sur, which she founded a few years later (in 1933), acted as a bridge between South American and North American intellectuals and those of Europe. Born to one

---

1 Keyserling, *Travel Diary*, 7.

DOI: 10.4324/9781003266099-1

of the wealthiest Argentine families of the turn of the century, Ocampo used her power and her fortune to promote culture – literature, music, architecture, photography – on three continents, and she was instrumental in publishing in Spanish not only Jung and Keyserling but Aldous Huxley, Paul Valéry, Virginia Woolf, Marguerite Yourcenar, Albert Camus, Graham Greene, and many others. An indication of her perceptive eye is that, for instance, her magazine published an issue on Canadian literature in which she included Marshall McLuhan and Northrop Frye, years before they became household names.[2] She would ultimately become the first woman elected to the Argentine Academy of Letters.

At first an enthusiastic reader of Keyserling, Ocampo initiated an intense epistolary exchange with him in 1927. She later arrived in Paris, paid for his room in the Versailles hotel, and attended devotedly to (and was bemused by) his many demands for things that should be made ready for him there – red ink, a ball of string, blotting paper, large envelopes. But their encounter in room 250 would prove so explosive that Keyserling would turn to Jung as he tried to assimilate it, and Jung would offer analytic interpretations and advice. The encounter would inform Keyserling's *South American Meditations* in such an offensive way that Ocampo would be appalled by his views and Jung would counsel him against publishing the book unless he extensively revised it.

The crossing of these three figures' paths had professional repercussions for all three and significant personal repercussions for Ocampo and Keyserling. Ocampo would bring Keyserling to South America, the trip that led to his *South American Meditations*, but soon thereafter she would end contact with him even as she remained fascinated by Keyserling's spiritual prose. Later, Keyserling's widow would publish posthumously Keyserling's memoirs, including chapters on Ocampo and Jung, and both of them found themselves arguing in print with the persistent ghost of a dead man. In her response, Ocampo refuted both Keyserling's writings on Argentina and his published portrayal of her.

Ocampo and Jung would also meet in person, if briefly. In June 1934, as she was mid-Atlantic on an ocean liner making her way from Buenos Aires to Paris, Ocampo wrote to Jung at his house in Küsnacht on the edge of Lake Zürich. Ocampo says she has read Jung's book *Psychological Types* in an English translation, and she passionately expresses her gratitude to him for whatever psychological serenity she can claim. But while she says, "We have common friends, I believe," she tentatively adds, "and maybe you have heard my name, maybe not".[3] She carefully avoids mentioning Keyserling,

---

2 Norman Cheadle connects the innovative vision of Canadian pianist Glenn Gould's "The Idea of North", a documentary CBC Radio aired on 18 December 1967, with the quasi-mythical "South" that Ocampo mapped in *Sur*. See María Rosa Lojo, *Free Women in the Pampas*, xii.

3 Ocampo to Jung, 12 June 1934 (Part Four).

Figure 1.1 Victoria Ocampo; permission to reproduce from Fundación Sur.

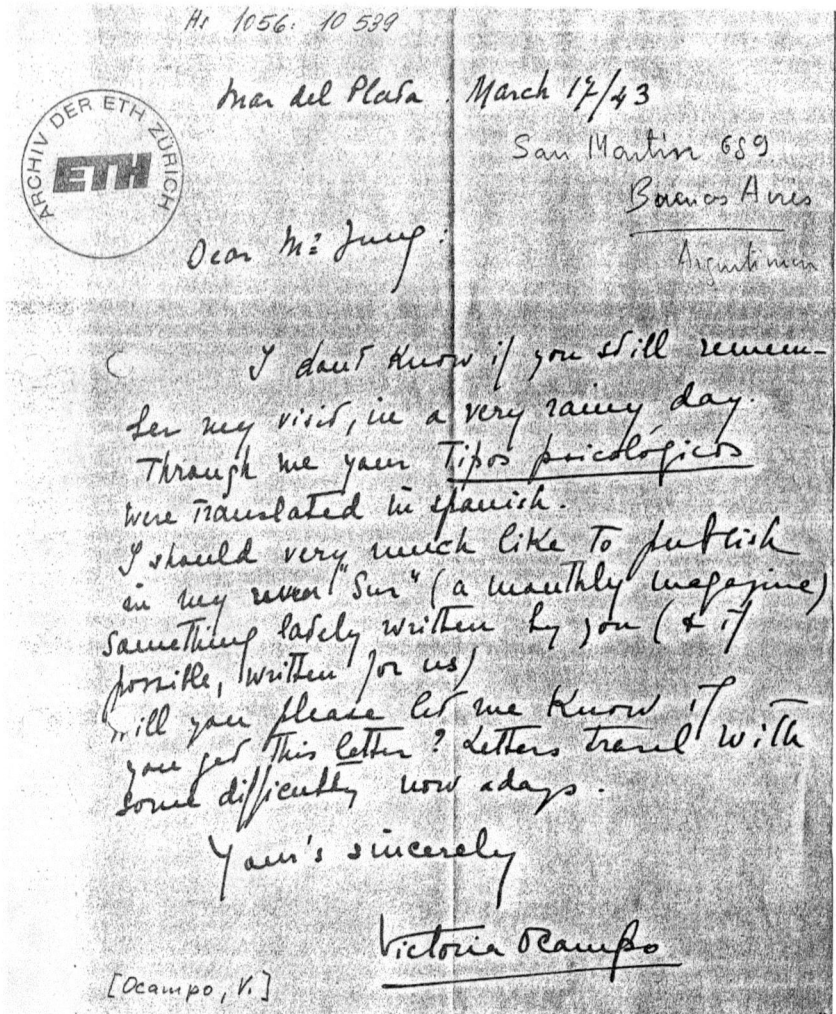

Figure 1.2 Ocampo's letter to Jung, 16 October 1934; permission to reproduce from the Foundation of the Works of C. G. Jung.

though she mentions Ortega y Gasset, another mutual acquaintance. If we read between the lines, we might understand that Ocampo assumes that Jung has heard about her, in complaints from Keyserling.

Writing her letter, Ocampo couldn't know that her meeting with Jung, in October of that year at his Küsnacht house, would be brief and singular. Jung agreed to see her for a few minutes between patients; later, she would write about the meeting (and appreciatively about him) for the newspaper

Figure 1.3 Hermann von Keyserling and Gödela von Bismarck-Schönhausen; author's collection.

Figure 1.4 Keyserling's letter to Jung, 31 March 1931; permission to reproduce from the Foundation of the Works of C. G. Jung.

Figure 1.5 Carl Gustav Jung with his dogs; permission to reprint from Bridgeman Images.

(An Hermann Graf Keyserling)  20. XII. 1929

Verehrtester Graf,

Von V.O. habe ich noch nichts vernommen. Selbstverständlich werde ich Ihren Brief als nicht existierend behandeln. Ihre ausgezeichnete Beschreibung des schicksalhaften Intermezzo mit V.O. lässt deutlich erkennen, dass es sich um einen bedeutungsschwangeren Zusammenstoss mit dem "Erdweib" handelt. Darin hat sich Yin und Yang gemischt und gemischt, eines der schönsten Animus-Animaabenteuer, das ich je gehört habe. Leider enden die Dichtungen in der Regel mit Enttäuschung, denn, wenn man seiner eigenen Seele begegnet, erkennt man sie nie, sondern verwechselt sie mit dem armen Menschentier, das unbewusst als Symbolträger funktioniert hat. Die Sehnsucht V.O.'s nach Identifikation gilt eigentlich dem Animus, dessen sie sich in Ihnen bemächtigen möchte; sie verwechselt aber Sie persönlich damit und ist infolgedessen natürlich aufs Tiefste enttäuscht. Diese Enttäuschung wird sich stets und überall wiederholen, bis der Mensch gelernt hat, seine Seele vom Menschen zu unterscheiden. Dann kann seine Seele zu ihm zurückkehren. Diese Lektion ist eine Höllenqual für Beide, aber äusserst nützlich, das Erlebnis, das man Ihnen gewünscht hat, und sicherlich die allerpassendste Tortur für V.O., die noch von ihren Erddämonen besessen ist. Sie zieht es vielleicht vor, von den Titanen zerrissen zu werden, wie es vielen solcher Animafiguren passiert. Darum sollen Sie immer in Andacht und Devotion dessen gedenken, das in der menschlichen Hülle einer V.O. Ihnen geoffenbart wurde, damit Ihre Seele unverlierbar bei Ihnen bleibe, und damit der Zugang zur Erde Ihnen nie verschüttet werde. Hoffen wir dasselbe für V.O., dass neben Tigern und Schlangen und ewigem Geiste noch ein Mensch in ihr vorhanden sei, der sich dankbar der Offenbarung ihres eigenen Geistes in Ihnen erinnern kann. Allzuleicht aber machen wir persönliche Tragik aus dem, was im letzten Verstande "Divina Commedia" war, und dann ist ein Funke vom ewigen Feuer in einem Tümpel verloschen.

Mit besten Grüssen
Ihr stets ergebener
C.G.Jung

P.S. Entschuldigen Sie bestens den Petroleumflecken auf dem Papier. Meine Lampe hat plötzlich Incontinenzsymptome bekommen

Figure 1.6 Jung's letter to Keyserling, 20 December 1929; permission to reproduce from the Foundation of the Works of C. G. Jung.

La Nación of Buenos Aires, and she included that piece in her memoirs. She would publish Spanish translations of Jung's books and introduce his work to Argentinians, indeed, to all Spanish speakers. Ocampo and Jung would not meet again, but Ocampo would declare Jung's critical psychology important to her experience as a South American.

As his memoirs attested, Keyserling remained fascinated by Ocampo and felt fatefully connected to her; in his collision with her he avowed he had experienced everything, "the whole history of Creation". Jung too remained a significant figure in Keyserling's life. In the memoirs he described Jung as "not only psychologically, mythologically, and theologically, but humanistically ... the most educated man of his time". In turn, Keyserling may have caused Jung to articulate his own cultural arguments more carefully.

Despite her enthusiastic advocacy of his earlier work, Ocampo read Keyserling's *South American Meditations* from what we would now understand to be a decolonizing and feminist stance. Coming to the end of the book, she realized that the count had toured her continent as her guest, projecting his European psyche on everything and perceiving almost nothing. He had transcribed anecdotes about Argentina that she had shared with him and then presented them in the book, distorted beyond recognition, as his own insights. And animating the book was what he has called the "South American spiderwoman", Keyserling's image for his negative experience of Ocampo herself perversely personalized and absurdly generalized. He was like Christopher Columbus seeing manatees for the first time, believing them to be mermaids and complaining that they were "not half as beautiful as they are painted".[4]

To understand how the encounter in Versailles affected Keyserling's views of both Ocampo and South America, and to see the affinities between the philosopher and the psychoanalyst, it helps to go back to the moment when Keyserling wrote to Jung asking for help interpreting the fateful meeting, a letter in which he predicts that Ocampo will be one of the strongest and strangest personalities of the twentieth century.

Keyserling and Jung

Keyserling's School of Wisdom at Darmstadt and Olga Froebe-Kapteyn's Eranos conferences at Ascona appear to have emerged out of a similar spirit-oriented European aesthetic. Indeed, the opening theme of Eranos was "Yoga and Meditation in West and East". But while Jung identified with the mandate of Eranos, he cautiously distanced himself from Keyserling's school. Reading Keyserling and Jung on the psychology of religion and on gendered

---

4 Columbus, *The Four Voyages*, "January 9 1493".

(as well as racialized) notions of spirit and matter reveals their apparent affinities. Keyserling writes:

> Man absolute is as originally "seeing" as woman absolute is originally "blind". This is why he is the original bearer of Spirit; this is why the word "history" is instinctively understood by each and all to be man's history.[5]

Jung says:

> Women are increasingly aware that love alone can give them full stature, just as men are beginning to divine that only the spirit can give life its highest meaning. Both seek a psychic relationship, because love needs the spirit, and the spirit love, for its completion.[6]

In their attempts to track collective trends in spirituality and psychoanalysis and to prognosticate, both Keyserling and Jung could generate absolutist principles without apology.

However, Jung's responses to Keyserling's school at Darmstadt were perhaps one way in which Jung recognized the need to articulate more carefully problems inherent in his own universalist arguments, acknowledging for instance a dichotomy between what he came later to describe as the psychologies of West and East. Jung argued: "Consciousness is by no means consciousness in general. It is rather a historically conditioned and geographically confined dimension, which represents only a part of mankind."[7] Gradually Jung qualified, and at times cautiously contextualized, his psychological commentaries on texts from India, China, Tibet, and Japan. For example, in his seminar, and also in an essay on the psychology of Kundalini yoga, he emphasized the limitations of his European perspective: "I will remain silent on the subject of what yoga means for India, because I cannot presume to judge something I do not know from personal experience. I can, however, say something about what it means for the West."[8] In other words, the notion of culturally contextualized consciousness was fundamental to his analytical psychology.

Jung could deal somewhat duplicitously with Keyserling. On the one hand, when before his encounter with Ocampo Keyserling wrote to Jung describing his somatic sufferings, erotic problems, and dreams, Jung wrote back offering friendly, detailed interpretations and advice. Jung noted in Keyserling's repeated dreams of execution by hanging, evidence of a conscious

5   Keyserling, *South American Meditations*, 165.
6   Jung, "Woman in Europe", *Collected Works*, Vol. 10, §269.
7   Jung, "Commentary on *The Secret of the Golden Flower*", *Collected Works*, Vol. 13, §84.
8   Jung, "Yoga and the West", *Collected Works*, Vol. 11, §866.

one-sidedness and an unconscious wish for a change of attitude, an assessment with which Keyserling agreed.[9] He hypothesized an exaggerated extraversion that the dreams compensated with an inner voice favouring "stillness".[10] He advised Keyserling that his superior function of extraverted intuition with its "stretching over continents" would deplete his energies. In a distressed tone that puzzled and irritated Keyserling, Jung wrote to the philosopher during his travels in America, admonishing him to pay careful attention to his body's sufferings as an enforcing illness, an attempt by the psyche to return him to himself.[11]

On the other hand, in his correspondence with his analytical colleague Oskar A. H. Schmitz (with whom Keyserling analysed for a time) Jung expressed scepticism about Keyserling as a philosopher. As Jung explained to Schmitz in a letter dated 26 May 1923, in his opinion the problem with Keyserling's School of Wisdom as an institution was that it had sprung from an attempt to build a new spirituality on a European foundation that was rotten.[12] In this regard, Jung was convinced that the only way for Europeans to progress spiritually was not so much by going out but by going down. That is to say, Jung wondered if Western fascination with Eastern spiritualities was a manifestation of resistance to the collective unconscious and a flight from the difficult work of confronting a murderous madness at the base of the European collective psyche. Again, we would refer to this today as precursive to a decolonizing insight.[13] For Jung, the problem with Keyserling personally was that he employed his eclectic musings about his spirituality in an evasive manner.[14] In the same letter to Oskar Schmitz, Jung writes: "Do you know Keyserling's dreams? And do you think he could safely stand the shock of glimpsing the face of his own shadow? I have yet to meet a man who has done so without shuddering, and who did not talk a little deliriously afterwards".[15]

9   Jung to Keyserling, 21 May 1927; Jung, *Letters*, Vol. 1, 46–47.
10   Jung to Keyserling, 19 June 1927; Jung, *Letters*, Vol. 1, 47.
11   Jung to Keyserling, 2 January 1928; Jung, *Letters*, Vol. 1, 49–50; quoted in Part Three. See also Keyserling's memoir, Part Seven.
12   Jung, *Letters*, Vol. 1, 39–41.
13   Rolando Vázquez describes this approach as follows:

> Decolonial thought cannot ignore the historical reality in which the metaphysics of modernity unfolded: how colonialism meant the objectification of Earth, peoples and their worlds to put them at the disposal of the subject that defined himself as the Human precisely in and through this relation. The appearance of the 'western man' as the Human is the expression of an anthropocentrism that brought Earth at his disposal, and a eurocentrism that brought other worlds at his disposal.
>
> *Vistas of Modernity*, 40

14   In this regard, see Robert Segal on Keyserling in his review of Richard Noll's *The Jung Cult*, 597–608.
15   Jung, *Letters*, Vol. 1, 39–41.

Jung was asking what it would require for Keyserling, like the hero in the Grimms' tale,[16] to learn how to shudder.

In his three reviews of Keyserling's books, Jung explicitly defined as a cultural phenomenon the problems he discerned in Keyserling – the best-selling writer, the guest speaker, and the director of a "wisdom institute" – and observed in Keyserling's work evidence of a progressive psychological development. Critiquing Keyserling's *Das Spektrum Europas* (1928), Jung warned the thoughtful common reader neither to dismiss the monocled aristocrat as a joke nor to be misled by the author's attempt to employ a humorous tone in order to lend his book lightness. Rather, *Europe* was Keyserling's very serious effort to classify a spectrum of European national psyches, "a psychological view of the world where nations are seen as functions". Employing his own psychological typology, Jung identified Keyserling's argument as extraverted and intuitive, as spiritual and archetypal rather than rational and philosophical, informed by a perspective that is elevated and collective, distanced and megalomaniacal in its solitude. It is a cosmic view that sees humanity from the outside and, as a result, is limited to daylight and vast surfaces, without addressing the opposing possibility of night or interiority. Still, Jung praised the specific descriptions of Italy, Holland, France, and Spain, as brilliantly precise. And he noted his counter-transference response to the description of Switzerland: "As soon as I became aware of my ruffled national pride, I read the chapter on Switzerland as though Keyserling had been writing about me personally, and behold! my irritation vanished."[17] The brunt of the review then plays with the oppositions between aristocratic Keyserling as an extravagant spendthrift man of "the spirit" and the Swiss as curmudgeonly aristocrats of "the earth", his idealistic fiery lightness versus the solid and conserving darkness of the Swiss, yang and yin each implicated in the other. One can observe Jung working hard to transpose Keyserling's take on Switzerland into a compliment.

Later, in his review of Keyserling's assessment of the American psyche, *America Set Free* (1929), Jung concurs with certain of the count's impressions of the United States, disagrees with others, and claims now to see evidence of psychological progress in the writer. According to Jung, Keyserling continues to function out of extraverted intuition as a "mouthpiece of the collective spirit",[18] but in contrast to *Europe*, in the new book Keyserling has also allowed the American earth to have its say. Curiously, as a result of listening to the earth, Keyserling concludes that America has not yet acquired a soul: "No gods have yet sprung from its union with man" (§926). Jung emphasizes how much Keyserling articulates a secret spiritual hunger in the American earth and intuits the implicit presence of "silent ones in the land". Jung is intrigued that Keyserling has again worked to discern intuitively, from above, as it were,

---

16   Grimm and Grimm, "The Boy Who Went Forth to Learn What Fear Is", *Complete Fairy Tales*, 14–22.
17   Jung, "The Swiss Line in the European Spectrum", *Collected Works*, Vol. 10, §910.
18   Jung, "The Rise of a New World", *Collected Works*, Vol. 10, §933.

the collective attitude of the United States, its genius or *spiritus loci*, but has also tried to "listen below" for the gods in the land. If he hears only chthonic silence (where the indigenous peoples of America can hear so much from which they derive wisdom and peace), at least, Jung seems to say, in leaning down, Keyserling has opened within himself a psychological receptive space.

Four years later Jung reviewed *La Révolution Mondiale et la responsabilité de l'Esprit* (1934), which was based on Keyserling's Paris lectures, and he again warned Keyserling's readers to adjust their expectations by explaining what precisely Keyserling is good and not good for. He said Keyserling voices well the Zeitgeist for the spiritual man, "condensing the utterances of the collective spirit, speaking through a thousand tongues, into a single discourse".[19] But readers need to re-orient themselves towards these ideas to comprehend them not as concepts but as images. They are symbols and symptoms to be interpreted psychologically, not hypostatised. And Jung questions the Enlightenment assumptions that inform Keyserling's stance. As Veronika Fuechtner puts it, Jung "described Keyserling's call for 'creative understanding' as stuck on a historically outdated mind-set of always wanting to understand everything. According to Jung, there were times when spirit was completely obscured, when the experience of this power should not be weakened by an attempt at understanding".[20] In the end, Jung expresses scepticism about the feasibility of Keyserling's solution for humankind's spiritual dilemma, if read literally. Jung observes a power dynamic in Keyserling's imagining of a kind of cultural monastery for the dark ages ahead (it is 1934), and concludes that it would only work if the aristocratic Keyserling assigns himself to labour daily in the kitchens; that is to say, in typological terms, if he integrates gradually, personally, his inferior function, his introverted sensation.[21] In this regard, according to Jung, the fact that Keyserling wrote the book in the "refined, cultured and elegant" French language did not bode

19   Jung, "La Révolution Mondiale", *Collected Works*, Vol. 10, §945.
20   Fuechtner, *Berlin Psychoanalytic*, 111.
21   In *The Original Protocols for Memories, Dreams, Reflections* (forthcoming Philemon series/ Princeton University Press), Jung states,

> When I was with Keyserling I was completely flooded. His words cascaded over me like a torrent. I could never get a word in. I saw him several times, and he always talked without stopping. I remembered that famous meeting between Professor Windelband and Carlyle in Heidelberg. Afterwards they asked the professor: So, Herr Professor, how was your visit? He replied by saying that he had spoken for two hours on the matter of holy silence! That was Keyserling! Part of his talk was always brilliant. But one was snowed under. When he held forth, from sheer exhaustion I could no longer give ear to that constant torrent, Why did he have to spout, I wondered. Does he want to prove something to himself? As if there was an urgent need for him to make other people realise that he was present and that he absolutely wanted to show something. But I wouldn't say that I found a thread to follow anywhere. I'd be unable to summarize a single exchange nor recall what he had spoken about. Because it was simply too much. It was completely amusing or brilliant, but always torrential, so it was futile to converse with him."
>
> Sonu Shamdasani, personal communication, 1 August 2022

well. But in that case, what has happened to Keyserling's nascent capacity to lean down low enough to let earth have its say? Jung seems to know but doesn't tell.

Taking up Jung's assessment, one might describe Keyserling as having used his philosophizing to avoid the psychological work of wrestling with his own shadow when travelling in Asia. Similarly, he undertook a publishing project that may have both addressed what he characterized as the marriage problem and avoided it at the same time. In 1925, Keyserling solicited papers for an anthology to be entitled *The Book of Marriage: A New Interpretation by Twenty-five Leaders of Contemporary Thought*, from writers such as Rabindranath Tagore, Richard Wilhelm, Thomas Mann, Havelock Ellis, Beatrice Hinkle, and Alfred Adler. Jung agreed to submit a piece and wrote "Marriage as a Psychological Relationship".[22] Keyserling begins his introduction to the book by quoting Bernard Shaw's reason for not contributing: "No man dare write the truth about marriage while his wife lives. Unless, that is, he hates her, like Strindberg; and I don't. I shall read the volume with interest, knowing that it will consist chiefly of evasions; but I will not contribute to it."[23] Keyserling quotes Shaw's letter of refusal admiringly, as an ironic quip with which to start things off lightly. But he could have taken Shaw's warning more seriously. Instead, in addition to editing the book, Keyserling penned not one but two essays: "The Current Statement of the Marriage Problem" and "The Proper Choice of Partners". Was this an act of hubris on his part? After all, Keyserling was married to Maria Gödela von Bismarck-Schönhausen, granddaughter of the first chancellor of the Wilhelminian empire. In his first essay, on the one hand he advocated the women's movement and the notion of woman as equal in a marriage; on the other hand, he recommended to readers his own personal solution to the marriage problem: "Adultery existed all through the ages and was never looked upon as a real danger to marriage ... The more gifted and developed a man is, the greater the variety of emotions he is capable of feeling, and the more numerous the persons and things he has the right to come in contact with ..."[24] Given such views, how would he fare in a confrontation with the problem of the anima and intrapsychic marriage that would arrive fatefully in the shape of a flattering invitation to visit South America?

Ocampo and Keyserling

Victoria Ocampo was born in 1890 and died in 1979. She was the eldest of six sisters, born into an aristocratic and rich family of Buenos Aires. As a girl, she was raised by a French nanny, so her French was as good or better

22   Jung, "Marriage as a Psychological Relationship", *Collected Works*, Vol. 17, §§324–345.
23   Quoted in Keyserling, *Book of Marriage*, iii.
24   Keyserling, *Book of Marriage*, 27, 45.

than her Spanish (she would quip, "I'm writing to you in French because I'm in a hurry") and she travelled often with her family in Europe, even auditing courses at the Sorbonne and the Collège de France although she was never permitted a formal education, much to her regret.

One of Ocampo's biographers, Doris Meyer, delineates genealogically the oligarchical power into which Victoria was born, as an Ocampo on her father's side and an Aguirre on her mother's, but at the same time emphasizes that this legacy of patriarchal power was compounded by the social restricting of women in Spanish colonialism and Catholicism. That is to say, as the eldest of six daughters, from a psychological point of view, she grew up in a privileged atmosphere of both expectation and limitation. Politically Ocampo could trace back in her lineage conflicting connections to both General José de San Martin, the South American liberator, and Juan Manuel de Rosas, Argentina's first dictator; she positioned herself as wishing to identify with the idea of liberation but feeling forced to acknowledge also the tyrannical element in her blood. In the shadows of her maternal line she discovered late in her life a link to the Spanish conquistador Irala of Asunción, who chose to recognize legally his Guaraní concubine and their daughter, Agueda. Says Meyer: "Victoria could rescue Agueda from 'history's back room', as she referred to the place where so many women's stories had been traditionally shunted, and Agueda, in turn, could provide Victoria with a blood link to Pre-Columbian America that complemented the spiritual link she had felt all her life."[25]

In 1924, Ocampo published in French her first book, entitled *De Francesca à Béatrice*, about the female muse. In some sense, the book was both personal and public, in that she had been a sort of platonic muse first for Ortega y Gasset and then for the Bengali poet/artist Rabindranath Tagore, who had fallen ill while making a stopover on his trip to Perú in November 1924 and convalesced under her care at her relative's house[26] in the Buenos Aires suburb of San Isidro until January 1925. Tagore was utterly smitten; "She was both shy and bold by nature, the Latin American upbringing encouraging in women a combination of coquetry and puritanical retreat", writes the literary historian Ketaki Kushari Dyson.[27] One problem with the role Ocampo

25   Meyer, *Victoria Ocampo*, 9.

26

> Victoria's father forbade her from hosting the widower Tagore (dressed in rags, to make things worse) so she had to sell a diamond tiara she famously wore during her honeymoon in order to pay the rent for her relative's house. Victoria and her tiara were mentioned by the Modernist writer Ángel de Estrada Jr (1872–1923, a cousin of Victoria's husband) in a novel taking place in Rome, whose main character is Victoria, and her tiara is an example of the owner's beauty as well as her fatal attraction, as it works as a scythe.
>
> Juan Javier Negri, personal communication, 4 April 2022

27   Dyson, *In Your Blossoming Flower-Garden*, 106.

had defined for herself in her first book was familial: the dedication on the first page drew public attention to her failed early marriage to Luis Bernardo de Estrada. Another problem with the role she enacted with both Ortega and Tagore was the degree to which she, as a privileged young woman, was projecting her authority in meek devotion to older male writers rather than experiencing it responsibly as her own.

In similar fashion, in 1927, Ocampo read Keyserling's *The Travel Diary of a Philosopher* and wrote to him to express her admiration. As a result of their correspondence, Ocampo agreed to travel to Europe in January 1929 and meet Keyserling at the hotel in Versailles. Both she and her family experienced this departure to Europe as a psychological sundering: her father unexpectedly gave her a large gift of cash; she experienced the departure as tearing herself away from Buenos Aires, even if her lover Julián Martínez had agreed to travel on separate business to Paris and share an address with her discreetly there.

Had Ocampo read a satirical piece about Keyserling (penned in part by James Thurber) in *The New Yorker*, she might have at least felt forewarned:

> Persons who were to entertain him in New York received written instructions, including: "He has absolutely no geographic sense. It would appear that he would be lost in his own home. He becomes extremely nervous with fear of not being met at the station when he arrives. He must be taken to the station and placed inside his Pullman or parlor chair car … He is helpless as far as tickets, baggage, etc., are concerned … He is nervously and physically exhausted after finishing a lecture. If he is to meet anyone after his lecture, he would enjoy doing so at somebody's home, under the following conditions … he is famished and must eat immediately after a lecture. Therefore he does not want to meet anyone unless he can have a sitting-down supper at which he will be served French wines or champagne … He cannot eat raw fruit, salad, vegetables, etc. He lives chiefly on fresh fish and fresh oysters, dozens of them on the half shell, and beef, lamb, and white meat of fowl … The Count refuses to attend dinners with men only…[he] enjoys very much being in the company of young people – providing girls or women predominate.[28]

Ocampo set herself up in Paris and immediately occupied herself with preparing a luxurious room at the Hôtel des Réservoirs in Versailles according to Keyserling's demands, where he could finish writing *America Set Free*. But when he arrived, she discovered that Keyserling had interpreted her epistolary enthusiasm and spiritual forthrightness as a sexual overture. She vehemently rejected his advances, and he was outraged.

---

28   *The New Yorker*, 31 March 1928, 8.

Nevertheless, they carried out the plan they had made. As prearranged, each day during his weeks in Versailles, Keyserling worked on his manuscript and then met with Ocampo. Many years later, he explained that, as spiritual practitioner of a wisdom tradition and a proponent of open marriage, and as the recipient of Ocampo's effusive letters and monetary benevolence, he had expected her in her role as hetairi-muse-courtesan to be sexually available. He described her refusal not only as a rejection of him but as an impediment to what he could offer her in return, the possibility of spiritual redemption.

Residing in Paris during these weeks, Ocampo visited Versailles each day, feeling violently conflicted. Outwardly, how should she best fend off his assault? Inwardly, how to reconcile feeling so moved as a reader by the power of Keyserling's words and so revulsed bodily by the man (not only physically, but also emotionally, witnessing him pathetically deflect his apoplectic rage at her onto a passing waiter over a dish of mashed potatoes he judged badly prepared)?

Still, she did not retract her invitation that he come to South America to lecture. When he did eventually travel to Buenos Aires, it was under a cloud: the trip was constantly threatened by anger and misunderstanding. Characteristically, Keyserling processed his psychological confusion by philosophizing about it in the book that was eventually published as *South American Meditations*, in which he purged himself of his anger and shame by generalizing his attacks on Ocampo as a spiritual reflection on Argentina, and on all of South America. He called South America "The Continent of the Third Day of Creation", a continent that apparently had progressed only as far as the point in Genesis at which land becomes differentiated from ocean and then plant life forms; that is to say, for Keyserling, South America was God's retarded vegetative backwater.

South American Meditations (1932, Spanish edition, 1933) is the oddest of travel books, curiously lacking in concrete details – place names, modes of transportation, regional foods, cultural references – and suffering from a supercilious top-down propensity to generalize:

> The masses of cattle of the pampa can only be understood in terms of the "Yeast of Creation". And the same holds true of the animality of Argentine Man. However much he may differ from the South American of the tropic zone – he is yet a special expression of the general type, so that *from a high point of vantage* one involuntarily includes in a single glance the Brazilian, the Venezuelan and the Argentine.[29]

Even worse, identifying himself with a gendered notion of "high" masculine spirit, he explains why he thrived in his travels to the spiritual Far East but suffered terribly in his confrontation with South America as Other, as

---

29 Keyserling, *South American Meditations*, 27; italics mine.

low feminine matter. This confrontation manifested itself first as somatic symptoms:

> South America has given me far more than India and China. The Chinese as well as the Hindu is closely akin to me, for he, too, lives out of Spirit; thus his difference from me means no more to me than does the difference of the French and English language. Now the South American is entirely and absolutely Man of the Earth. He embodies the polar opposite of the man conditioned and permeated by Spirit ... Just as the Bolivian *puna*[30] threatened to disintegrate my body, even so the vibration in tune with the foreign rhythm of the Argentine for a long time endangered the balance of my soul. This found its expression – for the body is the dial of the time-piece of Life – in protracted attacks of arrythmia perpetua, this being the symptom of the interference of incompatible melodies.[31]

Referring to his typology, Jung had already warned Keyserling during his earlier travels to North America that a one-sided reliance on such a strongly spiritualized extraverted intuitive function might constellate in him its opposite, that is to say, a compensatory enantiodromia into a shadowy introverted realm of somatic weakness and physical suffering. In South America, Keyserling experienced this *puna* as "Original Fear".[32]

From a conversation with Ocampo, Keyserling also learned about *gana*, a local term indicating a feeling of disposition, or more frequently indis-position or lack of will, to do something. Specifically, she shared with Keyserling a personal anecdote recounted by her sister in which Silvina offered to pay a poor boy to caddy her golf clubs and he refused, saying he wouldn't. When she asked why not, he said, "*Porque no me da la gana*" ["Because I don't feel like it"]. Ocampo related the story to explain how for Argentinians money is not the primordial drive, that they are not ser-vile. But Keyserling reworked *gana*, generalizing this lack of disposition in Silvina Ocampo's story and applying it to the whole of Argentina: "whose world of *gana* manifests itself more impressively than anywhere on earth, because its intrinsic passivity is concomitant with outward progressive-ness, intellectual alertness and great refinement of feeling. This nation lives a primordial life, and yet appears thoroughly modern."[33] He then characterized all South Americans as primitive, as prone to *gana*, as identi-fied with undifferentiated vegetative and animal matter. And going further he attributed to women, in particular to South American women, abysmal lives of primitivistic original wisdom. They are, he wrote, "cold-blooded

---

30   A debilitating altitude sickness.
31   Keyserling, *South American Meditations*, 33.
32   Keyserling, *South American Meditations*, 35.
33   Keyserling, *South American Meditations*, 185.

vipers in the primal slime" in need of a violent awakening to the masculine, to spirit, to consciousness:

> The women are of a great sweetness, and since the whole order of life is rooted in emotion, the warmth of atmospheres ought to pervade the continent. This conclusion seems so obvious, that for a long time my imagination construed the existence of this warmth. I was wrong nevertheless. Here tenderness, gentleness, sweetness and friendliness are essentially qualities appertaining to the cold-blooded creatures ... South American women have a horror unknown elsewhere of all hardness; anger to them is a vice; in warm passionateness they sense foremost the violence underlying it, and violence they cannot bear. But on the other hand in their heart of hearts they desire to be violated.[34]

> Nowhere else do the emotions of the women so easily turn into their opposite on the slightest provocation. Nowhere is the subsoil of the strongest passion so cold. Withal I do not in the least dispute the high qualities, and most of all, the possibilities of South American woman: what I have said merely goes to prove her primordial womanhood, which makes her particularly seductive.[35]

> Thus, the South American sweetness and considerateness does not mean warmth. What seems to be warmth, is in reality the need of warmth; thus, the lizard seeks the sun. Hence the typical coldness of those women who most excite and disturb men.[36]

Keyserling's rape fantasies are deeply troubling, forming part as they do both of the wild psychoanalysis within which he imagined himself relating to women and of his depiction of his European colonizing gaze on South America. Having analysed for a time with Georg Groddeck, the originator of the concept of the "id", he could also employ the trope of violation intrapsychically, describing how he could rape his own thoughts. For the record, Jung could also describe men's emotional inclination towards violence in response to power, specifically to the dynamic of women whom they experienced as animus-possessed. Jung writes, "Often the man has the feeling –and he is not altogether wrong – that only seduction or a beating or rape would have the necessary power of persuasion."[37] Jung hedges, hoping to metabolize the image of psychic violence by tracking the prospective function of such a fantasy towards an integrative outcome.

34 Keyserling, *South American Meditations*, 30.
35 Keyserling, *South American Meditations*, 44.
36 Keyserling, *South American Meditations*, 222.
37 Jung, *Aion, Collected Works*, Vol. 9.ii. § 29. For a feminist commentary, see Susan Rowland, *Jung: A Feminist Revision*.

During the time of drafting these meditations, Keyserling complained about Ocampo in a series of letters to Jung. He emphasized his somatic sufferings – heart and lung trouble and something he called "devitalization" – and wasn't the encounter with Ocampo the cause? In his replies, Jung diagnosed typologically the descriptions in *South American Meditations* as "the activation of the inferior function, which because of its contamination with the contents of the collective unconscious always drags up" the primeval slime. Jung read the not-yet-published manuscript and told Keyserling that his book was really about a destabilizing inner confrontation via the inferior function and anima possession with the collective unconscious. On the one hand, Jung tried to encourage the count in his encounter with the daemonism of the earth, saying "it has never yet been described better". On the other hand, he advised Keyserling to "cut down on the cultural speculation" about South America in the book and realize that he was writing about an intrapsychic experience.

On the surface, Keyserling acknowledged Jung's advice, even incorporating Jung's letter of support into his book. He included a short paragraph very near the end that reads: "C. G. Jung has shown that one of the typical ways of psychological development is to elevate things from the level of the object to the level of the subject: according to him, man begins by experiencing his inward reality as something outside of himself, and he draws this reality back into himself in the course of integration."[38] But as much as he could cite Jung's integrative model of the psyche, he did not know how to take Jung's advice to sink his ego consciousness down into his inferior function, to speak to his anima and then to listen, to write down the anima's words and to wrestle with their implications in intrapsychic dialogue. Instead, he regressively returned to the monologue of the Travelling Philosopher tracking Spirit in the world from a great height. Indeed, he entitled the final chapter of *South American Meditations* "Divina Commedia", perhaps in response to Jung's editorial observation that Keyserling's book was less a travelogue like Laurence Sterne's *A Sentimental Journey* and more a Dante-esque mapping of an individuation process. But again, Keyserling's extraverted intuition co-opted Jung's reflected insight about Dante and rendered it an inflated utopian vision for twentieth-century readers. Doing so, he reversed the negative power dynamics inherent in his experience of feeling anima-possessed and overwhelmed; instead, he defensively declared, with a grandiosity that he experienced as benevolence, that with this book he "gave to South America its soul".[39] In this way, Keyserling misappropriated, misused, and mistranslated South America,[40] much as he had Ocampo.

But neither Jung nor Ocampo could easily dismiss Keyserling. As noted above, Jung as a reviewer admonished readers to discern with care the value of

38   Keyserling, *South American Meditations*, 418.
39   Landau, *God Is My Adventure*, 213.
40   Garcia, *Signs of the Americas*, xv.

Keyserling's extraverted intuitions as an accurate articulating of a Zeitgeist, as psychological fodder for a diagnostic of the European psyche; according to Jung, Keyserling always struck "close to the mark".[41] And Ocampo herself confessed her dilemma, continuing to feel fascinated with Keyserling's spiritual prose even after she felt physically and emotionally revolted by the actions of the man she met at the Hôtel des Réservoirs.[42]

Keyserling's *South American Meditations*, published with the subtitle *On Hell and Heaven in the Soul of Man*, had a curious history with its readers. For instance, what Amy Kaminsky calls "the Keyserling effect" holds a deleterious place in the Argentinian *imaginaire*. Kaminsky asks, "Why the great minds of the nation [Argentina] fell for Keyserling's delirious writing in the first place, and then repeated and magnified each other's solemn agreement with his pronouncements is a good question."[43] She points to the historical argument that, from the establishment of its independence onwards, Argentinians identified with one of two opposing political camps and nationalistic impulses: the Unitarians, who attempted to construct a country through immigration and education by transplanting European doctrines onto Argentinian soil; and the Federalists, who offered an autochthonic political vision, claiming their soil as homeland. Neither party effectively acknowledged the presence of indigenous peoples. Curiously, caught in this irreconcilable collective split, in what Thomas Singer and Samuel L. Kimbles would diagnose as a cultural complex,[44] Argentinian readers were psychologically primed to collude with Keyserling's racialized, genderized power-fantasies superimposed on their continent and their nation.

Ocampo, for her part, in her first letter to Jung, hinted at her predicament as a privileged Argentinian living in a state of psychic exile or dispossession both from Europe and the Americas, at home nowhere. Was she attempting to address these collective dilemmas by forming erotic spiritual attachments to older intellectual men whom she deemed wise because they knew something about the power of words? In the days they spent meeting together at the Hôtel des Réservoirs, how close to the mark did Keyserling come when he intuited a psychic split in Ocampo, even if he described it ineptly as both medieval and schizophrenic? By launching, maintaining, and defending *Sur*, and by identifying herself as both reader and writer,[45] she was working to

---

41 Jung, "The Spiritual Problem of Modern Man", *Collected Works*, Vol. 10, §195.

42 Veronika Fuechtner, historian of psychoanalysis and culture in Weimar Germany, writes: "Given Keyserling's dialogue with Jung and Freud, his impact on Italian psychoanalysis, and his seminal writings on nation, religion, philosophy and the exotic, it seems high time for a critical rediscovery of his work" (Fuechtner, *Berlin Psychoanalytic*, 112). For a recent reassessment of Keyserling's wish for a new aristocracy, see Walter Struve, *Elites against Democracy*.

43 Kaminsky, *Argentina: Stories for a Nation*, 74.

44 Thomas Singer and Samuel L. Kimbles, eds., *The Cultural Complex*.

45 With regard to Ocampo as writer, see Hugo Beccacece, "Victoria Ocampo, Escritora", 43.

bridge the conflicting elements in herself personally and also to transform the Argentinian collective *imaginaire*.

Meanwhile, consider the following statement: "Precisely the lack of intellectuality and the passivity of South America, at this turning point, may have a mission for all mankind."[46] Here, where Jung was advising him to see a compensatory personal fantasy wish for change within himself, Keyserling intuits in an externalized inferiority a kind of messianic hopefulness that he generalizes as a potential for collective spiritual renewal. He hadn't arrived at this optimistic envisioning of a New World when writing about the moral pragmatism of the United States in *America Set Free* because he considered Americans to be spiritually bankrupted, their chthonic gods as silent. But now, writing about South America in a prophetic mode, he declared:

> South America's cultural future seems to me to be externally secure. First, it is true, Spirit must descend upon this continent. It cannot produce an original culture true to its style before. But all the conditions for its growth are there. It is possible, even probable, that the next rebirth of that spirit which once made possible the wonders of Greece, which rose again first in Provence, then in the Italian Renaissance, and ultimately in the French culture of form, which, alas, has already grown rigid – that the next rebirth of that spirit will take place on South American soil; for the salvation of all men, for the redemption of all from brutality.[47]

Some readers may have felt ambivalent about Keyserling's book, but others enthusiastically mined what they regarded as this promising vein. For instance, Stefan Zweig, after meeting Keyserling and reading *South American Meditations*, wrote in Keyserling's wake the hyperbolic utopian tract *Brazil: Land of the Future* (1941).[48]

Jung eventually agreed to endorse Keyserling's book with a blurb, but one notes how carefully he qualifies his faint praise:

> In my opinion, Keyserling's *South American Meditations* are one of the most important manifestations of the re-birth of the spirit of the age. Keyserling's adventure means a descent into the nether world, out of which, amidst desperate struggle, a great light tries to free itself. Keyserling has tackled the same spiritual sphere which Goethe tried to master in his second Faust. These Meditations are a unique synthesis of inward experience and outward manifestation.[49]

---

46 Keyserling, *South American Meditations*, 237.
47 Keyserling, *South American Meditations*, 241.
48 See "Keyserling, the Philosopher Who Envisioned Paradise".
49 Dust jacket of Keyserling, *South American Meditations*.

I mentioned earlier that Jung could be duplicitous regarding Keyserling. In contrast to this blurb's complementary reference to Goethe (though the second *Faust* is generally considered much inferior to the first), Jung complained in another letter to Schmitz by contrasting Keyserling with Faust. He writes: "Keyserling starts from Cagliostro, not Faust."[50] Jung is identifying Keyserling more with Count Cagliostro, that is to say, with change fuelled by an amoral unconscious Mephistophelean element, than with Faust and consciousness. As much as Jung supported and sympathized with Keyserling's experiences of negative anima-possession as a tragic collective longing for spiritual renewal, he judged Keyserling as lacking the requisite psychological sophistication or the ego strength to "drop down" into the berserker-like madness at the base of the collective European psyche and emerge again with a symbolic pre-figuring of a new paradigm. Again, Jung hypothesized typologically that Keyserling's over-identification as a writer with extraverted intuitive speculations led him to disregard consciously the inferior functioning of introverted sensation that manifested so dystonically: in his disorientation in time and space, in his voracious insatiable appetite, in his litany of somatic sufferings, to say nothing of his explosive complaints in response to what he experienced as the contradiction between Ocampo's bounteous generosity and her sexual unavailability.[51]

For her part, Ocampo emerged from the painful encounter in Versailles with profound insights into her own psyche. She struggled thereafter to take back projections and to look for ways to claim more of her own authority as a writer, a feminist, and a businesswoman, as much as that was possible at the time. However, she did continue to publish Keyserling in *Sur*, and she waited for many years to reveal her views about *South American Meditations*.

Ocampo and Jung

In June 1934 when Ocampo wrote to Jung to ask for a meeting, two years after the publication of *South American Meditations*, she knew that he would know who she was, that she was "the Argentine poetess" cited on page 307 of the *Meditations*, the author of *De Francesca à Béatrice*, Keyserling's "spiderwoman". She described to Jung that she felt liberated from her own oppressive intrapsychic cosmogony, in part by his critical psychology of type,

---

50 Jung to Schmitz, 21 July 1927, quoted in Emma Jung, *Psychological Perspectives*, 79.

51 It's interesting to note that Keyserling also mentions how Jung identifies emotion/feeling as a rational function, and how Keyserling as an extraverted intuitive and thinking type strongly disagrees; he emphatically corrects Jung by stating "emotion is essentially irrational". Here he has misread Jung, failing to differentiate between feeling as emotion and Jung's feeling function that rationally assigns value or importance to objects and experiences. See Keyserling, *South American Meditations*, 267.

and how important it felt to her to publish his book on psychological types in Spanish:

> Since I read the English translation of "Psychological Types", I have been wanting to meet you, to know you. Your books have been a great help to me. I admire them, and I am grateful to them, to you, for all I have found in them. I feel I owe you half of my actual serenity ... perhaps more than half! And I shall always be indepted [sic] to you for it ... I hope the Spanish translation and publication of "Psychological Types" will be an "*affaire conclue*" when I get to Paris.[52]

In an article for *La Nación* (5 March 1936) and later in her memoir, *Domingos en Hyde Park* (see Part Five), Ocampo recounts her meeting with Jung in October of that year.[53] She had come to Zürich from Rome, where she had just interviewed Mussolini.[54] In that meeting, she recognized the dangerous personal and political implications of projecting authority outwardly onto men, encountering as she just had the father of fascism who wanted to confine women to the passive role of breeders. Ocampo explains how, entering the house of yet another "great man", she experienced her inferiority constellated. But, as she waited for Jung to appear, she chanced upon a collection of detective novels on his bookshelves and a weight lifted off her mind. She, as a fellow enthusiast of the genre, depotentiated the negative complex by imagining the favourite authors that they might share in common. Later she describes admiringly Jung's "elephantine intelligence", and how he caught with wonderful adroitness whatever comment she threw to him. But she also recalls her shock that when, after inviting him to lecture in Argentina, he replied, "What for? They could not be interested. They would not understand."

Ocampo asks herself silently, "Because they are Latins? Because they are Catholics?"[55] She was trying to process the negative turn in the conversation, Jung's rebuking claim that Argentinians would not understand his work. Since she was working so hard to publish Jung in South America, no doubt she felt disconcerted by his response. Was he revealing a colonizing prejudice similar to Keyserling's, as if he too were characterizing South Americans as rooted in the *gana* of a Continent of the Third Day of Creation?

---

52   Ocampo to Jung, 12 June 1934. See Part Four.
53   William McGuire and R.F.C. Hull anthologized that article in their collection, *C. G. Jung Speaking: Interviews and Encounters*, 1977, 82–84.
54   Ocampo, "Living History", 217–222.
55   At this point in the English-language McGuire/Hull edition of Ocampo's account (in *C. G. Jung Speaking*), there is an editorial or typographical error. Clearly Jung did not ask the two questions that follow in the English text, nor did Ocampo speak these words aloud. Rather, as is clear in the original Spanish version, these are Ocampo's interiorized questions in response to Jung's immediate and emphatic negative response.

Reading this account now, how do we interpret Jung's reaction to Ocampo's invitation? The Argentinian scholar Beatriz Sarlo, commenting on Ocampo's memoir, describes Jung as "ironic, uninterested and rude" and Ocampo as naively not perceiving this.[56] It's a fact that Jung could express scepticism about the effectiveness of lecturing to the general public about the unconscious: "There is too much talk in the world anyway" (Part Four). Or, having read Keyserling's letters about Ocampo's propensity to project her authority onto men whom she published and invited to lecture, was Jung refusing to collude with Ocampo's possible animus projections? Was the elephantine Jung abruptly tossing Ocampo's invitation and her own authority back at her? His question, "What for?" is certainly coldly enigmatic.[57]

After Ocampo's short conversation with Jung, she waited a week in Hotel Baur au Lac, Zürich, for a second meeting, for the opportunity to discuss a new preface for the Argentinian edition of *Psychological Types*, as well as to speak about the possibility of doing an analysis with him. But she never received a reply from Jung to this request. She left Switzerland, expressing in a letter (Part Four) her frustration and disappointment. Jung fulfilled his professional obligation to her, sending his promised foreword for her Spanish-language edition of *Psychological Types* to her address in Paris. His brief correspondence with Ocampo reads oddly formal and business-like, as if knowing about her through Keyserling he had decided he would not or could not see her, neither as a patient nor as an individual.

But Ocampo's account of the meeting, written in 1936, is insistently positive about the importance to her of Jung's analytical psychology. In a kind of prologue to the memoir of her meeting (not included in McGuire and Hall's English-language edition), she describes writing a piece for a reputable Paris magazine and movingly defending her inclusion of Jung's word "introversion" in her text, even when this led the editor to refuse to publish her piece. As Ocampo made explicit, she regarded the two attitudes of introversion and extraversion, and the four functions of thinking, feeling, sensation, and intuition as potentially available to her – some less, some more – as a gendered individual. And the "critical" aspect of Jung's model of psychic functioning, the fact that he emphasized this in the preface for Ocampo's edition of *Psychological Types*, proved useful to her. With his "critical psychology" as her compass, she could orient herself and assess any argument or situation to

---

56   Beatriz Sarlo, *La máquina cultural,* 116, quoted in Lojo 2004/2021 197.

57   In *The Original Protocols for Memories, Dreams, Reflections* (forthcoming Philemon series/ Princeton University Press), Jung again expresses himself enigmatically, remembering his response to Ocampo's powerful constitution:

> Keyserling had a lady friend, a very beautiful woman, but an absolute horse. A classical beauty. Though one cannot ever say "beautiful." She was a mare; no, better, a stallion. Strikingly beautiful and an important personality. She came to see me once.
> Sonu Shamdasani, personal communication, August 1 2022

identify its typological bias, to identify its strengths but also to assess what was being left out and ought not to be left out.

At the same time, Ocampo was savvy enough to know that Jung's critical psychology of type as an instrument for psychological understanding could be badly misused. In his new foreword, Jung himself acknowledges that psychologists misapply his typology by pigeon-holing people into categories, thereby shutting down and shutting out any possibility of genuine encounter with the Otherness of the unconscious. Elsewhere, for example in his Bailey Island seminars, Jung noted how Americans, for instance, had turned his psychology of types into a collection of moralistic "shoulds". In her memoir of her meeting with Jung, Ocampo notes these misuses of typology as well. One suspects she might be describing the dynamic between Keyserling and herself when she writes:

> When a man who believes himself to be extraverted calls you an introvert, you, lady, be on your guard. And you should be on your guard, sir, when a woman who believes herself to be introverted calls you an extravert. In the depths of their unconsciousness, these words are implicitly proceeded by the adjective "BIG". And yet, in any case if we can emerge benefitting from this, it is to our gain. Before, we would simply have called each other idiots.[58]

After struggling to throw off Keyserling's projections and stand her ground, Ocampo felt forever changed. When she travelled to Zürich to meet Jung, whether he would acknowledge her or not, it was to convey personally to him that, with regard to her own individuation, her reading of his analytical psychology had made the difference.

A New Lucidity

In the spring of 1939, at Keyserling's sister's request, Ocampo drove from Paris to Darmstadt to visit the count, whose passport the Nazi authorities had confiscated. For the most part, Ocampo and Keyserling spoke about Hitler. The aftermath of their meeting can be read as an instance of pathetic fallacy. On her return trip to Paris at night, near Sarrebrück, Ocampo suffered a serious car accident and a neck injury. Later, Keyserling recounted to her an uncanny synchronicity: at the time the accident took place, Keyserling's legs were swept out from underneath him. Obviously, he still experienced the feeling of being fatefully connected to her. For a time following the visit, they renewed their correspondence, wrestling with the language each employed to describe the dynamics constellated by their relationship. For instance,

---

58   See Part Five.

Ocampo questioned Keyserling's personal identification with tigers as spiritually totemic (shouldn't he identify with something less exotic, more Baltic?) and mocked his insistent use of the serpent to confine her in her feminine identity to the telluric as an earth-woman. In these letters, Keyserling describes himself as having been victimized by the archaic or medieval splitting in her personality that she displaced onto him, which she experienced either as positive spiritual idolatry or negative physical revulsion. For her part, Ocampo apparently questions his continued mistake of reifying spirit as masculine, and nature or matter as feminine. (Her side of this correspondence is missing.) In his letter dated 15 February 1939, Keyserling predicts to Ocampo that she will later in life realize her significance as a great personality of the twentieth century. He had already written this to Jung in 1929.

Nevertheless, in his 15 February 1939 letter, Keyserling admonishes Ocampo, insisting on the validity of his published narrative as it previously appeared in *South American Meditations* and inappropriately diagnosing her "psychoanalytically" as suffering from a schizophrenic-like splitting. In another letter he suggests, in a more conciliatory fashion, that they might simply agree to differ. Keyserling died in 1946. In the chapter on Jung and psychoanalysis in his posthumously published *Travel through Time*, Keyserling, as the founder of the School of Wisdom, compares and contrasts himself to Freud, Adler, and Jung: on the one hand, he praises the progenitors of psychoanalysis as important pioneers; on the other hand, he attacks Jung in particular as "humanistically" well-educated but destructively "unspiritual", as well as cold, even cruel.[59] In the chapter entitled "V.O.", Keyserling recounts his encounter with Ocampo in the Hôtel des Réservoirs and the lecture tour that followed, maintaining that she functioned as a symbolic and unsympathetic Arachne-Beatrice to his Dante on a journey through South America as hell, purgatory, and heaven. For a number of years, Ocampo remained publicly silent about Keyserling's use of her in *South American Meditations*. In 1951, however, Keyserling's widow published his memoir posthumously, including the chapter not so discreetly entitled "V.O." (See Part Seven). In her little book entitled *El viajero y una de sus sombras* [*The Traveller and One of His Shadows*; see Part Eight], Ocampo would definitively refute Keyserling's version of herself and of Argentina. She explicitly takes up the verb "to differ" to declare her intention. Ocampo carefully argues that Keyserling's memoirs once again misappropriate, misuse, and mistranslate her, to say nothing of his portrayal of South America. For example, she interprets Keyserling's gender bias, in which only the masculine is spiritual and the feminine is unredeemed

---

59   Jung writes, "Some while ago the readers of your magazine were given the opportunity to read a posthumous article by Count Keyserling, in which I was characterized as 'unspiritual'" (Jung, "Religion and Psychology: A Reply to Martin Buber", §1499). Keyserling's 1950 article in *Merkur*, "Begegnungen mit der Psychoanalyse", is a version of the chapter in Keyserling's posthumously published memoirs (see Part Seven).

nature, as fixed or intransigent because of unresolved parental complexes. Specifically, she pinpoints details from his memoirs about how the adolescent Hermann suffered, in what resembles a Hamlet-like oedipal dilemma, not only the early death of his beloved aristocratic father but his mother's re-marrying (in Keyserling's mind far too soon) his tutor, a younger man of a lower class. It's interesting to note that in 1928, at Keyserling's request, Jung had worked with Keyserling's dreams archetypally (rather than reductively focusing on the family history) and had come to a similar conclusion about a psychological skewing evident in the count's parental imagos. In his 25 August 1928 letter to Keyserling, Jung amplified:

> The negative relationship to the mother is always an affront to nature, unnatural. Hence distance from the earth, identification with the father, heaven, light, wind, spirit, Logos. Rejection of the earth, of what is below, dark, feminine. Negative relationship to material things, also to children. Flight from personal feelings.
>
> On the subjective level the "father" is an imago: the image of your relationship to the father and everything he stands for. In your dream this imago is dark, on the point of disappearing; that is to say a different attitude to the father imago is brewing (and to everything it stands for). Your *one-sided spiritual tendency* is probably meant, for anyone whose stature requires the size of a continent is not so very far away from Father Heaven (Zeus). This is too much for our human stature. It is an *inflation* by the universal, suprapersonal spirit. (Originally this was forced on you by the negative attitude of your mother). This spiritual inflation is compensated by a distinct inferiority of feeling, a real *undernourishment* of your other side, the feminine earth (Yin) side, that of personal feeling. Hence your feeling appears in negative form, as an obsessive symptom = *fear of starvation*. Because of your negative relation to the earth side there is a danger of actual starvation; you arouse enmity because you give out no warm feeling but merely autoerotic emotions which leave other people cold, also you are ruthless and tactless in manner. But your inferior feeling is *genuine*, hence anyone who sees behind your heavenly cloak with its ten thousand meteors has confidence in you.[60]

Similarly, in her assessment, Ocampo astutely articulates the contradictions she still experienced in pondering Keyserling: she admits her ongoing fascination as a reader with Keyserling's prose, especially in *The Travel Diary of a Philosopher*, while at the same time feeling negated by his skewed cosmology in which a spermatozoid is more spiritual than an ovule.

---

60 Jung, *Letters*, Vol. 1, 52–53. Gerhard Adler, the editor of Jung's published letters, notes that Keyserling dismissed as erroneous Jung's interpretation of his inferior feeling (Jung, *Letters*, Vol. 1, 53, n.6.).

She also revisits Keyserling's portrayal of her in both *South American Meditations* and *Travel through Time* as an indigenous warrior shooting at him with poison arrows. Reversing the negative power dynamic implicit in his primitivistic use of this metaphor, Ocampo co-opts the image and claims it as her own, identifying herself with it as evidence of what she names her "Penthesilea complex". As the Thracian warrior Queen of the Amazons, Ocampo portrays herself as feminine and regal and spirited and warring. Also, in an epigraph to her book in which she positions herself as standing in the shadow of the traveller, she cites Heinrich von Kleist's drama in which Penthesilea slays Achilles (as opposed to the traditional version of the myth in which Achilles slays Penthesilea at Troy).

At the 1977 ceremony in which she was admitted to the Argentinian Academy of Letters, Ocampo shocked the upper-class racist and gender assumptions of most of the audience by honouring the memory of her indigenous great-grandmother:

> On my mother's side, I am descended from Domingo Martínez de Irala, a companion of don Pedro de Mendoza, and a Guaraní Indian woman, Agueda. This Spanish man and this American woman had a daughter whom her father legally recognized as his. Given my feminist "prejudices", I sympathize more with Agueda than with the one who spoke to the founder of Buenos Aires on equal terms ... In my capacity as a woman, it is both an act of justice and an honor to invite my Guaraní ancestor to this reception at the Academy.[61]

In much the same way, in *A Traveller and One of His Shadows*, she ironically wields her Amazon complex as evidence of her South American spiritual pedigree.

Most important, she describes the difficult encounter at the Hôtel des Réservoirs and her subsequent interpersonal conflict with Keyserling as epiphanous "to a new lucidity". It was this state of feeling precursive to lucidity that Ocampo had wished to articulate to Jung. Had they met again, had they met within an analytical frame, she might have spoken to Jung of her tormented alienation as the eldest daughter of an oligarchical family, consigned by Argentinian convention to a privileged life. Her failed early marriage, her subsequent love affair with Julián Martínez, her book on love in Dante, and a frustrated passion to perform on stage, all combined to help her step off that entrenched familial trajectory. She might have described to Jung how passionate relationships with accomplished men (Tagore, Ortega y Gasset, Pierre Drieu la Rochelle, Waldo Frank, and later Igor Stravinsky and Roger Callois) as well as her inspirational friendships with women (Virginia

---

61   "Women in the Academy", quoted in Meyer, *Victoria Ocampo*, 283.

Woolf, Gabriela Mistral) were leading her to leverage more and more of her wealth and status to sustain the bridging artistic device that was *Sur*.

Assessments of the significance of Ocampo's life and achievements have only increased with the passing of time. She is the subject of a novel (by María Rosa Lojo), biographies (by Doris Meyer, María Esther Vázquez, María Soledad González, María Celia Vázquez, and Ivonne Bordelois) and a literary history (Ketaki Kushari Dyson). Her correspondence with Roger Callois, Albert Camus, Jacques Maritain, Gabriela Mistral, Alfonso Reyes, Drieu la Rochelle, Rabindranath Tagore, and Virginia Woolf has been published, much of this thanks to the enterprising efforts of Juan Javier Negri, as have six volumes of her *Autobiografía* and ten volumes of her *Testimonios*. She wrote what some considered the best biography of T. E. Lawrence, published in 1947. She advanced feminist agendas but could also campaign against women's suffrage in 1944 when Perón manipulated women's right to vote to his advantage. She opposed the Perón regime and was jailed for her stance in 1953. Until the end of her life, Ocampo continued to build cultural bridges between Europe and the Americas, as director of the literary review *Sur* and the publishing company. Jorge Luis Borges wrote of Ocampo: "In a country and in an era in which women were generic, she had the distinction of being an individual, she dedicated her fortune, which was considerable, to the education of her country and of her continent ... Personally I owe a great deal to Victoria, but as an Argentine, I owe her far more."[62] Borges described her as "the woman who was everything".[63] But, even though he owed to her recommendation his post as director of the National Library of Argentina in 1955, Borges could also privately dismiss her as an affected privileged poseur.[64]

Keyserling ends his memoir with this sentence: "it is possible to experience ... in the encounter and collision with one woman, the whole history of Creation" (Part Seven). In his 20 December 1929 letter to Keyserling, Jung wrote: "Hence you should always remember, with reverence and devotion, what has been revealed to you in the human shell of V. O., so that your soul may remain inalienably with you, and your access to the earth may never be blocked. Let us hope the same for her, that besides tigers and serpents and eternal spirit there is still a human being in her who can remember with gratitude the revelation of her own spirit in you" (see Part Three). That is to say, Jung was not clinically optimistic about a couple bound in a *folie-à-deux* by anima-animus possession.[65] His own personal experiences with anima images projected onto individuals were fraught.[66] But as John Beebe writes,

---

62   Jorge Luis Borges, "VO".
63   Alberto Manguel, private conversation.
64   Casares, *Borges*, xxx.
65   For a summative explanation of anima/animus, see Verena Kast, "Anima/animus", in Papadopoulos, ed., *Handbook of Analytical Psychology*.
66   See Mark Saban, *"Two Souls Alas"*.

psychotherapeutically "to put the conscious standpoint in regular communication with the inferior function, which may be symbolized by the anima in
a man or by the animus in a woman, is to establish a *spine of integrity* within
the personality".[67] Jung emphasized the animating but necessarily conflictual
quality of that relation between ego consciousness and the inferior function
symbolized as anima-animus, a function that can be rendered conscious but
will always partake of the collective unconscious.[68] Quoting the fourteenth-
century John Gower's *Confessio amantis*, Jung characterizes such a relationship, whether inwardly to one's soul or outwardly to another person, as an
erotic mystery couched in oxymoron: "a warring peace, a sweet wound, a mild
evil."[69]

Keyserling could not endure the contradiction he encountered in Ocampo
between the impassioned letter-writer and the beautiful tongue-tied socialite
who rejected his advances, and he projected erotically onto her his own one-
sided psychic split, his archetypal need for the life principle or soul to be
found in the earth, in sensation. For her part, in the emotions sparked by
their failure to meet on equal terms, Ocampo honed more and more keenly
her voice as a public intellectual, a feminist, an Argentinian who experienced
her America as vibrantly autochthonic and also creatively connected to its
European and North American counterparts and, most importantly, as spiritually linked to its indigenous peoples as she linked herself to her Guaraní
ancestor. Keyserling did certainly value her as a significant personality of
his time, but even in his late memoirs he missed the mark by designating her
as essentially telluric. It was the Mexican poet Octavio Paz who corrected
that error by praising Ocampo as the instigator, explorer, and defender of the
psycho-cultural-geographical collective imaginary idea of "South", the creative "founder of a spiritual space" called *Sur*.[70]

---

67   Beebe, *Energies and Patterns in Psychological Type*, 186.
68   Beverley Zabriskie points to Jung's *Visions Seminars* where he says,

> The animus and anima are unconscious factors which never completely disappear –
> there would be no object, no other human being, because you perceive differences only
> through that which is a likeness to the differences in yourself … If the animus or the
> anima could disappear completely, there would probably be no reason whatever for any
> sort of psychology, for only through disturbances and certain shocks do you become
> aware of having a soul.
>
> (Jung, *Visions*, 498)

69   Jung, "The Psychology of the Transference", §523.
70

> The literatures of freedom always depend on one or another idea of freedom: *Sur* is the
> freedom of literature in the face of earthly powers. Something less than a religion and
> something more than a sect … Victoria Ocampo is a Pillar, but she is not a mythological
> creature; she has arms and hands, will and imagination, anger and generosity. And with
> all this, she has done what no one before had done in America.
>
> (Octavio Paz, quoted in Meyer, *Victoria Ocampo*, 119)

Editor's Note

In the rest of this book, the three protagonists speak for themselves through their correspondence and other writings that preceded and followed their meetings.

In Part Two, an autobiographical account of the years 1927–1929 supplemented with several newly published letters, Ocampo recalls her early enthusiasm for the works of Keyserling, both as a reader and as his publisher. She describes writing to him with passionate fervour, inviting him to lecture in Argentina, and agreeing to meet him in France. With astonishing frankness, she recounts their stormy encounter in Versailles and its aftershocks, as well as his visit to South America and her decision to end contact.

Part Three consists of an exchange of letters between Keyserling and Jung from 1929 to 1932, concerning Ocampo and the problems arising from Keyserling's book manuscript on South America. Keyserling describes Ocampo as having come to him seeking spiritual redemption and portrays himself as having failed her. He notes that despite her severing their relationship, he still experiences himself and Ocampo as fatefully attached. Jung advises Keyserling to reconfigure his portrayal of the encounter with Ocampo by taking responsibility for his "anima projections" and to re-imagine his travels to South America as an inner journey to "the continent of his inferior function".

Ocampo and Jung's correspondence from 1934 to 1943 makes up Part Four. It begins with Ocampo's first letter to Jung, praising his *Psychological Types* and *Modern Man in Search of a Soul* and asking to meet. Their letters continue briefly after their short meeting, but the two do not meet again, though Ocampo writes to Jung later, during wartime, to ask for an essay for *Sur*.

Part Five is Ocampo's memoir of her meeting with Jung, published in 1936 in *La Nación* (Buenos Aires) and later collected in her *Domingos en Hyde Park,* translated here from the Spanish. In the first half of the article, Ocampo describes the disagreement with the French magazine editor over Jung's word "introversion". In the second half she describes her short encounter with Jung.

Part Six presents Keyserling's 1939 letters to Ocampo, translated from the French. (Her side of the correspondence is not available.) The exchange begins after Ocampo's visit to him in Darmstadt. In these letters, they again wrestle with how to make sense of each other using the languages of spirituality and psychoanalysis, as well as how to respond to the deteriorating political situation in Europe. (Ocampo will later provide refuge for many European intellectuals in Argentina.)

In Part Seven, translated from his memoir, *Travel through Time* (1949), which was published posthumously in German, Keyserling explains the importance in his life of both Jung and Ocampo, and he evaluates the contemporary significance of psychoanalysis for him as a philosopher and director of a spiritual school of wisdom. He insists on characterizing Ocampo as a telluric "*gana*-woman" and also considers her as suffering from a medieval psychic splitting that he could not heal.

Part Eight presents Ocampo's *A Traveller and One of his Shadows* (1951), translated from the Spanish, in which she firmly refutes Keyserling's portrayal of Argentina in his *South American Meditations* and rebuts his version of her as telluric.

By including her correspondence and her unexpurgated memoir, this book presents Ocampo's defence of South America and of women in historical context. It also supplies the contexts that informed her only meeting with Jung in 1934 and her championing of analytical psychology, including the translation into Spanish and publication in South America of *Psychological Types*.

Part Two

Ocampo and Keyserling, 1927–1929

In her autobiography, Ocampo excerpts and provides context for some of her letters from the years 1927 to 1929, when she read and published Keyserling, invited him to lecture in Argentina, met him in Versailles, and hosted him on his trip to South America. When she decided to end contact with him, she had Keyserling return her letters and she destroyed most of them. However, she transcribes into her autobiography a few extant letters, and with extraordinary candour her older self reassesses the younger's infatuated tone. The following selections from her autobiography are supplemented with additional letters from the Keyserling Archives at Universitäts- und Landesbibliothek Darmstadt, published here for the first time.

Upon his return, Ortega renewed his friendship with me as a comrade and started to call me again by *tu* ...[1] He[2] judged that I put Keyserling on far too high a pedestal, even though he found traces of genius in *The Travel Diary*. Without underestimating the talent (a word that made K. indignant) of the great Baltic writer (I refer now to his size), Ortega would warn me about his defects. I was guilty of not believing his judgment. I was enthused by reading the *Travel Diary* and *World in the Making*. I couldn't see in those books more than what I needed to find in them. I wasn't reading Keyserling, I was reading myself in those books. Even before the arrival of Ortega in January of 1928, I had reached out to him to satisfy certain of Keyserling's demands. But I had to go through María[3] because I hadn't written to Ortega since our "break" in 1916. So I wrote to María in December 1927:

---

1 Selections from Ocampo, *Autobiografía, 4: Viraje*, 123–158. Translated from the Spanish by Alberto Manguel.
2 José Ortega y Gasset (1883–1955), a Spanish philosopher. Ocampo befriended him during his first visit to Argentina in 1916. He returned in 1928. At the start of the Spanish civil war he lived in exile in Paris and he spent time in the Netherlands and Lisbon, where he became a resident between 1942 and 1946. He founded the Spanish-language magazine *Revista de Occidente.*
3 María de Maetzu (1882–1948), a Basque Spanish writer and founder of the Residencia de Señoritas in Madrid to promote women in higher education and the Lyceum Club to support

DOI: 10.4324/9781003266099-2

You know that the works of Keyserling interest me very much. I'm told that you are not enthusiastic about them. I believe they accuse him of not being "serious" or something like that. Well, I adore his *Travel Diary* and his *World in the Making*. I am in correspondence with him. Confidentially, he talks to me about his latest book *Das Spektrum Europas* that should come out in German on January 10th. He will send me the proofs. We have spoken (in writing, I mean) of a possible and immediate translation into Spanish. I've told him that I would willingly undertake explaining to my Spanish friends the hurry we are in and the wish to entrust the new book to a perfect translator. He has given me full powers to decide everything as I please. I sent Ortega a telegram. He must have been surprised. Beg him to pardon me. I was in a hurry to put this matter in the hands of Morente,[4] in my opinion the only translator possible. Keyserling wishes that this translation would be one of the seven marvels (Ortega would be a dear if he checked it a little). I'm sending you the contract. I'm putting it in the same envelope. Urgoiti[5] has seen it and finds it reasonable. If there are difficulties of cash, I'm willing to advance, to lend the publisher, the 4500 pesetas that Kapmann is demanding (or half that amount). It would be reimbursed to me as the book sells.

I have telegraphed Darmstadt to beg K. that he send directly to Ortega *Das Spektrum Europas*, therefore I suppose that he will know what this is about when my letter reaches you.

That is to say, in short, what we need to know is: can Morente be in charge of the translation? It's necessary that it be Morente, no matter what the cost. When can he start to work? If he has other translations on the go, couldn't he do K's first? If it means compensating Morente or paying him more (this between Ortega, you, and me) count me in. And since I know that Morente is not a millionaire and has a number of children, he will welcome this. Would Espasa-Calpe accept the contract? I think the book will be successful but I insist on *advancing the 4500 pesetas and accept all risks and perils*.

It seems *Das Spektrum* is full of humour and is the most untranslatable thing in the world. Ask Ortega to forgive me for my telegram. He must have thought: what impertinence! Tell him that I owe him thanks for *everything* and that my debt towards him would increase if he deigns to busy himself with *Das Spektrum*.

professional women in the exchange of ideas and protection of rights. After 1926 she lived in exile from Spain and taught in many places, including the University of Buenos Aires.

4   Manuel García Morente (1888–1942), a Spanish philosopher, translator, and university professor.

5   The publishing house Espasa-Calpe was created in 1925 by the union of Editorial Calpe founded by Nicolás María de Urgoiti in 1918 and Editorial Espaca founded by José and Pau Espasa Arguera in 1860.

This letter is one of the countless letters that I wrote to Maria about Keyserling, his translations, his demands, up to the day I broke off with him. I always took his side and defended his interests and his point of view.

I also said to Maria:

> Claudel writes, I don't know where, in French, 'Every artist comes into the world to say only one tiny thing, and this is what must be found, gathering everything else around it.' I realize more and more that I have never written anything except this one tiny thing. And that I don't write to make literature but in order not to drown. No doubt it's as old as the hills but because I have had to discover it in myself, having had to re-cognize it, I have the feeling of having invented it, of creating it as I speak. This tiny thing is in me like a splinter and as long as I haven't pulled it out of my flesh, out of my soul, by explaining it, I will bear it with an ineffable pain.

I thought that Keyserling's books would help me in this undertaking. I started to swear by them.

Looking for what had enthused me in 1927, I pick up now the *Travel Diary*. I find there again pages that I have never turned my back on and whose insight is indubitable. There was much there to fire up the person I was 25 years ago. The person I am now finds in them subject for reflection. The strange thing about the human condition is that it mingles in a person so much intuition and so much impermeability (which he showed in Versailles), so much refinement and so much vulgarity, so much knowledge and so much ignorance when faced with the woman I was then. And what troubles me, as much in him as in me, even more now, is the ability to grasp a spiritual truth of the highest importance, together with the incapability of enjoying it fully, of living it out. That is to say, to understand a spiritual truth of which one is not yet worthy, since one is below its *realization*. As if there existed in us levels of maturity different in each zone of our being and that the manifest and dazzling maturity of one of these zones does not necessitate that of the others. One explains to oneself that the branches of a tree that are more exposed to the sun bear fruit that mature more quickly; that one side of a peach (the one that tends its cheek towards the warmth) becomes ripe before the rest. But what cruel star matures our intuitions, transforms them into thoughts before it makes us capable of living them out? And is this cruelty indispensable for our health?

When I read *Travel Diary* in 1927, I believed that this stage of imperfection, well known to me, must have been overcome by the unknown man from Darmstadt. The ideal of a *personal* perfection, *different from that of professional efficiency*, to which Keyserling returned insistently, seemed to me a central problem. To which should we grant priority, to *being* or to *doing*?

To attempt to accomplish perfection in oneself, or to place it in an object, a work of art outside oneself? The artist can content himself with this perfection placed in the object he is making. But the saint (or whoever, for whom without being a saint, saintliness exists and elicits an attraction) cannot disperse the dreamt-of perfection, cannot give it, cannot render it sensitive to the heart, efficacious, without living it inside himself as much as in his works.

The response of Keyserling to this problem was:

> Unfortunately it is not true that all forms of perfection lie in the same direction; the perfection of a work of art demands conditions different from those required by the perfection of personal existence. Now, whenever the choice has to be made between a mediocre realization of one's self in life and an important one in one's work, the latter is always to be preferred. A profound recognition discovered and expressed by an imperfect being may benefit the whole of humanity. To place human perfection in this sense above everything else, as is usually the case, is a proof not only of the most primitive form of egotism but also of a fundamental misconception.... There is no difference in the sight of God between the man who strives after personal perfection and the man who lives for his work or for his fellows or for his children. Everyone aims at something beyond the individual.[6]

Martha and Mary! This wish to go beyond what is individual, from Francesca to Beatrice, was starting to obsess me more and more. I could not conceive of another salvation. And yet, I was so terribly tied to the more individualistic forms of life!

Underlined with thick pencil I find on almost every page of the *Travel Diary* sentences in which my preoccupations at the time found their echo.

> In what way ought one to love one's neighbour more than oneself and sacrifice one's ego? Not in the sense that other lives are more valuable than one's own, but in so far as the highest ideal is, like the sun, only to give and not to take. In how far is inferiority to be preferred to greatness? Not in so far as the lowly are more pleasing in the sight of God, but because the latter feel induced to cling to appearances in a lesser degree, and so on. The true, that is to say the objectively correct, significance of Christian teaching has hardly been understood by Christianity up to the present. Christianity has, therefore, given us, apart from treasures of good, also a rich harvest of evil.[7]

---

6 Keyserling, *Travel Diary*, Vol. 1, 32.
7 Keyserling, *Travel Diary*, Vol. 1, 65–66.

Every time I read the book, which became in 1927 my favourite one, I was plunged into endless interior discussion that I would have wished to continue with its author. But when I had the opportunity to speak with him, I understood that he did not live according to the truths that his mind so easily constructed. And that he was wise only in print. I refer, for instance, to this passage:

> But only a sage can permit himself the luxury of looking down upon prejudice. He who throws away his prejudices prematurely does not gain his freedom, but rather bars his way to it. Our own times illustrate this truth with terrible clarity. Modern humanity has destroyed the form whose development made our ancestors profound, and since it has not invented any new one to replace the old, men are becoming more superficial and more evil from year to year.[8]

I am of the same opinion. But when I met Keyserling, he did not show respect for what, *in his eyes*, were prejudices *for me*. And if there is something worse than challenging prejudices prematurely, it is to pretend to rip them out by force from those who hold them when they have not matured enough to be cast far away. It is all well and good that K. should have tried to attempt this with me, when he took "my revulsion" which he inspired in me physically, as a prejudice. I was far from imagining that he could behave in a manner so different from that he manifested in his books.

"Non-consideration of the feelings of others is better than consideration of them so far as the former are foolish ... And this is not due to lack of feeling, but because we begin to grow beyond the stage of being conditioned by emotional circumstances, because we are ceasing to identify ourselves with our empirical nature, and only recognize as absolutely valuable not what satisfies a given individual, but that which helps him beyond himself irrespective of the pain it costs him."[9] I would have proof that at least in this, Keyserling behaved according to his theories. He didn't take into consideration the "feelings" of others. And that this lack of concern that can be achieved when applied to one's own "feelings" risks becoming catastrophic when applied to the feelings of a fellow human being. At times dazzled, at times reticent, I would read the *Travel Diary* and when I would reach considerations such as "There are no such things as good habits. It is not true that any routine of life produces freedom of spirit. A saint by routine is no saint at all",[10] I would feel stunned, tremulous, the ear alert, like a hound sniffing a trail. These affirmations did not seem to me irrefutable. As far as the saint is concerned, yes, up to a certain point. Cocteau also thought this but in other

8   Keyserling, *Travel Diary*, Vol. 1, 115.
9   Keyserling, *Travel Diary*, Vol. 1, 166.
10 Keyserling, *Travel Diary*, Vol. 1, 194.

terms: the speed of a bolting horse does not matter. The saint is the exception, and sainthood cannot depend on a *habit*, far less on *bolting*. But is that so for the rest of us mortals? Evidently, no more-or-less comfortable life routine can lead to spiritual freedom. Rather, it can stifle it. However, there are bad and good habits, and it would be absurd to deny that man is a creature of habit. In any case, his body is, quite clearly. To tear from a body an acquired habit is almost always painful, even when it concerns very simple things. If to be in full health one imposes upon oneself a diet to lose weight, the first week is torturous. It is necessary to acquire a new habit before being able to endure being deprived of the food (in quality and in quantity) which one has abused. One acquires the habit to go to bed early or late, and so on. Tobacco, alcohol, drugs: all habits. It is useless to insist on the importance of good or bad habits acquired by babies, dogs, cats ...

Might there not be good and bad mental habits? It's true that virtue, unlike vice, cannot become a habit, because virtue is always an ascent, not a sliding down a slope, a descent, an obedience due to the laws of gravity.

To what degree was my life on the edge of routine? The *Travel Diary* forced me continually to ask burning questions, to seek a foundation for this or the other belief, to affirm myself in this or another me. Why that book in particular? Perhaps a matter of circumstance, occasion, chance. It had fallen into my hands at the right psychological moment, to coin a phrase, at a crucial moment in my life. The same would happen later with *Seven Pillars of Wisdom* (T. E. Lawrence), as had happened before with *The Divine Comedy [Dante]*. I don't know if the order of these readings could have been modified. I doubt it. They were stages that I had to cross.

My correspondence with Keyserling began with the invitation I made him to give a series of lectures in South America. About that, I have nothing to add to what I wrote in *El viajero y una de sus sombras* [*The Traveller and One of His Shadows*]. When, after our quarrel, I sent him back his letters and he returned mine, most of the ones that came back from Darmstadt I burnt in horror. I kept some as reference points, to recognize myself in that *selva selvaggia* [dark wood] of my life, if ever I felt like casting a glance at the past, if I ended up "establishing myself in my memories as in a great library".

These letters reached their peak of exaltation *before* Versailles. Rereading them, I was not surprised that K. had been mistaken from the very start. I had not hidden from him any of the circumstances in which I found myself: separated from a husband I detested, joined to a lover by marital ties. (He believed that I could behave with J.[11] as he with G.[12]) But in spite of the School of Wisdom and his intuitions of genius, Keyserling lacked the imagination he believed he possessed, or did not have more imagination than in the sense of 'wishfull

11   Julián Martínez, with whom Ocampo had a long, intense relationship.
12   Maria Gödela Gräfin von Bismarck-Schönhausen (1896–1981), the wife of Hermann von Keyserling.

thinking' [*sic*, in English]". For the rest, the turn that the events at Versailles took were suspended when faced with a banality: Cleopatra's nose. If mine, too short, had repulsed the count (a descendent of aristocrats accustomed to paying for their fantasies and having themselves rocked to sleep by Bach or tutored by Kant) or if the count's *plumage* had seemed to me as handsome as his *branches*, the face of the world (of our world, ours) would have been changed without the shadow of a doubt. In any case, our behaviour, that of one with the other, would have varied. I would consider myself a great hypocrite if I did not consider this hypothesis. A curious thing: the look, or rather the real *presence* (in the mystical sense of the term) of Keyserling revealed to me an important facet of his personality that I had dodged in his books and his letters (where I read only what I enjoyed reading in them) and faced with which I felt an undefeatable distancing. I called his feature an *interpretative elephantitis*.

My correspondence with Keyserling made my wish to return to Europe even keener, a wish that my passion for J. had placed on a back burner for many years. Europe had tormented me dully for a long time. Ah, to see my Paris, my London, my Rome once more! Those cities of my childhood and of my immature youth! I spoke with J. I told him that I wasn't resigned to leave on my own and yet the urge of that trip burned inside me. J. promised me that he would take a long enough vacation to be able to get away.

Even though our relationship had changed *de mode*, and the amorous passion had turned into tenderness and the exultation to which my books and music led me (and those with whom I shared it and spoke about it) absorbed me to the point of making me often forget (the rest: that form of love that is making love, simply, in the throes of a great passion), the notion of leaving J. did not enter either my head or my heart. The fact of leaving alone, before him, caused in me a sort of panic that I could only overcome with difficulty, with a great effort of will. During the month that preceded my departure, I faced with terror this tearing away. And indeed it was a tearing away that led me to a definitive crossroads in our life. It was then that we started to separate in order to follow each his or her own journey (the great one, the one that leads to death).

I entrusted a friend with renting an apartment for me in Paris so that J. could also live there. She found what I needed at 40 rue d'Artois.

Here are some of the letters addressed to Prinz Christiansweg 4, Darmstadt during the period from 1927 to 1928, just before boarding the *Cap Arcona*. I repeat that it is not surprising that the Baltic count should have imagined (a less passionate man might have fallen into the same error) that my passion for his work would easily embrace his entire person. However, these high-school-student letters, feverish with enthusiasm, signed with my soul, my intelligence, and *above all my imagination*, were not signed with my body. And my body has always had a say in regards to love and even the *right to veto*. On this occasion it had not pronounced itself, it had not had the chance to do so, and had not been consulted in regard to what was happening in the other realms of my person. This is what Keyserling would later call my *medieval split personality*. However, the reading of his *Travel Diary* had produced in me exactly the same effect that *La genesis del siglo XIX* [*The Foundations of the Nineteenth Century*] by Houston Chamberlain[13] had produced in him. He had spoken of that book and of its author with the same passion:

> Suddenly it became clear to me that if I had been able to meet the man who had written that book, I would have immediately discovered what was the goal of my life … in truth I went to finish my studies in Vienna in order to meet Chamberlain,

wrote Keyserling.[14]

Was I condemned, by the simple fact of being a woman, to not being able to feel what Keyserling felt without it being labelled (if the body did not follow the soul at an equal pace) medieval split personality and schizophrenia? Come on, Mr Philosopher!

Buenos Aires, July 25, 1927

To Count Hermann Keyserling, Darmstadt

Sir:

On the last page of *The Peter's Pence of Literature*,[15] I read a note you have written; "I don't have time for personal correspondence". Neither must you have time to read the letters addressed to you. Therefore, I'll try to be brief, but it will be extremely hard for me because I would wish to speak with you all the time (all the time you don't have).

The Travel Diary and *World in the Making* absorb me in such a tyrannical way that it would be difficult for me to be silent about what they mean to me. For my own satisfaction I will at least tell you that the discovery of your books has given me a joy of such quality and intensity that I have spent several days without resigning myself to relinquish them, not even in the material sense. When I wasn't able to read them, their material presence was necessary to me. I felt the need to have

---

13   Houston Stewart Chamberlain (1855–1927) was a British-born philosopher who wrote political philosophy that advocated anti-Semitism and the racial superiority of "Aryan" culture, influencing Hitler's National Socialist movement. Chamberlain naturalized as a German citizen and married Richard Wagner's daughter, Eva von Bülow.
14   See Keyserling, "Houston Stewart Chamberlain", *Riese durch die Zeit*.
15   Keyserling, "The Peter's Pence of Literature", *The World in the Making*, 92–103.

them at hand. I took them with me to the table. I went for walks with a volume under my arm.

At the time of this discovery I was launched on a project that was headed in a bad direction, and this worried me very much.[16] But your thinking was such an illumination for me, such a warmth, that my worries literally disappeared. In the morning, before being completely awake, I had the feeling of a vague well-being such as one feels when, on the previous evening, a happy event has filled one. And when, awake, I tried to give a name to that contentment, I would find it in one of your pages.

A certain music especially close to our sensibility seems to follow with surprising fidelity the outline of our joys and sorrows, so much so that when we hear it express with marvellous precision that which is inexpressible in our dark mood we exclaim: "I needed that! This frees me and suffices!" Your books bring me an analogous feeling of liberation and fulfilment. One finds in them certain passages in which your thoughts have such a solid base that it causes in us the blossoming of what we carry but cannot yet put into words. But I promised to be brief.

As regards your lectures in Argentina (1929), the president of the German Argentinian Cultural Institute, Ricardo Seeber, together with the Sociedad Amigos del Arte, of which I am presently the current Vice-President, will write you a letter that you will find, I hope, perfectly clear.

You would not have to pay your travel expenses, nor those of your lodging. If you and Countess Keyserling would accept to come to my house and stay there during your time in Buenos Aires, it would make me very happy. *My house is at your disposal.* I trust that you would not feel uncomfortable because everything in my house that might disturb you in the slightest (myself included) is susceptible to disappearing.

As far as a fee is concerned, whatever your answer might be to this project (it would be seven or eight lectures) I beg you not to doubt that I will defend before anything else your interests.

Thank you for sending me your *World in the Making*. I had read the Spanish translation published in *La Revista de Occidente*, and it was through that translation that I got to know you. But it does not include *My Life and My Work* that I never stop reading. Thank you for

---

16   Ernest Alexandre Ansermet (1883–1927), a Swiss conductor, was to give concerts at the Asociación del Profesorado Orquestal. He conducted in Buenos Aires often from 1924 to 1927. In 1925 Victoria Ocampo performed as a reader in his production of Honegger's oratorio *Le Roi David*.

having had the thought of giving it to me. That book is for me doubly precious.

I must apologize for having sent to Darmstadt a trifle on *The Divine Comedy*. It was written, as everything I write, *"in order to learn"*; but it was sent to you *in order to write the dedication*.

Thank you and until soon, I hope.

V.O.

Buenos Aires, November 10, 1927, 11:00 p.m.

Three letters.

It's evident that if I had not lived through and suffered certain things (or to be more precise, the lack of certain things) with a certain sharpness, I would not feel in this moment the joy of having three of your letters. This joy is all my exchanged pain that disappears around you.

The sun of your letters! Let me fall asleep in them, rest in them. And I will later bloom through them. Ah! How good it makes me feel and how sweet it is. I love them so much! I would not know how to speak to you reasonably tonight. I have a headache, but at least I want to write to you because tomorrow there is maritime post. And also, I'm *so close* to you in this moment that your *material* presence, if it were suddenly possible, would do no more than distract me from your profound existence within myself.

I think I'm so full of what you are that the slightest movement would make me exhale a delicious scent. And if you were here I would not lift my eyes to your eyes for fear of losing that *you* that is beneath my jealously closed eyelids.

"I am there", you write to me. It is you who is saying that to me. Isn't it beautiful, isn't it miraculous that these three words resting on my heart would comfort me more than a hand stretched out in the midst of a great danger? When I'm not able to resist the need to send you a telegraphic SOS, "I am there" will be your answer. That's what it's about, being there, *somewhere in the world*.

I don't really know how to address you. "Dear friend" repulses me as much as "Dear sir". And it's also false because it's just a fragment of the truth.

I don't know if you had time to read the idiotic article by C. that I sent you. This individual (who makes vain attempts to seem spiritual) says somewhere, alluding to my admiration for you: "her Keyserling". Perhaps that is the first time that a possessive adjective has been placed correctly by this poor devil. Indeed, it's of *my* Keyserling that I speak, and it is to *my* Keyserling that I am writing now. In truth, this is the only name that I can, in all sincerity, give you. *I don't know Keyserling.* I only know *my* Keyserling. Except, would you wish, wish for that name?

Don't allow yourself to be disheartened by that *my*. *My* means simply the sum total of everything that is yours, of everything that, inside me, bears your name ... even if it is, in essence, myself.

V.

Monday, November 14, 1927[17]

Yesterday I spent the day in the *estancia* of one of my cousins, one hour from Buenos Aires. I thought of you. That is to say, I thought that you would like this immensity and solitude, these fields of flax in bloom that make a blue ocean undulating in the wind! By saying I thought of you, I mean I thought that too. Because I think of you constantly. Yes, constantly. I think about it too much in this sense: the things you're not in, the things I imagine I can't get you into with me, I'm not there anymore, I don't enter there anymore myself. For it to be possible for me to be really interested in any work, there must be you at the end of this work. Take an example: a month and a half ago a great friend of mine died in Paris after a terrible illness. This friend is the Argentinian poet and novelist Ricardo Güiraldes.[18] Argentina loses in him not only an authentic talent but an authentic man and an authentic Argentinian. He was young (41 years old), belonged to one of the oldest families in the country and when he was not wandering around the world, he lived at La Porteña, his estancia, as a gaucho. No one before him, no one like him has so loved and translated the meaning, the emotion of our wild and fertile pampas, of its inhabitants the gauchos (on the eve of their disappearing) and of the harsh and masculine life led there. Much has been said about Ricardo in the newspapers. The works will

---

17   Letter from the Keyserling Archives, Universitäts- und Landesbibliothek Darmstadt, KEYS-169-0184-0190. Translated from the French by Craig Stephenson.

18   (1886–1927), most famous for his 1926 novel, translated as *Don Segundo Sombra: Shadows on the Pampas.* Translated by Harriet de Onís New York: Signet Classic, 1966.

appear in the editions of *La Nouvelle Revue Française*, translated by Valéry Larbaud, Miomandre, etc. But I know that we haven't said, that we haven't explained what Ricardo preferred in his work, for the simple reason that we don't know. And I also know that Ricardo would have been happy for me to talk about it.

For a month I have been trying to detach my mind from you to fix it on this duty. Impossible.

And yet Ricardo's death is deeply heart-breaking to me. In a way, we got along admirably. We were both of the same race, of the same country, of the same heart. We had lived from the same horizons, from the same childhood, from the same youth. We had for each other one of those unalterable friendships that even differences (and there were some between us) cannot destroy.

Ricardo had a fervent, beautiful soul, the likes of which I have rarely encountered. I would have liked to let you know it; through it you would have come into contact with our land, with all that it has that is harsh, generous, vast, primitive! With all the *cortesías de su corazón* [courtesies of the heart] too. It was the Lord of Pampas that you would have known in him. *El gran Señor de la Pampa.* Although you do not like verse, I will transcribe for you one in which Ricardo, without thinking about it, has drawn his own portrait. It's called *"El hombre que pasó"* …

Tomorrow, on the steamer *Avila* "what was" Ricardo Güiraldes arrives. And going in front of him it seems that I will see again his broad smile which looked mocking and which was only tender! It seems to me that I am going to hear him say to me, as he would have told me if he had been alive, *"¡No has tenido tiempo para mí! ¿En qué andas?* [You've had no time for me. What have you been up to?] And I will repeat to him: *"Te esperaba para hablarte de Keyserling"* [I've been waiting for you, to talk with you about Keyserling].

When I think that I'm never going to be able to talk to him about you and that you aren't going to know this beautiful side of our country that he represented, I tell myself that it's really too sad and too absurd. Among the books I intend to send you there will be one of his, *Don Sombra*. It is the life of the gauchos in the middle of the Pampas, told by the man best placed and gifted to feel it. It's a story, hardly a novel. Only I'm afraid it's extremely difficult to understand, because of so many *argentinismos*. Spaniards do not understand most of these expressions. The book will be translated into French (but I'm afraid that it is essentially untranslatable). Perhaps it will be better for you to wait for the translation.

To come back to what I said to you at the beginning of this letter: the pull, the attraction that your mind exerts on mine is so strong that it tears me away from everything that is not you. I am like a swimmer caught in a whirlpool and who feels physically unable to fight against the pull of the water. Your mind absorbs mine. I have fallen deep inside you.

Don Segundo Sombra is a gaucho who was, so to speak, photographed alive – whose soul was photographed – by Ricardo. Don Segundo Sombra is an old gaucho from the Güiraldes estancia. The naive admiration that Ricardo as a child felt makes him say, about Don Segundo and his own state of mind as a little boy, amazed by the strength, the address, the courage, the roughness of the gaucho: *"[Pensé en don Segundo Sombra que en su paso por mi pueblo] me llevó tras él, como podía haber llevado un abrojo de los cercos prendido en el chiripá"*; that is to say, "He took me with him as he might have taken a thistle hanging from his *chiripá*" (the chiripá are the wide trousers of the men of our countryside). This is how Don Segundo Sombra won Ricardo's heart. Bearing witness to this, a year before his death Ricardo proved it to us in a book full of beauty.

Don Segundo is also Ricardo himself.

V.

November 18, 1927[19] 1 a.m.

I went to *La Nación* this afternoon. Unfortunately, Jorge Mitre[20] – who can do and undo everything in this and who I know how to push in the direction I want – is in Europe at the moment. I wanted to find out what prices we pay, etc., before talking to Luis Mitre. A friend of mine told me about it and took it upon himself to announce to L.M. that I will be going to see him on Monday (I am leaving tomorrow for Mar del Plata and returning on Sunday).

My dear Keyserling, I will take the liberty of acting in this matter, as my instinct and my desire to serve you, in the best sense of the word, will dictate. The friend I am speaking about told me that they will probably offer 250 pesos for each item. I seem to remember that we paid 300 pesos for Tagore's pieces (and Jorge Mitre assured me, at that time, that we had never paid better for such a collaboration). If Jorge Mitre were

---

19   Letter from the Keyserling Archives, Universitäts- und Landesbibliothek Darmstadt, KEYS-169-0191-0193. Translated from the French by Craig Stephenson.

20   Bartolomé Mitre (1821-1906) was the first constitutional president of Argentina and founder of the newspaper *la Nación*. His grandson Jorge Mitre (1884–1966) directed *la Nación* from 1912 to 1932. Luis Mitre (1864–1950) also worked there.

around, I'd get that for you too (hopefully he'll be back soon). But I'm afraid I'll have less control over who I talk to on Monday. I will try to seduce them … but I doubt that they will be sensitive to the charms of my eloquence! How about 250 or 300 pesos per item?

Another story: *La Nación* and *La Prensa* (our two major newspapers) only publish and accept unpublished articles and are very strict about this. I'm sure we shouldn't run the risk of getting into trouble about this. Above all, you must not expose yourself to this. The friend I spoke to asked me about it, and so far I haven't answered anything; I acted stupid. But when Luis Mitre asks me this question and imposes this condition on me, I will have to answer! I therefore believe that it is better that I consult you before acting. *La Nación* would quickly find out that your articles have already appeared elsewhere, and I don't want this kind of fuss with this kind of people.

When I have spoken with Mitre on Monday, I will tell you the result of the conversation and you will tell me what you think. The newspapers here aren't very generous. I got into trouble with them when Tagore was here with me.

See you later, my dear beast, and please bear no grudge for my acting for you as I would act for myself.

I'm sad – a little – tonight. It seems to me that you will never understand what you are to me! What I am for you is so different!

V.

---

8 a.m.

It is absolutely certain that I have lost the taste for sleep.

Buenos Aires, July 10, 1928[21]

The day before yesterday Moner[22] came to visit, and we spent the afternoon speaking of you. I discovered: first, that he is less intelligent than sensitive (as far as your work is concerned); second, that he understands you but that he is very unskilled as regards translations (he ignores that enterprise, as he himself admits).

But I'm delighted because as well as he could, he translated for me *Wiedergeburt* [*Rebirth* (1927)] and *Philosophie Als Kunst* [*Philosophy as*

---

21   From Ocampo, *Autobiografía, 4: Viraje*. Translated from the Spanish by Alberto Manguel.
22   Dr. Gabriel Moner.

Art (1920)]. And he's capable, like I am, of speaking about you for a whole day. We both adore you, it's as simple as that.

We spoke as well of your vision, so precise, of Spain. *Europe* is a truly extraordinary book. I'm impatient for it to appear in Spanish. It will be necessary for you to ask Urgoiti to send a telegram to Madrid to get precise information. I think that it's best for me to abstain from doing it myself. People feel that I love you too much, they believe that I exaggerate. That bothers them.

Ortega? He will leave by ship in the first days of August. I know nothing more for the time being.

In the preface to *Wiedergeburt* (according to Moner), you write, approximately (is this correct?): "In *Symbolic Figures*, I rooted my conviction that no one can do other than *incite*, that there are no ethics superior to fecundity and also that all progress takes place only through the influence of *Logos Spermatikos*, the creator in its masculine form. Therefore this book is written in such a way that, before giving some definitive wisdom, it incites them as new in the reader, thereby justifying the justness of the meaning of the title *Renaissance*: that which I believed I knew and was cognizant of for myself has to sprout from the reader as his own personal discovery."

God! How I wish I could speak with you!

Your preface to the French edition of the *Diary* will appear this Sunday in *La Nación*. All the copies that Calpe had received (of the Spanish edition, of course) have been already sold. Thank you for the one you sent me. It gives me great pleasure that it has passed through your hands.

V.

Buenos Aires, July 18, 1928[23]

Yesterday we spoke with a friend about our future president, Hipólito Irigoyen.[24] I remembered and repeated those words of his about Primo de Rivera: "Primo de Rivera embodies the complementarity to the eternal Don Quixote. And who is that? The no-less eternal Sancho Panza. In a chauffeur age, the latter, as the authentic ruler, is absolutely in the right place. Thus Primo de Rivera, too, belongs to eternal Spain". I believe that Irigoyen "belongs to Argentina" *quoique par d'autres côtés*.

---

23   Letter from the Keyserling Archives, Universitäts- und Landesbibliothek Darmstadt, KEYS-169-0196-0200. Translated from the Spanish by Craig Stephenson.
24   Hipólito Yrigoyen (1852–1933), president of Argentina 1916–1922 and 1928–1930.

I don't know if you know that Irigoyen is the idol of the people. This gentleman is the grandson of Turco Alem, the friend of our tyrant Rosas; nephew of Leandro Alem, founder of the radical party and friend of my grandfather. Leandro, who died years ago, was a man of a different stature, they say, than our current Hipólito. This, as his surname indicates, is Basque as well as Turkish. These two mixed nationalities on Argentine soil have produced a man who confounds some, infuriates many, and ignites an extraordinary fanaticism in the people. What can be called amongst us the aristocracy hates him.

I don't know if I've already told you what gestures make him so immensely popular: he gives away his presidential salary to the poor (publicly); he lives badly, in a dirty, ugly, and poor neighbourhood; he dresses poorly; his henchman is a shoemaker; he promises a lot and continually (he delivers little); he surrounds himself with a certain mystery and speaks like a fifth-rate prophet; he is illiterate and corny. Some good conditions he will have, I imagine! But since I only know him from giving him a hand, by the way, and since all the people I meet can't stomach him, I really don't know what virtues he hides.

However, a friend of mine, a man of letters, Argentina's minister in France during the war, has become an Irigoyenist for a few years (causing a great scandal) and it is precisely this friend, Enrique Larreta,[25] with whom I was speaking yesterday. We both agreed that you should know Irigoyen. And we agreed that he would arrange an interview ... Because you will know that it is not easy to reach Irigoyen when he is not just a simple bum! Having money, name or intellect are not exactly good recommendations for him. I believe that this "myth" of ours will be of interest to you, if only as "weird".

I received a letter from a great friend of mine, a Swiss, who finds everything you say in the *Spektrum [Das Spektrum Europas]* admirable. What refers to his own country seems very accurate. But he tells me that the majority of the Swiss do not agree with him nor with you. *Et pour cause* [With good reason]!

In which month do you plan to embark for America? May? Peru, Uruguay, and Chile are countries that can be counted on in advance (I am already being diligent in this regard). Brazil will not be difficult. But when would you go to Brazil? June, July, and August are the months in which you would not suffocate in that magnificent country of macaques. In your telegram you do not mention Uruguay. However, in Montevideo you could easily give some conferences (well paid). Anyway, I'll handle it.

25   (1875–1961) Argentine writer and diplomat.

I have looked up Zermatt. I can't find it. Where is it? (I know it's in Switzerland). I hope the letters will not be lost. It is true that Switzerland is a handkerchief.

I think of you literally from morning to night.

This concern already has something of a fixed idea, of mania, of madness and I am looking forward to meeting, so that I can think of something else! I say this half as a joke, half seriously. You don't think of me, in this distant corner of America, living off your letters, your books; waiting to learn your wishes; waiting to learn your likes or dislikes; with no other aspiration than to serve and please. Don't you think, I repeat, that this is already past "dark brown" (as we would say here)? This is the work of enchantment, no more, no less ...

I know you deserve all this and much more, but sometimes it makes me want to buck like a wild colt and not be worried about you anymore because you deserve it, but because of something else, I don't know what it is either.

Buenos Aires. August 23 1928[26] 11 p.m.

I spoke with L.M. (Louis Mitre, *La Nación*) today. As I expected, it was impossible for me to corrupt him. But J.M. [Jorge Mitre] will be back in April. And I'm going to make him do – pretty much – what I want.

So, here it is: your articles will be paid 250 (L.M. said 200, but understand that it will be more if you insist, that is, if I insist). You should plan to send the things you write for newspapers or reviews in North America or Germany, etc., so that *La Nación* has time to publish them a few days after they appear in North America, Germany, etc. That is to say before these newspapers or magazines have time to arrive in Argentina. We will write under your articles – as we do for Ortega, etc. "*Especial para La Nación*".

If you become a contributor to *La Nación*, they will advertise you a lot – especially when you come. I repeat, when Jorge Mitre returns from Europe I hope to be able to put things better. For the moment, is it okay? I told L. Mitre that I was going to consult you, that I could not commit myself to anything – or commit you to anything – before explaining things to you. What do I do with the items you sent me?

26   Letter from the Keyserling Archives, Universitäts- und Landesbibliothek Darmstadt, KEYS-169-0208-0210. Translated from the Spanish by Craig Stephenson.

L. Mitre told me and recommended (the idiot!) that he only wanted new things written in the present moment.

I await your orders. I will do what you want.

So, it is understood that if you write for North America or Europe you can send me those same articles for *La Nación*. Does this seem acceptable to you? I did what I could. Given the absence of my friend J.M. and the stupidity of people, if I disappoint you, if you expected more and better from me, excuse me. Of course, I'm never happy with what I can offer you!

Do not forget to send me a dispatch when you have received the letters that leave tomorrow on *Cape Polonio* for Hamburg. I will be on hot coals. Let me at least know, by a word, that you don't blame me, that I don't bother you with my endless letters, or that I do bother you and that you blame me.

Good evening, "my" dear Keyserling, and sorry for not having the land in my hands to offer it to you.

V.

Buenos Aires, October 22, 1928[27]

I'm waiting impatiently for your letter, without expecting too much that it will arrive ... so soon (so slowly!). Since we corresponded, I open *La Nación* every morning on the page titled *Sea Travel*. *"Ships from overseas"*. I know by heart the arrival and departure dates of the fastest *postal ships*. The names of the steamers that I believe will bring me your news fill me with emotion like the name of the street of the house of someone you love.

How lucky that you exist! I bless the Lord (just in case) for that. I look in vain around me for someone to whom to communicate the kind of happiness I feel knowing that you exist. I feel assured that all that is left for me to do is to address God in order to speak with the feeling of being *exactly* understood. I need to believe in God to thank Him.

When your letters arrive, I always have the feeling that a moment before I was drowning, and I understand you all the better because of the immediate relief that this oxygen grants me. I read you with my lungs.

You ask me to send you frequent telegrams (have I read correctly?). I can't believe that it's because my telegrams please you. I suppose it's because in my ignorance I must have transmitted to you, assisted by

---

27   From Ocampo, *Autobiografía, 4: Viraje*. Translated from the Spanish by Alberto Manguel.

I don't know what semaphore signs, that the cry of a telegram is necessary to me.

Spontaneously, this is not an idea that would have occurred to you. In any case, it makes me happy. Tell this to the Keyserling of Darmstadt.

V.

Buenos Aires, November 1928

My dear Keyserling:

Your last letter (October 29th) makes me a little angry.[28] You ask me if I'm the kind of woman "who never gives a clear answer, except sometimes in a PS (an impossibility in the case of a telegram)". I don't know what kind of woman I am, and I was precisely depending on you to find out.

What is absolutely certain is that *there exist subjects that cannot be discussed in a letter* at the distance at which we find ourselves, you and I, at the present moment.

I hate mundane life and the mundane world as much as you do, and perhaps more. I don't go to Paris to wallow in these delights. I'm not at all interested in seeing you "with others", as you suppose. It's with you that I want to talk. It's you I want to hear. Also, you should have noticed that that is all I do since June 1927.

It's possible and even probable that I am an absurd person and that my absurdity disgusts you; but it doesn't let me forget that you want to lodge at the Hôtel des Réservoirs in Versailles. I have already written and telegrammed to you that all this would be arranged upon my arrival in Paris (your stay in Versailles is at my expense). If you wish to stay at the Hôtel des Réservoirs for more than two weeks, you will be welcome to do so.

I will go and see you every day and whenever you want. But it would be good that you know that I am, probably in more ways than one, *perfectly unworthy of occupying all your time*. In a word: as the moment of our meeting approaches, I feel an inferiority complex developing in me (not *unravelling* as you wrote in your article on Tolstoy). I believe that I truly don't possess the necessary conditions for you to find my company in large doses interesting. And of course, this makes me suffer. If you write to me in a certain tone, if you write certain things … it's worse.

---

28   Ocampo changes from the formal *vous* to the informal *tu*.

Then I feel the wish to vanish from the surface of the earth. I haven't received an answer to my last telegram, and today I'll send another to have news of your health.

V.

"The impulse which drives me into the wide world is precisely the same as that which drives so many into monasteries: the desire for self-realisation,"[29] Keyserling had written in his *Diary*. I don't know to what point this was true for him. Perhaps it was. In any case when I left for Europe in December of 1928, I had nothing more than that to lend me the necessary strength to abandon the life I was leading, a life that was sweet and seemingly protected. But a life in which certain unemployed faculties that I believed I possessed were demanding more and more to be put to use. It is also true that I ardently wished to be in touch again with the great capitals that I adored because of their beauty and their intellectual atmosphere. But I doubt that this attraction could have overcome, on its own, the apprehensive anguish of travel, just at the moment in which I was beginning to rid myself of so many difficulties, to enjoy a freedom laboriously earned and paid for at a very high price, the years of sacrificed youth (as I thought).

In order to build for myself a house in Buenos Aires, following that ideal of renunciation that had led me to build the house at Mar del Plata, I sold this last one. I made the mistake of addressing myself to the architect Bustillo,[30] simply because I had had occasion to see, when I visited houses that he had built, that he employed excellent materials. Bustillo detested what I loved, and we fought before reaching an agreement. I won in part, making him build at least partly what I had in mind. It was not without suffering that I did it, and he, who used to put his name on the facades of the houses he built, refused to put it on mine. Therefore, "she" (the house) had gained a good deal, *inside* at least. Bustillo had a certain sense of beauty and order and above all a sense of quality (as far as his profession was concerned). He loved good quality wood, quality stone, good bricks. That was at least something. Uniquely distracted, one could not help finding him terribly exasperating yet amiable. When I left for Paris, my house in the neighbourhood of

29 Keyserling, *Travel Diary*, Vol. 1, 14. Ocampo notes, "This is the impulse that led Lawrence of Arabia to enter the RAF."

30 Alejandro Bustillo (1889–1982), an Argentinian architect and painter. In 1929 he was responsible for the construction of Victoria Ocampo's house (according to her design specifications) in Palermo at Rufino de Elizalde 2831, Buenos Aires 1425. See: www.galin sky.com/buildings/victoriaocampo/index.htm

Palermo, half built, remained in his care, with a thousand interdictions and recommendations.

I left. To calm my parents who always looked upon my comings and goings with worry, I took with me José and Fani.[31] My father had made me a gift of one hundred thousand francs (ten thousand pesos at the time), which in those days was a very agreeable sum to receive. It cost me a lot to leave my family. On the day of my departure, I was crying like an unfortunate creature, and in the morning I awoke feeling like someone condemned to death.

J.[32] would come meet me in February. I was going to see Keyserling in January and Keyserling, of course, was aware of this. At first he had suggested that I meet him in Germany. I answered: No. Then he agreed to travel to Versailles on condition that I would also live there. I answered: No. He could settle in Versailles, and I would go visit him every day during his stay. In the end, that is how it was arranged. I won't repeat what I have already told in my book about this affair. In it I speak of his demands that amused me and almost flattered me at the time: I was not to see anyone but him during his stay in Versailles, etc.

I arrived in Paris just in time to attend an Ansermet concert at the Salle Pleyel. I felt as if I were dreaming. Paris, that music, the chance to meet writers (apart from Keyserling), musicians that I worshipped ... In my comfortable orchestra seat I melted with pleasure. The ground under my feet felt as if it were made of rubber. In Paris and free for the first time. Everything seemed delightful to me, tea at Rumpelmeyer's, the arcades of the Rue de Rivoli, the Place de la Concorde (beloved of my childhood), the Champs Élysées, the Seine, the Pont Alexandre, the Arc de Triomphe, the familiar outline of the Eiffel Tower, the pale winter sun, the scent of Paris breathed in on a street after a concert. I was trembling with happiness.

I went to Chanel to order two suits. Chanel had had an affair with J. in 1913, and I had been jealous as of other women as well. But that feeling now was stifled by my happiness.

So much stifled that I barely remembered it. When I met Chanel (the next year) she told me, among other things, that she didn't like to have sex with men (with each man) more than two or three times. After that it became a chore. The men became jealous, demanding, and offered little in the way of novelty. I asked her, "Do you know, I was very jealous of you?" She asked me, "Because of whom?" And then she added, "Stravinsky?" I said: "Oh no!" And we spoke of something else. My conversations with Coco Chanel made me understand the folly of certain jealousies, "so much mud for a two-minute

---

31   José was her butler. Estefanía (also called Fanny) Alvarez, a maid who travelled with Ocampo, was with her for 42 years.

32   Julián Martínez.

fit" as the poet put it. So much jealousy for a spasm; because Coco didn't seem to give more importance than that to erotic transports. Physically she was full of grace, charm, elegance, even though the wasteland of her heart (that her words did not at all attempt to conceal) was too visible for one to feel tempted to fall under her spell. How could I ever have suffered because of her and because of similar things! But what is the mechanism of these states of idiotic torture? And how to pull it apart? Also, is jealousy not inseparable from certain love affairs, and something like the price we have to pay for them? It is love that can be transformed, not the jealousy derived from a certain kind of love.

[...]

I went to Versailles to reserve the rooms (a sitting room, a bedroom, and a bathroom) for Keyserling immediately after my arrival. The Hôtel des Réservoirs, old fashioned and charming, with its interior windows opening onto the "solitary and frozen" December park,[33] seemed to me a décor worthy of the most refined of Baltic sensibilities. There reigned there a provincial calm, barely disturbed by Sunday strollers and tourists about the palace and the Trianons. Snow cottoned the silent streets.

Keyserling, a guest of his mother-in-law Bismarck in Schönhausen, was supposed to arrive from Germany to Paris on January 5th without stopping over in the capital. Two of my letters were awaiting him at the Hôtel des Réservoirs with the ball of string, the large envelopes, the red ink, and the blotting paper that he had asked me to get for him. During his stay, he proposed to finish *America Set Free*.

To send to Count K. upon his arrival, Hôtel des Réservoirs

40, rue d'Artois, Paris, January 2, 1929

My dear Keyserling:

I trust that your rooms won't displease you too much.[34] The furniture is uglyish, but I suppose that this kind of thing doesn't bother you; and furthermore, you have the whole of the Versailles park coming through your bedroom window.

Don't reproach me for being sad. It is true that I suffered terribly throughout the month that preceded my departure from Buenos Aires. But if you knew how happy I am to have come, to be here! If you only

---

33 Paul Verlaine, "Dans le vieux parc solitaire et glacé/ Deux forms ont tout à l'heure passé", "Colloque sentimental", *Fêtes galantes*, 1869.

34 Ocampo reverts from *tu* to *vous*.

knew how grateful I am to you for having somehow torn me away from my corner! Because without you and your terrible insistence (how pig-headed you can be), I would not have left the American continent ... at least for the time being. I would have left it later, it was fated ... too late, perhaps. Thanks to you, I have gotten through a pain of which I was fearful.

But I'm happy to have come. And I await you with joy. You are totally mistaken if you believe that my psychology differs from yours as regards the epistolary effects of our relationship. I feel like writing to you *now* as I did when I was in Buenos Aires.

I hope that, thanks to the red ink, the ball of string, the blotting paper, and the envelopes, nothing will be missing from your room at the Hôtel des Réservoirs.

Why do you ask me not to be conventional? Were you not ready to *take me as I am?*

I will not tell you if I am tall or petite, conventional or not. These are things that a man of your penetration should have guessed earlier. Furthermore, to be "tall" for you is harder than being tall for anyone else: you are a giant. And the same thing happens, I suppose, as regards conventions. Doubtlessly I will not be at your level. And above all, above all, don't forget that I express myself with difficulty; that in this sense, I'm the contrary of you. I'm convinced that I will seem an idiot if you ask me any question.

Until tomorrow, dear unknown.

V.

Paris, January 3, 1929[35]

Dear Keyserling,

Why haven't I heard from you since Boulogne? Are you mad at me? The address of the bank was serious – whatever you think – and you could have used it perfectly. I want to see you right away, because this prolonged state of waiting is spoiling my sleep and I'm afraid I'll look terrible on Saturday. I would like to telegraph to be sure of your existence (I have my doubts) but I no longer know where to reach you.

35 Letter from the Keyserling Archives, Universitäts- und Landesbibliothek Darmstadt, KEYS-169-0223-0224. Translated from the French by Craig Stephenson.

I assume you are in Berlin today. I'm sorry because I won't have a new dress on Saturday, and I had counted on that a lot so as not to feel too moved. Nothing brings one to the surface like a dress one is wearing for the first time (if it's pretty). So, I won't even have that *"burladero"* [joker]! It's awful! But why haven't you been in touch anymore? What is happening? I hope you are not sick. Now your disease would come to my senses, and consequently, it would be impossible for me to remain indifferent to it, as when I was in Buenos Aires! I don't know how to live the hours that separate me from our meeting. It is impossible for me to read since I left Buenos Aires. *Vivo en el aire,* [I live floating on air] do you understand? I will go to Versailles tomorrow to take the ink, the string, the envelopes, and the blotter. I will also phone your editor. I could have sent you my car to take you to Versailles, but unfortunately it's not there yet – and I don't think I'll have it on Saturday – I can't tell you anything right now, I'm counting the minutes.

V.

To send to Count K. upon his arrival, Hôtel des Réservoirs

40, rue d'Artois, Paris, January 3, 1929, 7:00 p.m.[36]

My dearest giant,

News at last!

Yes, I suffered from a terrible melancholy, on New Year's Day. It's silly, it's silly, I will not speak further of this.

I'm happy to have received your news because I felt somewhat uneasy. I did not write to you at Schönhausen Elba, because the address did not seem serious to me ... [Bismarck Castle].

But yes, I'll look after you, and you won't have to worry about anything. Don't do it. If Monsieur Delamain (your publisher) has cracked his skull skiing, that is of no importance (except to him) because in spite of this you will have a car waiting for you at the station. A friend will lend it to me. I have explained to the chauffeur what you look like ... He will recognize you amidst a thousand faces. And so that the matter is

36   From Ocampo, *Autobiografía, 4: Viraje.* Translated from the Spanish by Alberto Manguel.

even more certain, I will send to the station my "butler" who will recognize you as well because he knows you from photographs.

I knew beforehand that you would not feel like meeting me upon getting off the train. I know you because I know myself.

I've placed soap, eau de cologne, and flowers in your apartment in the Hôtel des Réservoirs. Do you need anything else?

(At this very moment, your postcard has arrived, so Schönhausen really exists!)

Why do you say that I'm an extraordinary woman? Don't make fun of me or I'll go back to the American continent. You are right to suffer on my behalf ... I also suffer, and more than you. But you would not like me to have a sobbing fit.

Midnight. I've come back from seeing the Diaghilev ballet. I loved them in 1913. I love them more now. I find Serge Lifar very handsome: he is the most handsome dancer I have ever seen. But the show bored me after fifteen minutes. Last night, for instance, I had more fun. I was at the circus. There was a juggler whom I found enchanting. After five minutes I had forgotten all about you.

After tomorrow at this time, what will you be thinking, and what will I be thinking? I'm much overcome by emotion. Don't make fun of me. Why do you make fun of me? On Sunday, you can make fun if you want. But not on Saturday. I'll be too intimidated by your presence.

May God keep you.

I feel as if *I'm almost saying goodbye to you on this piece of paper, goodbye to the person you were to me* and who will stop being that person a few hours from now, in Versailles. How will I manage without that Keyserling of mine, made up by me?

But let's return to practical matters. My phone number is 33-10 Élysée. If you wish to send me a message, I'll be home at 4:00. If I don't hear otherwise, I'll come to you at 5:00 or 5:30. Won't you be tired?

Goodnight. Until tomorrow.

V.

On January 5th 1929, towards four o'clock in the afternoon, I was examining the mirror of the wardrobe, in the apartment at 40 rue d'Artois.[37] I was wearing a new blue, pink, and brown sweater (Chanel), a navy blue *suit* very well cut, one of those very simple *suits* that are very expensive and more

---

37 From Ocampo, *Autobiografía, 5: Versailles-Keyserling Paris-Drieu.* 9–62. Translated from the Spanish by Alberto Manguel.

difficult to obtain than a ballroom gown. On my head I wore a felt hat pulled down to the eyebrows. Lucienne (Reboux) had cut it and moulded it on my head with cries of delight. She liked combing my hair. I wore it short. The hat suited me. The sweater tones made the bronze hue of my face (the eighteen-day crossing of the Atlantic) stand out. A grey sky. It was snowing. The sun seemed to shine only on my skin. In the car that was taking me to Versailles, I checked myself many times with my pocket mirror for last inspections. The company of my face quietened my nerves. For no reason. I should have had doubts about that face; made up by the sea breeze, it could cause me diffi-culties on that day and turn into my enemy. I thought I was establishing a relationship with the founder of the School of Wisdom, and I couldn't guess that I would be met at the Hôtel des Réservoirs by Genghis Khan. From the first handshake, from the first greeting – which was a cordial embrace (for the time being) – I had the feeling that I had wandered into a hornets' nest. Imprudently I had proffered sweet nothings like "kitty" or "puss", I had offered a saucer of milk without knowing what species of carnivore he was, that with a strike of his paw could tip the innocent beverage and shatter the delicate porcelain.

As in a film that one can stop when one wishes, I leave Keyserling and myself, the two of us frozen in the instant of that first greeting standing in the middle of a small sitting room, to go back to the *Travel Diary* before carrying on. There, Keyserling stresses that "only women with polygamous tendencies, who possess a vast emotional horizon, women with assorted sympathies and many profiled features, are destined to the position of queen, muse, and sibyl. The virtues of a housewife forbid great efficiency of huge dimensions ..." etc. Fine. As far as Keyserling is concerned, I was evidently classified amongst those women. He also insists on the need for an erotic tension in the life of men who are not made in the image and semblance of most Germans: in the realm of love, they know nothing but vice and matrimony (like most Argentinians of my youth). And this tension cannot come except from a fem-inine type who is neither the whore nor the wife. In classical antiquity this was the role of the courtesan. Today (it would be best to say yesterday), of the Grande Dame. Only they have been capable of polishing a man and making him reach a higher stage of refinement and culture.

How many things they owe to commerce with such women, Keyserling exclaims. Of course, these *elite* women must know their *métier*. The great periods of Latin civilization have known this, and it is thanks to these women that the culture of these periods reached such an exceptional level. It is thanks to them that, on the thick loom of sexual appetites, man has woven such exquisite and silky tapestries.

No doubt, there's much truth in these considerations. But if in a first instance they seem free of certain prejudices (Keyserling seems, in a word, to find that the type of the courtesan, the sibyl, the muse is more exceptional, superior in a certain sense to the others), we always perceive a background note infamous for our sex. Most of the time, it seems that he cannot speak of women unless it's in relation to men, as far as she can be useful to him materially, affectively, intellectually, no matter in what way. He needs her in certain conditions to reproduce himself in others, to procure him pleasure or to perfect him spiritually. He needs the one who is so very prolific, the mother with a guaranteed *pedigree* (the *tota mulier in utero* [she is a womb] par excellence) in the North; the prostitute, the courtesan for the moments in his life of rough style in the South; and dominating this panorama in the East and the West, the muse and sibyl, doubling as Grand Dame or courtesan for those moments in his life of exalted, inspired, or sublimated style.

And the woman? Can she not find such things exactly in the opposite sense, logically, and see man, if she so wishes, only in terms of her needs?

To begin with, it seems that she must be the supreme judge in the question of the multiplication of the species. She must choose because it is she who will pay with her person under those circumstances. It is not the stud who is supposed to choose but simply serves the purpose that nature assigns to him. His role is *episodic*. The role of an *accompanist*.

Yes, to choose. It is said that individual preferences do not guarantee the excellence of the fruit of a coupling. Leaving aside cases of aberrant preferences and other abnormalities (that would lead to mental deficient individuals), is it not so? The physical (sexual) attraction and repulsion, as intense and irrefutable as it was in my case, for example, are pointless? Is it a simple whim? Is it a gratuitous instinct? What do they mean, the useless remains of an atrophied organ, like paps on a male body? Is it inconceivable that in certain individuals it is preserved with a strength similar to that of the homing instinct of messenger pigeons? I cannot believe that a sustained physical attraction is meaningless. That the individual and the species are in frank contradiction. I'm sorry not having been able to give (at least in my case) a testimonial to the contrary (not having had a child). I have not wished to have children except with one man. What would these children have been? Perfect, mediocre, frustrated? Maybe I have been fated to have no children other than those of the spirit, those born of a spiritual rather than a physical attraction. Maybe my destiny was to sacrifice the former for the sake of the latter. But I am not at all convinced. However, I also know that we can only see the reverse of our fate, the very reverse of ours, as Arkel[38] says.

And so, to begin, choose. And I continue to do so *(cum grano salis)* [with a grain of salt]. Together with those fathers who would guarantee the procreation of fine-quality children and according to the preferences of the woman as far as the human type is concerned, why should she not have as well her inspirational prophets? If there was a Cumaean Sibyl, there also was – to balance this out – the Delphic oracle. Why can a woman not have her oracles

38   Possibly a reference to Reginald Arkell (1881–1959), the popular British novelist.

as well? Why can she not assume that men exist only in relation to her? As far as the propagation of the species is concerned, the role of the man is becoming that of an accessory that can be purchased in medical clinics. In the United States, test-tube babies[39] have already appeared. Semen will perhaps be sold in vials, in boxes, with all the other pharmaceutical products. For the full believer in eugenics (and I believe in the need for eugenics but not in its intrusion into everything else with regards to the propagation of the species) for whom the attraction that one human being feels towards another means nothing, means absolutely nothing (while a combination of this man here and that woman there seemed to offer them ideal possibilities), artificial insemination must seem the solution of their dreams. The bettering of the race, planned by the intelligence of respectable scientists bent over their vials, their syringes poised over inert human bodies, produces in me nothing more than a sad scepticism. To decree, in questions of procreation, that instinct, attraction, carnal affinities, the pull of the blood (I don't know what name to give this thing) are trifles, will not lead us, I fear, to anything of value.

If this be error and upon me proved
I never writ, nor no man ever loved.[40]

I'm aware that in many countries and at many times the attraction of which I speak and matrimony (the union, institution, and sacrament that indeed point toward the reproduction of the species) have not gone hand in hand. Furthermore, I have never doubted the need for certain rules dictated by eugenics. I was already thinking about this in my adolescence. It's necessary to guarantee a child a healthy soul *in a healthy body* and also that these advantages are likely ...
But there's something more. There is:

Make thee another self for love of me ...
That beauty may live in thine or thee.

One of the deepest, most mysterious, most poetical, most transcendent impulses between a man and a woman. This thirst to immortalize in the flesh the being one loves, which no woman truly in love cannot have felt. The thirst that, for me, is the touchstone of a great love (carnal love).

Now stand you on the top of happy hours[41]

39 Artificial insemination; in-vitro fertilization did not exist at this time.
40 This and the subsequent couplet are from William Shakespeare, "Sonnet 10".
41 This and the next quotation are from William Shakespeare, "Sonnet 16".

What conscious woman has not thought this, looking upon her young lover-husband-friend sleeping next to her?

And you must live, drawn by your own sweet skill ...

It is, for me, only, that you can survive; that this fleeting moment, in time that destroys you, can be fixed, halted. It is in me that you will design your eternal youth. Now or never. There is no other barrier between devouring Time and you, than me, than us. We cannot vanquish it except together.

And I go back to my starting point in this digression that has (apparently) led me too far astray. Keyserling believed that procreation "is a matter of *racial concern*" and should be regulated in such a way that individual preferences should not play a key role in it, etc." I suppose that, based on this, he married Gödela Bismarck. In that marriage which he often proclaimed to be a complete success, two families rather than two individuals were united. From what I can judge at a distance (I don't know Countess Keyserling except through correspondence), Hermann had chosen his wife well. She admires him, and he is devoted to her. She accepted him just as he was. She accepted me as *inspirational muse*, sibyl or Grande Dame (that is to say, a courtesan). Gödela had the intelligence that led her to know what the situation was. She moved with ease in the world created by her husband. Her case provokes in me a great curiosity. I do not have her flexibility.

To try to explain what happened between Keyserling and myself from our very first encounter (or collision) in Versailles, I have to continuously reach for the *Travel Diary*. I admit that if I had read it in a more strictly objective way, certain attitudes of its author would not have taken me by surprise at our meeting. For that, mea culpa. But nothing of what I might have found in that book, supposing I had read it with exemplary objectivity, could have prepared me for the turn things took at the Hôtel des Réservoirs. Keyserling revealed himself there to be in flagrant disagreement with some of his theories. He shares with the whole of humanity the impossibility, or near impossibility, of not falling into this contradiction. What is important is to admit this willingly.

The division between one kind of woman and another, which Keyserling makes in his chapter on Udaipur[42] doesn't seem true to me, except in part, and *mutatis mutandi* [with the necessary changes], it is applicable also to men, in as far as it might be valid. A woman is not necessarily limited by this or that predominant trait of her character, of her nature.

A woman, like a man, can feel that she is several things at the same time: muse, artist, scientist, wife, and mother. If motherhood, like the religious orders, demands that one devotes oneself to it, leaving aside other concerns *for the time being*, it isn't enough to fill the life of a woman who has desires

42 Keyserling, *Travel Diary*, Vol. 1, 178–183.

of another kind, intellectual curiosities, artistic tastes, etc. Once the children have left her care (and children do this soon in our days), what will she do with her time, no matter how much of a "housewife" she might be? In what conditions did Emily Brontë[43] find herself when she found herself writing in the Yorkshire presbytery? Did she not knead the dough for her bread in the kitchen, at the same time studying from a book open at her side? Did she not fulfil the humblest cleaning tasks, like a servant?

But I'm drifting off again. Let's go back to our subject. Was I what Keyserling believed I was? Yes or no. Yes, in what concerned the type of woman "who possesses a vast emotional horizon with varied likes and many drawn-out traits …" Polygamous? If polygamy is measured with that yardstick, certainly. Though it is true that the sexual act in itself had carried for almost fourteen years a warning sign, "Hunting Forbidden" (forbidden to all except one) in my domains, I could not boast of having limited my *affections* to J. Other men had moved and interested me. I had engaged with them continuously and had enjoyed the pleasure of moving and interesting them.

The men I truly admired did not particularly attract me from the point of view of *sexual appeal*. Some of them provoked in me a *distancing* in that regard. Another kind of man, those who did not arouse admiration (in me, at least) might have appealed to me physically. Their *sex appeal*, their beauty or charm, did not pass unremarked by me. But soon I found them stupid, or infantile, or with fake wit, or gifted almost exclusively with an animality. Unbearably conceited, on top of everything, in spite of their obvious inferiority. Very notable hunks of *meat* from which I soon would turn my eyes impatiently with that vague unease that the window of a butcher's shop produces in me … (except W.P. whom I knew in my youth).

The fact is that J., sensual and tender, sensitive and handsome, not at all vain (a defect I would not have borne well), wishing to see me succeed in my aspirations, full of faith in my "talents" (as he called them), was a too-perfect lover. There was between us a true understanding. Happy coincidences rarely repeated. The path of our lives that we walked together, from a certain moment to another, was what it had to be, not thanks to my virtues but thanks to that understanding and to his merits, to him. Had we been limited to physical and sexual attractions, my relationship would have lasted *what a rose lasts, a morning*. Now I can speak of this with first-hand knowledge, having had other experiences. That love-passion as such was unique in my youth. Unique, as it is in my discovery of music, the passage in which Wagner expresses the inexpressible: Isolde, waiting for Tristan, her arms around the great pine tree. Bach, Chopin, Debussy, Schumann, Purcell, Stravinsky, etc., have spoken to me of other emotions. I will not deny one or the others. They are not interchangeable in me and cannot be added up. One cannot

43 Ocampo lectured on Emile Brontë on June 14, 1938 at the Women's League Library, Buenos Aires. See Ocampo, "Emily Brontë", *Victoria Ocampo*, 150–159.

add a cloud to a fruit, the sand of the desert to a rosebush. Each of these things makes *one*.

She who was looking at herself in the mirror, on rue d'Artois, on January 5th, 1929, was a woman who had reached the end of a stage in her life by the force of things, by an inexorable push (and here I use that word *poussée* in the sense of inexorable progress). I was about to leave a haven that had sheltered me for years, that had fortified me and made me languish, as contradictory as that might seem, these two effects of the same cause. It is true that I had not been stultified by the delights of Capua,[44] because a powerful passion is always accompanied by strong pinpricks and vigorous tremors. That passion had put me on the trail of a great spiritual truth, the grounding of all religions. But this gradual and fatal display was as if dulled by the attenuating effect of time on these tumultuous preoccupations. The hungry and ardent impulse had given way to an amiable habit. That feeling could not absorb me nor fence me in more than the tenderness I felt for my family.

All transitional crises are painful. I was entering a second phase of my adult life. And I couldn't do it with a rending.

Like the two Tartarins, one saying, "Cover yourself with glory" and the other, "Cover yourself in flannel",[45] two voices were giving me different orders. One spoke to me of seeking refuge at whatever price in a happiness without surprises, in which it wasn't necessary to shatter the apparent calm; the other shouted: "Preserve us, O Lord, from languishing in sheltered havens. Force us, O Lord, to set sail, to return to the high seas from whence we came." As much as I was a *creature of habit*, a slave to routine, the latter voice often overwhelmed the former.

When I was very young, one of my friends came on her honeymoon to Paris, where I was living then. In the morning I went to see her at her hotel. I was imagining that she would be wrapped in happiness. The young couple received me in the bedroom in which reigned the disorder of open trunks and an unmade bed. Everything had the warmth of waking up in that room. My two lovebirds held each other by the waist, tenderly, and the breakfast tray with two cups was awaiting them on the table. There was such a feeling of being locked up in that atmosphere, protected from the winds outside, in a material and spiritual sense, that I was overcome with a furious attack of claustrophobia. I remember leaving as if I had been drowning, and walking with great strides down the Champs Élysées, breathing in the cold air that was freezing the tip of my nose. And I thought to myself: "What a prison, that room! I will never get married."

44   Allusion to Hannibal Barca's decision, after the triumphant battle of Cannes in 216 BCE, to winter partaking in the delights of Capua, the easy living softening his soldiers to their ultimate detriment.

45   "The Two Tartarins" by Alphonse Daudet (1840–1897) recounts how the two aspects of Tartarin's personality, represented by Don Quixote and Sancho Panza, so oppose each other that Tartarin never leaves home.

It was the languor in that haven that was already terrifying me. The atmosphere of a hothouse that protects happiness from the winds of spirit. Being penned up in the contentment of barnyard fowl. The lulling of domestic beatitudes. And yet I was also a homebody, attached to the gods of the hearth … In my twenties I was many things at the same time, and also none of them. Those things that would in the future impose themselves were little by little pushing the weaker things out or repressing them in me, whatever the case.

I go back to the film of my life at the moment that I was standing facing Keyserling at the Hôtel des Réservoirs, wearing my pink, blue, and brown sweater, uneasily asking myself if I were not going to be once more disappointed (as with Father A.)[46] in my search for the absolute. A woman with all the power and scope of that word, through the sacrament of a happy and rending passion, a passion that revealed itself as a springboard. I was quivering, elastic, like the end of a springboard suspended over the void under the feet of a swimmer who is about to jump into the water. I was on that springboard and after having run its length breathlessly, I felt catapulted into the void by my own impulse and condemned to a perilous jump, the *dépassement* [overcoming]. Towards what? And at what risk? At the risk of falling into eternity?

Had I once again mistaken the door? What would be the consequences this time?

Obviously, the man I had in front of me did not belong to the category of wise men, as I understood wisdom, nor of the saints who don't reject life, like Tagore. Rather, on the contrary, the warnings that my Spanish friends had given me regarding his character welled up in my memory.

Keyserling at forty showed his age. Very tall, hands and feet to match, high forehead, clear small slightly slanted eyes with a penetrating and alert look, a well-proportioned rather aquiline nose delicate and beautiful, a big brutal mouth with lips swollen by appetites and ready with an easy Homeric laugh, greedy for food and drink. The whole accompanied by a moustache and a pointed beard that lent this Russian-Mongolian face a touch of gravitas. His speech was incredibly quick. Eisenstein would have loved to include him in the landscape of his *Alexander Nevski*. A primitive man (though he did not believe he encountered fully that facet of the human being until his trip to South America, however he had stated in an autobiographical essay of 1927: "From 1898 to 1900 I was beyond a doubt the least spiritual, the cruellest and most bestial of the *Korpsstudenten* of Dorpart") and genial, earthly, and spiritual, overflowing with himself and casting glances upon the world that were at times blind, at times canny, skewing and clairvoyant, the author of the *Travel Diary* carried in his blood a feudal lineage of Livonian Russian lords, enamoured of art and culture, mixed with that of the *boyars* [the highest

---

46   Ocampo notes, "A story never told of a preacher then *à la mode*".

rank of feudal aristocracy, second only to ruling princes] of Tartar origin and of the Ungern-Sternberg, one of which was the famous Mongolian *condottiere*, a character in Ossendowski's book.[47] In his youth, Keyserling had felt, as a sensitive being, inferior to the extremely violent men on his mother's side; as an avid and healthy animal inferior to the intellectualized men on his father's side. This brew in the Keyserlings, benefactors of Bach, Kant, Voltaire, friends of Frederick the Great, and of the Ungern-Sternberg, "feudal commandeers and also buccaneers" (Léonie, K.'s sister, married one of them), produced this exemplar of humanity called Hermann. An Orpheus who carried within himself his wild beasts ... and who was torn apart not by the Bacchae but by Eurydice.

Why did this Baltic man get into his head the idea of seducing me? Why did he persist in spite of my resistance and my refusals? Why did he insist on building up theories to justify his attitude and at the same time explain mine away in a manner that would please him? Did he not declare in his memoirs that he was not in love with me but *bewitched* by me? Profoundly bewitched.

The fact is that I presented myself at the Hôtel de Réservoirs with my "cakes" (take this as a play on words or not) and my pot of butter for my Grandma, following in the tradition of Little Red Riding Hood. And I found myself facing a carnivore who demanded a more substantial meal. How ridiculous, my innocent provisions! I immediately, indignantly, objected to the behaviour of the philosopher-wolf. I was determined not to let myself be devoured by him, but neither did I want to hurt him, to wound him (fool that I was). My guffaws were stifled by this concern (everything that Keyserling says about South American delicacy has its roots in this. The delicacy that in order "not to cause distress, stabs one in the back"). This produced an equivocal situation, given this man's character. Keyserling's personality interested me profoundly. But his domineering and violent manners were repulsive to me. Also, they made me afraid. Disappointed by the elephantine quality of his skin – speaking metaphorically, enraptured but also indignant with his brilliant imperative manner of claiming his lordly rights over the daughter of a servant (as it seemed to me), keen to read the manuscript of *America Set Free* on which he worked day after day, flattered by his attention, humiliated by his deafness towards my interdictions, marvelling at the homage offered to my intelligence and to what he called my beauty, I didn't know where to turn to get out of the situation. I had ardently wished to awaken the interest of this man, and he was going way beyond my wishes. My situation was becoming more and more unsustainable.

---

47   Nikolai Robert Maximillian Freiherr von Ungen-Sternberg, known as Baron Roman Ungen-Sternberg (1886–1921), was a general in the Russian Civil War and a warlord in Mongolia. Ferdynand Antoni Ossendowski, (1876–1945) was a Polish writer and anti-communist who in 1922 wrote *With Baron Ungen in Urga*.

Keyserling seemed to think or imagine that to establish our relationship on a solid base of spiritual communion, carnal intercourse had to be included. This consideration did not touch me except with its absurdity. Without giving the sexual act too much importance, he assigned it *a great symbolic value.* He saw something essential in having intercourse with a woman (this is a supposition) and having her offer guarantees to the man. This is true in certain cases and not true in others. Concerning him and me, it was completely false. Our relationship could have had no other character than a spiritual one, at least on my part. From a physical point of view, nothing in Keyserling attracted me, and that lack of attraction, which could have remained as something neutral, took on the aggressive action of a repulsion when the object of my admiration made every effort to leave it aside and reach his own ends. I began to ask myself if my physical repugnance did not reveal *some mistake in the spiritual attraction* that Keyserling inspired in me. And at times I got impatient with the reaction of my body that allowed itself to reject, uncrowning at its pleasure beings that I had crowned as kings because of their intelligence.

In that way I swung from one extreme to the other, alternatively doubting the testimony of my intellect and of my flesh, following at one time the first, at other times the second.

As far as my feeling of repulsion towards Keyserling, the existence or not of J. did not play any role. I think those feelings led in me an autonomous life. The mechanism of attraction and repulsion worked independently. In Keyserling's case, the repulsion was sparked when he thought he could dictate his laws to this clockwork mechanism, so simple and yet so complex. If he had had the tact not to insist, I repeat, the aversion would have remained latent. But Keyserling really lacked all tact and prudence. Was it my fault if he now regretted it?

I blame myself for not having known how to moderate the exultant tone of my letters when I did not know him. But in what way did this tone differ from that when he used to talk about Houston Chamberlain? Would it be called amorous? I will be told that the case would be different between a young woman and a man who is still young. That depends. Let's not forget that the fact of writing certain things in a certain tone, giving oneself as an example, carries a certain responsibility. That was the case of the author of the *Travel Diary,* which was the reason that led me to write to him those letters so full of enthusiasm. Letters that I never would have thought to write to Louis Jouvet[48] whose physical aspect I was so fond of. Let's not forget that Keyserling had said and repeated ad infinitum: "Salvation can never be imposed on others; we can only help them by showing the acceptable symbol of their own achievement. He who has already reached his goal can never help directly; he issues his assertions from premises that the others lack. He who wants to help must be

---

48   Jules Eugène Louis Jouvet (1887–1951), a French actor/director.

equal to those he wants to help, but he must be above them as far as truth, courage, and honesty are concerned ... My life is caught in the uttermost immediacy of my work. Whatever I might write, say, or do, is always nothing more than the partial expression of what I am." I knew these statements, and I had taken them at face value. And now the man who proffered them made the success of our friendship, of our spiritual communion, depend on an act that was repugnant to my body, to my conscience, to my heart. On an act that could have no meaning, no repercussions, unless it was consented to happily. Did I not then have reason to become exasperated? However, the furious rebellion did not explode at that very moment because I was still too entrapped in the two years of admiration I had felt for Keyserling. That prevented me from being brutal with him in spite of his showing himself imperative and proving that he didn't have – didn't use – any tact with me. The fault was mine. I lacked the courage for a quick capital execution. A mixture of weakness and pity led me to extend it (see the chapter entitled "*Delicadeza*" in *South American Meditations*). I should have told him immediately that not only did I not agree with him regarding *those* feelings, but that I *could* not be his lover under any pretext. I couldn't, as if we belonged to two different zoological species. In this lack of desiring him, Keyserling thought he saw "self-inflicted" prohibitions, taboos, superstitions regarding sexual fidelity that were not important for him (his relationship with Gödela Bismarck was, I believe, very free in this regard). Even if this hypothesis was justified, his behaviour was no less unjustifiable. If my "stage of evolution" did not allow me to shed these convictions, these false obligations, he was not going to free me of them by force. A trauma is not a liberation. Better than anyone (according to his writings), he understood that taboos and superstitions cannot be cured from outside but through an internal transformation that cannot be provoked by I don't know what *moral violation*. Had not he vigorously condemned missionaries, saying, for instance: "How narrow-minded are the missionaries!" Had he not written: "How tactless are all the people who insist on improving their fellows"? Had he not criticized: "the imposition of your own view upon another human being"? Had he not proclaimed: "He who throws away his prejudices prematurely does not gain his freedom, but rather bars his way to it. Our own times illustrate this truth with terrible clarity ..."?[49] Furthermore, in this case it was not prejudices but revulsion (unless that feeling were classified by the Darmstadt philosopher as a *prejudice of the body*: in that case, I have my prejudices). Let's leave aside that which depended, as I have already pointed out, on Cleopatra's nose, on a fortunate or unfortunate physical fact. Let's leave aside the circumstances. In a word: let's go to the prejudice, "the decadent taboo of sexual fidelity", "of erotic property". His jealousy, which even children and animals feel spontaneously, is *a prejudice*? To tell the truth,

---

49 Keyserling, *Travel Diary*, Vol. 1, 51–2, 115.

I do not find it respectable either in me or in my neighbour. Nor do I consider it "intelligent". But the fact is that it *exists* and because it exists, it transforms and dramatizes an act that cannot have any other importance than that of a passing hunger; a taste for this or that human treat or dish devoured and immediately forgotten.

Fine. In the meantime, and however solid the arguments that contradict the legitimacy of this feeling, or ridicule it, might be, jealousy refuses to allow for the distribution of passion as far as passionate love is concerned. This distribution can be exciting when it consists of simply a pleasure, a luxury, like so many other ways of restoring life to dulled feelings.

We Argentinians, especially the men, are still a race with very primitive reactions as far as these matters are concerned. The French find arrangements, and that's that. Can it be said of Proust that he was primitive? And who ever analysed the mechanism of jealousy with greater skill? Can it be doubted that he was a victim? On the other hand, unless I am mistaken, none of Gide's pages on the subject have particularly moved me. I ask myself if Gide interested himself in the subject, because I can't remember anything of his on this question. Why? Because for Gide, the sexual act is almost exclusively associated with lust, with pleasure, even with prostitution. It consists in one of these "creature comforts". You pay, you savour it like a juicy fruit. Then, enough. It's over. Jealousy cannot play a role in this kind of commercial transaction. Is it because those who feel like this have reached a superior evolutionary state? *Nothing in me will admit it.*

[...]

Let's return to jealousy. The real fact is this: it exists. The pain it causes exists for all those for whom the whirlwind of passion exists. Here also stem taboos, the superstitions of the heart, the prejudices (if prejudices there be) of sexual fidelity. It's easy to measure, when it is experienced, the inanity of an instant of transitory voluptuousness. "So much abject emotion because of a passionate two-minute whim!" It's difficult to measure it with the same yardstick if applied to the other, to the person we love. For the lover, everything has a consequence.

Let it be understood that I'm speaking of men and women susceptible to feeling a strong amorous passion (doubtless something rare these days). Passion is dramatic or is nothing at all.

In Versailles, looking at Keyserling, to whom I had devoted a veneration of two years, I asked myself: "Have I the manners of a wolf in a sheep's clothing? Do I behave in daily life like one?" Horrified, I tried not to act with total honesty. Horrified and with cowardice. Everything seemed impure regarding Keyserling in that matter. And the sexual act *inconceivable, impossible, hateful as a rape.* He ended by understanding that he would obtain nothing and that he would not force me to relinquish my passive resistance. He gave up little by little his intentions: that perfect union, crowned (my God!) by that of the flesh. In the uttermost depths of his thoughts, I believe that this was nothing more than a postponement ... He must have thought that things could be sorted out in Buenos Aires. As he gives to understand in the chapter "V.O." of his memoirs. In any case (and he says this too) he did not notice the change, the turn that his attitude had provoked in me. As a reaction I started to doubt everything that issued from his pen, everything that he stood for or had stood for in my eyes. (In the same way Catholics drew me away for a time from the great Christian truths). I felt soiled by the slightest caress: a kiss on the cheek.[50] Contrary to T. E. Lawrence (who I was to admire so deeply in spite of our notions of things related to carnal love that were so different), for me the body had never been a lowly *despisable object*. Especially concerning love. I had seen in him an almost supernatural beauty.

In his chapter on Singapore (in the *Travel Diary*), Keyserling wrote: "And beauty? In the face of plants its meaning jumps to the eye ... They wear a festive garment when the time of perpetuation draws nigh; then they are resplendent in the most glorious decoration of bloom. Scholars have endeavoured to explain this by consideration of utility: how blind intellect is! Beauty is everywhere a purpose unto itself; it is the ultimate expression of potentiality. The whole of creation becomes beautiful during the season of love, *because then infinite, superindividual possibilities manifest themselves for a while in the individual, because then the spirit of eternity transfigures what is mortal.* In the case of man, it makes his soul blossom; its gloriousness beautifies, as long as the blossom lasts, the plainest face. In the case of plants, being is exhausted in corporeality, the spirit puts forth corporeal blossoms.

"The contemplation of the plant world gives one a key even to the darkest and most tragic problem: the one-sidedness of every direction of development. A being is either a monad or an element; as a monad it is doomed to death, as an element it is, though immortal, impersonal."[51]

I had known those moments in which the spirit of eternity possesses us and transfigures what in us is ephemeral; I had known the extraordinary beauty that passion lends in the season of love to the flowering flesh and the things of the flesh. That season in which "superindividual possibilities" manifest in the individual. I had known the demands to:

> Make thee another self for love of me
> That beauty may live in thine or thee.[52]

I had known, once and for all, love. I had a reference point with which to recognize, therefore, the places to which life and chance led me. Versailles was *something else.* And wanting to mix the genres, allowing entry into the realm

---

50   Ocampo notes, "I remember a music teacher (I was ten years old), a very nice man but who disgusted me. One day he brushed from my cheek with the tip of his finger a pie crumb, and I ran like a lunatic to soak my face in the bathroom."

51   Keyserling, *Travel Diary*, Vol. 2, 19–20.

52   Shakespeare, "Sonnet 10".

of carnal love that which belonged to a different zone, disfigured a land-scape that could have had a beauty by itself. This was something Keyserling wouldn't or didn't understand.

As I launched myself in search of my soul, I had fallen in I don't know what trap. My soul was degrading itself through a degrading vision of the body. My body felt as if soiled by the fact of being desired. If I felt these things with such intensity, how would I have been able to bear *what he had decided to call brutally* "possession". And yet I repeated my cowardice with disgust; it was a question of degree, not essence. Why not cry out my truth? Why this pity that led to nothing more than sacrifice? Why these *alms*? I was horrified of Keyserling and of myself.

I had felt guilty (because I was lying and violating a pact established by me) in the case of Captain A. Guilty, NOT DEGRADED. Even if it was something different because the sensual attraction was entirely absent, I felt myself degraded. My body seemed to dictate to me an inflexible code, a code that would not admit that the rest of my person should underestimate it in the slightest.

This savage pride, which T. E. Lawrence employed in degrading the body, I had partially known. I could have experienced it in full if I had given myself over to the man I so admired. I don't know what T. E.'s abasements were. But this would have been mine. And yet, I could not conceive *giving one's body except for love*. Except for *the attraction to another body* (even if love itself did not exist). For me, there was *something sacred*, something secret in the body. I cannot forbid it to free itself, but I cannot oblige it to do so without its consent. If one had told me about a man for whom I felt disgust in this sense, "he will die if you do not belong to him", my first impulse (and also per-haps my second) would have been to answer, "*Let him die*. I can do nothing." Malraux[53] asked me the question last year with regard to Keyserling, and those were my feelings then.

My kindness towards Keyserling turned against me and also ultimately against him. It would have been better to be brutal from the start. I ended up being brutal when he came to Buenos Aires. In Versailles I was too much afraid of hurting him. I also feared his anger, a nervous fear like that which thunder inspires in me.

In order to explain such a savage attitude and so many contradictions in this South American woman from the Third Day of Creation, Keyserling resorted (when he returned to Darmstadt) to astrology. He consulted the greatest astrologer in Germany after a previous questioning about the day, hour, and minute of my birth.[54] Although under the sign of Aries (I don't

---

53   André Malraux (1901–1976), French author, art theorist, and statesman.
54   Ocampo notes: "It was only two years ago that I learned Keyserling had written to Jung about me. Jung's answers are in his *Letters,* which have already been published." According to Juan Javier Negri, Fundación Sur, the publisher Soledad Ortega of Revista de Occidente,

understand anything about astrology) it seems that the sign of Virgo has much importance in my life and destiny. This discovery seemed to clarify something about me for Keyserling. He sent me the horoscope so that I could judge his perspicacity. He assured me that he had translated it word by word, but I imagined that he had "condimented" to his own taste this analysis of the stars' influence upon me. That allowed him to "put me in my place", without appearing to be responsible.

Could the richness of Keyserling's points of view, his humour, his mental dexterity, his partial resemblance to the author of the *Travel Diary*, counterbalance the differences, the aggressive defects of his character? Could the subtlety of his intuitions make me forget the vulgarity of his nature? I don't think so; I emerged from this experience as if skinned alive. I thought: my God! What a lesson! And I also thought that this time I couldn't begin to imagine telling J. the story. Perhaps I did not feel for him the passion that would have led me to inflict a suffering that earlier to me would have been the price for the right to such a passion. It did not seem possible for me now to alleviate my conscience and make him suffer a painful rift.

The mental restriction that I imposed on myself with J. hurt my relationship with him. I myself felt hurt.

[...]

I had a qualm, that of not being a person anymore, of escaping others and myself with regard to the passions of love. Of taking again my life in my hands (however hard and sad this freedom might be), of breathing the air of freedom. The atmosphere of closed rooms, the rooms where people made love stifled me, like the one that stifled the young woman who ran down the Champs Élysées, vowing never to marry.

Yes, I loved J. (I believe I never have stopped loving him, loving the eternal moment in which we were so marvellously, so sweetly united). But at the same time I felt the need to make him my friend, my comrade. Being constantly on the warpath, as passion requires, shattered me. I dreamed of putting down my weapons and, together with them, abdicating my privileges and my crown.

This change in the psychological atmosphere, of the psyche (I don't know how to call it) needed to be born without words, without explanations. What words, what explanations would not have made our hearts bleed and have betrayed truth in the name of truth itself? On top of all that, we were too full of sentimental coyness. And yet there was something between us that resembled the tenderness one feels towards one's parents and that was avoided in a language that corresponded to the intensity of that feeling. In the most

wrote to Franz Jung, the son of C. G. Jung, on 2 April 1975 inquiring on behalf of Ocampo about the letters Keyserling and Jung exchanged about her. (Personal correspondence, 10 February 2022).

shattering moments of tenderness towards my mother or my father, I had not been able to articulate a single word to express them. And J. had become like a member of my family. My family, whom I had hurt so badly when I tore myself away from them in order to live according to my destiny. Also with my father and my mother I had gone through a stage in which my flesh loved their flesh, their flesh loved mine. The love of little children for adults and of adults for children is of the flesh, not of the spirit … barely from heart to heart. One is not *friends* with a child of three, four, five, six. What does that child know beyond the great carnal tenderness that he inspires and beyond that what is dreamt for him, about him? What does the child know about those who look after him, indulge him, protect him, except what his instinct dictates to him and makes him follow them like a little dog, bothering them sometimes and trying to follow their wishes, feeling himself darkly the master of their emotions? And when I say that I had gone through "a stage" of love from my flesh to the flesh of my parents, it must be explained that though my feelings for them evolved and drifted to the heart, they never quite abandoned the body, these feelings never entered the realm of friendship. I had adored my young parents with the adoration of a small animal that already perceived beauty. I found them handsome and good. I loved to go into my mother's wardrobes and hide my head in her dresses, because I found there the scent of her rice powder, of her youth, which for me then was her person. I liked the cologne and the tobacco that lingered on the clothes or handkerchief of my father, with which I wiped myself and dried my tears, because he was in them. And many years later when he would say to me: "Go and fetch me this or that from my wardrobe" and I opened it, I would find once again the scent of cologne and the box of Havanas so familiar and I stood still, wrapped in those odours, feeling a happiness that belonged to a season in my life: that of my childhood.

In the same way that I had not managed to turn my parents into my friends, I would not be able to turn what had been a great passion into a great friendship or into a great tenderness. What reasons could have frustrated, in the case of J., this wish? Even today I don't have a clear answer. Maybe as I write these pages in which I free myself, or I shed the "I" that I was (at least that is the illusion I have), I'll be better able to discern these motives.

When Keyserling left Versailles, he left, planted in my heart like *banderillas* intertwined, an anger mixed with pity that made me feel sick at every moment. Pity (a pity that said: "After all he is a poor man, a poor man like the others") gave way more and more to anger, to exasperation. I was furious with him. This occurred slowly and with his help, because of his lack of tact, his lack of understanding and his character.

In answer to his letters, here are some of mine that I wrote to Darmstadt at that time (these letters were returned to me after our quarrel. I had not kept copies of mine because that is not my custom):

Paris, February 7, 1929

Yesterday I welcomed your[55] Chestov[56] and Ortega. Chestov never stopped talking (even in Greek). Ortega and he launched into a discussion about phenomenology (is that what it's called?). Chestov wanted to explode it while Ortega pretended to extend it north, south, east and west ... All this in French that rrrrrrrolled over the Spanish and Russian r's like over badly oiled wheels. They also talked a lot about Heidegger.[57]

I have a thousand things to tell you. I went, preceded by your letter, to see Anna de Noailles.[58] After three minutes, she took me in her arms and throughout our conversation (which lasted an hour and a half) kept my hand in hers and said that I did her good. She was very affectionate with me and she repeated that I brought warmth to her life. She wishes to see me often, almost every day. We spoke of you. She regrets not having been able to see you *en tête-à-tête*. She begged me to explain everything about you, and I gave her *Symbolic Figures* to read. Tonight I returned to her house at 7:30 and we had dinner, she, Ortega, and I. I find her different from other women here, full of enthusiasm. With vain touches of a spoiled child. Something of a bird hopping about. Giving in too much to the pleasure of showing herself witty at all costs. But she is vivacious and effervescent. So much the contrary to the style of a Valéry.[59] Yesterday she sent me a book with the following dedication: "To you, who so fully deserves the name of Victoria and who in an instant of your moving friendship has conquered the most desolate of hearts, I offer this book as testimony of a great fondness. Infinitely moved. Anna". This dedication is in the purest of *Condesa [Comtesse] de Noailles* style, don't you think? But I love her just as she is. It's rare to find beings as determined as she is.

Berdiaeff?[60] Yes! ... But in the end I don't know what I think of him. I have to revise this. I believe that I understand him better than I understand Chestov. I will invite him with Ortega. I love these Russians because they are so earnest, so turned towards the depths of themselves, so tormented and sincere. All the contrary of the French, in general.

---

55   Ocampo returns to the familiar *tu*.
56   Lev Shestov (born Yehuda Leib Shvartsman, 1866–1938), a Russian philosopher who emigrated to France in 1921.
57   Martin Heidegger (1889–1976), German philosopher.
58   Anna, Comtesse Matthieu de Noailles (1876–1933), a Romanian-French writer and feminist.
59   Paul Valéry (1871–1945), French poet.
60   Nikolai Alexandrovich Berdyaev (1874–1948), a Russian philosopher who was forced into exile in Germany and France in 1922.

The Frenchman with his superficial attitudes tires me. But I cannot help falling back on the French with a certain voluptuousness (I don't know if I make myself clear).

Yesterday, for instance, I didn't experience any (voluptuousness) when I saw them reach the uttermost depths of intelligence. No, none. It made me angry. We were having lunch in a small restaurant (in honour of Ortega). This is the list of guests: Valéry, Supervielle, Ramón Fernandez, Isabel Dato, Drieu la Rochelle, etc.[61] In spite of *L'homme couvert de femmes*, Drieu is better than the others from our point of view, (yours and mine) because he is a boy who, like Pascal said, is in the category of those who search whiningly. He at least guesses the existence of things that the others don't care about.

Paul Valéry spoke all the time (he says that Foch, you and he are the three persons who speak French the quickest). Valéry declared that his motto was: to do without believing. He's charming. I wanted to curse violently in Spanish (even in Argentinian) and I felt ready to throw my disgust into the face of that mummy.[62] Happily I felt that Drieu, Fernandez, and the others were uncomfortable hearing France being spoken about by that mouth ... Drieu was exasperated: "This man belittles France", he said.

[...]

April 7, 1929

[...]

I'm extremely upset by your letter, believe me. If you think that things are not going well, it is not because of ill will on my part. For you and in your name I make sacrifices that I would not for anyone else.

V.O.

P.S. It is useless to beg you not to torment me and yourself. You wouldn't know how not to. Sorry if I'm harsh: I'm full of bitterness.

---

61 Jules Supervielle (1884–1960), Franco-Uruguayan poet; Ramón Fernandez (1894–1944), French writer and collaborationist; Isabel Dato (–1937), Spanish noblewoman; Pierre Drieu la Rochelle (1893–1945), French writer and fascist. See Ocampo, *Drieu*.

62 Ocampo notes, "The last part of this letter has been lost, and I hasten to add that I have changed my opinion about Valéry."

40, rue d'Artois, Paris, April 1929, Monday

I received many letters this morning. You always seem to reproach me because you say that I don't keep my promises. Then the simplest would be *not to do anything more*. If I did not *want* to, it would be because it was *outside my inclinations*. I have done everything, everything that I could.

Let's begin with your lectures: I don't think you should start speaking at the Amigos del Arte, because it is all of us, not they, who have invited you to travel to Argentina. There might be some difficulties there but they can be fixed *if you want*. Indeed, I believe that it would be the right thing that you should start with the subject of North America. However, it would be prudent to wait until you are in Buenos Aires to reach a decision. The university expects you to give four lectures, Amigos del Arte two, and of course they ask for one more.

You don't need to write to announce the subjects. I will do that for you. But send me the titles *typewritten*. Understood?

I will write to Ortega who is not in Madrid right now. But I have already made all the possible and imaginable recommendations on your behalf. It would be ill mannered to insist too much.

I will not travel to Spain until April 20th. I don't feel like it. I love France, and I'm not tempted, not at all, to go for a short while to Madrid where I have so many friends.

I will see that you are housed in Buenos Aires as best as is possible. *I stress that I cannot promise anything.* As I've said, as best as is possible.

Let's agree to differ [In English in the original]. I like the neighbourhood of l'Étoile; I'm charmed by old houses and old streets, but I don't like them from a physical point of view. I would not like to live in them. You will not like my house in Buenos Aires. Nothing of the past (the future, "sir", belongs to God) nor any patina. Everything is disgustingly "new", like the house of a saint. For the moment, that's what I like. Beyond that, I don't know if the house is well or badly built (in its genre). When I left Buenos Aires it barely existed.

Don't think too badly of me. Much love.

V.

40, rue d'Artois, Paris, Sunday, 1929

Dear K.:

You don't need to telegraph or write to Amigos del Arte to tell them what your subjects are. But if you would rather do it, here is the address of Señora Elizade: calle Ocampo 2832.

Don't try to imagine what is happening to me and what disturbs me. You will never guess. Above all, you'd guess wrongly.

Certain problems are not and will never be for me what they are for you. And I cannot accept "prefabricated" solutions that have not been created *in me*, not by me. Solutions don't come from outside. You know this better than anyone. When I say that you want to break me, it's because I have the feeling that you impose on me, perhaps unconsciously, things against which I rebel and that my entire being repudiates. I can accept nothing but what I discover in myself. I cannot submit to established laws that go against my instinct. But it's impossible to speak about these things in a letter.

I'm a very wild creature.

V.

40, rue d'Artois, Paris, Wednesday morning, 1929

Copy to Ortega

1) The new edition of *Travel Diary* will be published by Calpe immediately and therefore Keyserling will immediately receive the corresponding payment.

2) *World in the Making* will also be reissued immediately by Revista de Occidente and of course the stipulated amount will be sent. But Keyserling is mistaken in supposing that the first edition was made with nothing more than an *agreement by letter*. There exists a formal contract with a publishing company, Reichel, that stipulates the conditions and the following editions. For this contract Keyserling is to receive 250 pesetas and the same amount for the publisher. However, I will have Revista de Occidente send him 300, as stated in his letter. The sum owed to the publisher will be sent to him as soon as the edition is on sale.

3) Calpe will publish the *Philosophy of H Keyserling* in two volumes: *Schöpferische Erkenntnis* and *Wiedergeburt*. With this purpose, he will be sent a contract. Are you satisfied? Is everything in order? There you have it.

As far as González Garaño[63] is concerned, I have had someone write to him and I will write to him myself (which, however, is useless). Right

---

63   Alejo B González Garaño Peña (1877–1946), Argentinian art collector, bibliophile and historian. He was Director of the National Historical Museum (1939–1946), was a founding

now, he's travelling through Italy and has other things to do. What you want to get from the Argentinians (that they propose subjects to you) is as if the Argentinians wanted to force you to speak slowly and to write in a decent legible manner. *That's against their nature.*

However, I will try to please you; but it will be damnably difficult.

You should speak about MEANING and of North America. Don't blame me. I'm too blame-able these days. This is going badly. I feel terribly depressed and in a private hell. The smallest things demand a cruel effort from me.

Till soon. I will write to you about Spirituality when I'm no longer in the truly horrible state in which I find myself.

V.

P.S. I received the letter in which you list the subjects. I will do everything possible.

Paris, Friday morning, 1929

Dear K:

You are right. You don't say so, but I'm guessing. Enough complaints about people who don't busy themselves with anything other than what I do. Furthermore it's unhealthy. The more one allows oneself to hear these things, the more they overwhelm one and grow in importance.

Yes. It's awful to do business with my compatriots. They are lazy, extraordinarily lazy, with bouts of activity that follow one after the other without one being able to provoke them or extend them.[64]

As far as González Garaño is concerned, it's your fault. He sent a telegram to Buenos Aires saying that you demanded that they suggest subjects to you immediately. What else could he do?

What do you want? There exists an inertia against which one beats one's head. I know this by experience.

The president of Amigos del Arte is an intelligent woman who wishes to do things well; but she is incapable of understanding you, as she is incapable of understanding Ortega, about whom she is passionate.

The subjects that they are proposing are the ones I already proposed:

---

member of the Fine Arts Academy and shared with Ocampo a position on the board of *Amigos del Arte*, the institution that paid for part of Keyserling's fees while in Argentina.

64   Ocampo notes, "See *South American Meditations* in which this quotation appears without mentioning the source".

For Amigos del Arte:

1. The United States and the Material Conquest of the World.
2. The United States and Woman's Supremacy.
3. The United States and the Kingdom of the Holy Spirit.

It will be a wild success, and I'm certain that you will do marvels. I don't think that anything needs to be added. And it will be enough for you to speak about North America for people to hang on your every word. It's a subject that can interest and impress them most.

For the Jockey Club, "Concerning the Soul of a Nation", I think, is a good subject. And since by the time you give this lecture you will have had contact with Argentina, I'm persuaded that nothing too strong will come of it.

As far as the university is concerned, I think you don't have a choice, and they will have you talk about *your* philosophy. The subjects you propose are terrific, and I can imagine what you will get out of them.

I'll be in Buenos Aires *before you*. Don't keep insisting on doubting it. If my ship were to sink, I believe you capable of attributing the ship-wreck to my negligence. Consequently, I hope I will be spared this catastrophe.

"After all, you love your country and you don't wish for me to fail. Or will you fail?" I won't dignify that with an answer.

Until soon. I hope to see González Garaño tomorrow. I won't tell him that you wish for it terribly because he won't understand. But I'll beg him to write to you.

Pray pardon my offences as I pardon yours.

V.[65]

After Keyserling left for Darmstadt (what a relief!), I remained for a time alone in Paris in a state of mind very different from that which I enjoyed when I disembarked from the *Cap Arcona*. My ardour to continue to the uttermost point had become a dampened match from which no spark could any longer be obtained. I was full of doubt about others and about myself. But Paris was here within my reach at this time. And the possibility of gradually getting to know some writers. That had been my dream since my adolescence. And London was a stone's throw away.

65 Keyserling notes at the end of this letter, "She forgive my offences? My God, if she could see clearly. It's terrible to live in darkness."

True, I had lost my "state of grace". The idols of my youth (Anna de Noailles, for example) were no longer inaccessible deities. They were no longer gods. Keyserling had given me a letter for her, as well as for the Russians Chestov and Berdiaeff, for the English Shaw, Wells, Goldsworthy (sic), Lady Astor.[66] I found these letters of introduction ridiculous because I was playing the role of the "paragon" and a rare species of paragon at that. I told myself that I would necessarily disappoint these personages. I wanted to go to them as I was: an obscure self-taught South American, lover of belles lettres, of Europe, and young enough to be pleasing to the eye. The apartment on rue d'Artois, quite simple and old-fashioned, could accommodate two people (with separate bathrooms), allowing them full independence. When J. came to spend a few weeks with me, he was able to come and go without being seen. My friends didn't have to bother him. About Keyserling, I gave him the following report: I always found him extraordinary, but unbearable beyond description. His character, his pretentiousness, had considerably cooled the admiration I felt for his talent, without destroying it completely. Not to say, froze it. That was the truth. I didn't tell J. about this philosophical elephant's pretensions as a seducer and of my strategic contortions to dissuade him without hurting him excessively.

I went out a lot and saw many people. J. and I led different lives. My friends ignored his presence in the apartment. A sort of clumsy camaraderie was established between us.

I wished to reflect, to get to know myself in depth. I did not love myself. The Keyserling affair (the disappointment regarding his person) had sunk me into a universal tedium.

I wanted to draw away from certain forms of love. I wanted to take myself in hand, to analyse myself, or analyse my insufficiencies, my weaknesses. I wanted to be face to face with that dark "I" that kept escaping me with its tricks – as it seemed to me – and preserved no more than an appearance of dignity, to examine it under a microscope. I felt the urgent need to catch that "I" in the act, to test it, to figure out what it was capable of. That "I" that inhabited me and with which I did not identify, I longed to pull it out, to see it in a clear light. Because if I was who I wanted to be, then I was not that "I" that I carried within me. In the same way that I carried, without having chosen, the colour of my hair or of my eyes. That colour did not belong to my preference. It belonged to the chance of my birth.

And so, entering I know not what stage, fearing and searching my experiences with the truth, I wandered through Paris allowing my gaze to touch the beauty of that city that I had loved in so many different ways since

---

66   George Bernard Shaw (1856–1950), Irish playwright; H. G. Wells (1866–1946), English writer; John Galsworthy (1867–1933), English novelist; Viscountess Nancy (1879–1964), American-born British politician.

my childhood. I was hungry, not only for its stones, its trees, its air (in which I found, as in London, a particular flavour), but for its inhabitants. My curiosity drifted preferably towards those I already knew *through their writing* and whose perfection in their writing made me *now* fear their material, living imperfections. Versailles had taught me many things (scepticism teaches us so much) that I did not wish to forget.

I felt the need to escape in others. And at the same time I felt the need of an examination of conscience that requires solitude. I felt the need to fill my life with small things, because they seemed to empty me of the big ones.

Part Three

Keyserling and Jung, 1929–1932

Jung and Keyserling had exchanged letters from time to time before Keyserling and Ocampo met. Though Jung had previously helpfully and sincerely interpreted a dream or symptom of Keyserling's from as early as 1923, he expressly kept Keyserling and his School of Wisdom at arm's length. In 1929, Keyserling writes to Jung about his encounter with Ocampo and later about a dream in which she appears. Jung suggests he reframe the encounter with Ocampo, re-imagine his travels to South America, and rewrite the manuscript of South American Meditations. Keyserling revises, and the book is published in 1932 in German, with faint careful praise from Jung and superlative endorsements from Thomas Mann, Jakob Wasserman, and Max Rychner. Jung's letters to Keyserling appear in Jung's published Letters, but this book presents for the first time Keyserling's side of the correspondence, also held in the Jung Archives, Special Collections, ETH Bibliothek.[1]

Darmstadt, 25 November 1929[2]

Strictly confidential

My dear Doctor,

Today I would like to inform you in the strictest confidence about a case which concerns in the first place another person, in the second place me, but in which I see at the same time a possible object of research of the first rank and a possible task for you. I believe to be entitled to do so in all respects, since the person in question – originally at my instigation – will in all probability get in touch with you in the course of this winter, and if anyone, *you* can help her. *But she must never know what I have told you.*

---

1 Letters by Jung translated from the German by R. F. C. Hull in Jung, *Letters*, Vol. 1. Letters by Keyserling translated from the German by Achim Stanislawski.
2 ETH Bibliothek identifiers: HS 1056: 402/ HS 1056: 29 880.

DOI: 10.4324/9781003266099-3

I am talking about Victoria Ocampo who brought me to South America. She has long had the reputation in Europe to be the most important woman of that continent (she is now 39 years old) and is undoubtedly one of the strongest and strangest personalities in our era. In the summer of 1927, she suddenly fell in love with my work and literally leapt on me like a tiger. She wrote me daily letters of the highest spiritual and emotional beauty. But more and more they became real love letters, more and more the motive came to the fore that she had finally found the one who would understand her completely, love her completely, just as she is. And with wonderful perspicacity she immediately recognized the one insertion point at which she could grasp me: my concern for material survival, or in my usual image: my fear of starvation. She was completely one with me, she would say, my work was her whole task, and she would take away all my worries of an uncertain future. Thus, I, living predominantly a life of poetry, slowly weaved her into the poetry of my destiny, and even today, when everything is over, I can hardly imagine her as not belonging to me eternally. She swore to me that she would now do everything for me, and in particular took over the preparation of my entire South American trip. It was a novel in letters and telegrams, as I have never heard of, more beautiful and intense than any fairy tale. But I felt uneasy about bursting into such a fairy tale in a foreign country, and so I let her – *c'est bien le mot* [it's the correct word] – come to Europe the previous winter so that we could get to know each other before the joint campaign in South America began. So we spent a month together in France in January/February 1929. She lived in Paris, I in Versailles, but she was with me at least 12 hours a day. The personal encounter exceeded all my expectations. Victoria was not only highly spiritual, she was very beautiful, and in her role of *donna umile* [humble woman] she developed in me an inspirational power such as I thought impossible. I was working all the time on *America Set Free*, which I completed in Versailles, and if the chapters "Predominant Women", "Culture", and "Spirituality" are certainly among the best I created, it is to her credit. I felt as if I was living in a poem back then. But at the same time, this woman somehow stirred me in the consciousness of an unattainable depth in her, as none before her had ever done. I was never in love in the usual sense, it was always clear to me that as a "woman" she was not really my type, but her influence shook me so violently that I did not sleep a single night and yet I was fresh and inspired to the highest degree and, above all, most of the hitherto buried or repressed emotional primal energies in me were set free. Later, all my friends found me rejuvenated by 10 years and completely relaxed inside. But the woman was at the same time in an incomprehensible way unhappy, even close to despair. She could never tell me what was happening inside her, she only cried uncontrollably, declared that she was living in hell. She gave me all the signs of love, except the last one, which I could have had at any time. Today I thank all my guardian spirits that I did not force her. I saw a terrible conflict in her – the unsolvable conflict between pure spirituality and the wild nature of the tiger or the serpent. I was well aware that the latter bound me, but that V. O. at the same time suffered from it and had come to me quite actually to be redeemed from it. Of course, I believed she wanted to be redeemed and tried to give her clarity. But her suffering became bigger and bigger only, as *I* became happier and freer, even if inwardly more agitated, I never took it seriously in the last instance.

I left. We were to meet again in South America, where she wanted to return before me to prepare everything. As soon as I left, the letters became strangely different from before. I was very worried and urged her to explain herself, that I was not a good guesser, that I could accept everything if she could only make me understand her. Always only reassuring letters, I should not worry, it was completely useless, it would only make her sick, and I found such letters at every station until the encounter in Buenos Aires. But when I arrived, I was suddenly confronted with a different person: no longer a *donna umile* in the least, but a violent queen, a Semiramis,[3] of incredible strength and ruthlessness, sometimes a fury. Outwardly she did everything for me, I was not allowed to do anything on my part that she did not prepare, but inwardly there was no longer any connection, the past was as if erased. This was the strongest shock of my life. It manifested itself, as always with me, above all physically – in one month I had more heart attacks (arhytmia (sic) perpetua) than in the previous 48 years. For I could not give in. If I broke away from South America, which everything urged me to do, it would have been an irreparable fiasco of my work. On the other hand, I could not expose her – for she had affixed herself to me with all the generosity of a good nature, and in all of South America we were more or less considered one, and all the world, beginning with her family, saw me that way. So I had to overcome myself as never before. That irritated her, she began to abuse me publicly (in private she never dared), I put up with it smiling. At the same time I tried for a long time in vain to achieve a clarification. Finally she explained to me that she had never really loved me, that she had only played in Versailles for fear of losing me,

---

3   The historical queen Shammuramat was the wife of Shamshi-Adad V (824–811 BCE), who ruled the Assyrian empire for five years as regent. In fables and legends, she appears as Semiramis, the Babylonian wife of Onnes and Ninus.

that we were incompatible, except spiritually, accusing herself that her basic trait was nothing but moral cowardice. I immediately addressed the situation, took all the blame, tried to re-found our friendship – in vain. The more I tried, the more unpleasant she became, albeit with constant relapses into tenderness and continued possessiveness. One thing was clear to me: the turnaround meant the violent incursion of reality into 2 years of a dreamed-up life. In particular, it was the revolt of the born and accustomed ruthless ruler to two years of *donna umile*, which was not acted, because it corresponded to the *real need* for admiration of her nature, but nevertheless constituted only a small part. Above all, I was really *physically unsympathetic* to her – no matter what had been the case earlier. I found in her, who had hardly been denied a wish from her second year of life, the desire of a woman to subjugate a man. My ever-growing serenity irritated her more and more. Whatever the outward appearance may have been (in fact, no one, even Victoria only to a small extent, noticed what was really going on inside me) – I have never suffered anything even remotely similar. The continuing bond routed through the unconsciousness, the necessity to hang on for the sake of my work, at the same time to overcome myself again and again – for there were moments when I would have loved to knock this woman down publicly – created for the two months I spent in Buenos Aires a state of inner torment such as I wish only for a few of my enemies. But I held out, and also forced – as I must admit, often with statesmanlike harshness – Victoria, who constantly, as a spoiled woman, wanted to break out, to keep her commitments once made. But when I was finally able to travel to other countries and there gained the opportunity to reflect on my feelings, I realized that I had been so deeply hurt that I had to break with her for a time, *precisely in order not to think badly of her all the time*. I did this from Chile and asked her to allow me not to see her again on the return trip. This was unexpected for the poor woman who had always lived her caprice. She is said to have suffered terribly and admitted it to me in her farewell letter. This letter was, by the way, *the first explanation* of what had really happened inside her – no matter what the original truth was – this woman has little imagination, and only a few women can ever imagine that they ever felt differently than they did at a given point in time. She declared in the bitterest, most hurting words possible, that I had always been as repugnant to her from the standpoint of sensibility as I was to her spiritually; that she had *prostituted* herself at the time out of love for my spirit and work, but that I had *poisoned* all her devotion, her admiration, her enthusiasm, etc., by my attitude toward her (which was simply that of the uncomplicated lover, on the one hand, and of the poet, on the other, who sees his muse primarily as such). She told me, she was guilty only of one thing: to have been too cowardly to show me the truth from the beginning.

I understand the complicated nature of women too poorly to be able to overlook what the ultimate truth may be. But one thing is for sure: I am deeply in this woman's debt and therefore I want to do everything that could help her. In her debt not because of the many external things she did for me – she made up for that abundantly by moral torment. *But because, in the final effect, she has done only good to me, and at her moral expense.* It is one of the strangest coincidences that could really make me believe in Christian providence, that the difficulty in South America has done me more good than all expected luck could ever have done. By some process of mysterious soul chemistry, which you will understand better than I do, the adversity has not embittered me, but, as far as I can see, has finally freed me. This is not imagination, but proven fact. Not only did I talk better than ever before – that is natural with a fighter nature like mine. But the energies rejected by the meant object became "universal", objectless, free. For the first time in my life I not only felt almost only positive myself – I triggered *love* in all others, indeed in whole peoples, to an overwhelming degree. I was carried by an ever higher and wider wave of sympathy. I was praised as a human being, as *el gran enamorado de la vida* [the great lover of life], as a person of pure and rich humanity, as the "eternal child" of ultimate simplicity. And this love, in turn, triggered in me a love for the entire South American continent such as I feel for no other soil. Towards Victoria I have today no shadow of a negative feeling. The moment I cut the thread, all bitterness in me ceased, I only think of her with deepest affection and have only one wish: to help her, which unfortunately I cannot do anymore.

This is the point for the sake of which I am writing to you. I have to thank the woman regardless of whatever I have gone through at times. *But I fear that I have only harmed her.* And the thought that it will remain so is unbearable to me. Since she is now sure to come to you, and you are the only person who in my opinion can help her, I would like to inform you in advance as to *how I think* her case lies. She is really quite a good nature. But she is completely torn between heaven and hell – it is not for nothing that she has written the most convincing text, to my knowledge, about hell in her book *De Francesca à Béatrice*. She is essentially good and generous – but her soul is completely unintegrated – there is no possibility of unification between the femme fatale, which she is to the highest degree, the refined sexual being, the ruler, *and the servant of pure spirituality, with which alone she identifies.* However, since she is 98% a powerful earth-spirit, she is constantly disappointed by the fact that no one believes in the supremacy of the spiritual in her. Since she is also completely undisciplined and ultimately inferior to her own nature, despite a very strong will, everything in her life goes badly for her – so far she has lost every significant person, her marriage was a disaster (she is separated, they have not agreed on a divorce), and the only permanent thing in her life is a very insignificant but tolerating *amant sérieux* [serious lover]. Her condition only got worse, since she suffers like all South Americans from an "inflation of the ego in its passive modality" in an almost improbable way. In her mind everything is related to herself and the way it affects her. This results in a hopeless permanent sadness, a real state of hell – for how is one to become free if one's consciousness is always held in shackles? Since she has been pampered and spoiled throughout her life, since the most unbelievable things have been let through and forgiven her, she cannot bear the slightest contradiction. She holds a grudge for every bad word spoken against her, which she takes as "misunderstanding of her being". Finally, she is still *ultimately shy*, even to the point of cowardice; her regal demeanour is in part overcompensation. The case is thus pathological in the deepest sense of the word.

Surely, she came to me to be redeemed – and I disappointed her. She always claimed that she and I are the same, because she can't stand to love someone she doesn't identify with – in truth I am her exact opposite. And when I now hear that she wants to visit you – I think *you* are likely to become her exclusive interest (she is only interested in one person or one thing at a time, other things meanwhile no longer exist for her), this is probably the same instinct. Only this time it seems to me to be directed correctly. You can *really help her*. That's why I'm informing you here in advance, as best as I can. I beg you from the bottom of my heart to help her. *It is worth it*. She is really quite a good nature. Only she must not know how much you have learned through me, indeed anything at all through me. *That is my basic condition*. Surely she will blame me for everything. May she let off some steam. But perhaps after a while you can contribute to a conclusion where she does not remain my enemy and her – certainly justified – personal resentment no longer stands as her last word. For somehow she remains just as attached to me as I remain to her. And one should probably hold dear troubling memories, but never ugly ones.

Another very important thing: a dream accompanies Victoria throughout her life: she sees someone she loves, who makes her completely happy, she rushes to him joyfully, and all of a sudden he changes, becomes indifferent or even a complete stranger. This is what she has experienced in everyone so far, probably most strongly in me. It would be nice if she did not experience the same in you – surely this can be achieved by psychosocial techniques.

V. O. will probably come to Europe in December and I suppose she will write to you then. But perhaps she is already corresponding with you. If you wish to write to me about possible outcomes *concerning me*, which have aroused your interest, I would be very glad to hear from you. By the way, we will probably see each other in January, since I have finally accepted the urgent invitation of the Zürich Schauspielhaus, which has already been repeated five times.

With best regards.

Yours faithfully,

Hermann Keyserling

20 December 1929[4]

Dear Count,

I still haven't heard anything from V. O. It goes without saying that I will treat your letter as non-existent. Your excellent description of the fateful intermezzo with her clearly shows that it is an encounter with an "earth woman", fraught with meaning. Concealed and revealed in it is one of the most beautiful animus-anima stories I have ever heard. Unfortunately poetic stories usually end in disappointment because, when one meets one's soul, one never recognizes it but confuses it with the poor human creature who has functioned unconsciously as a symbol carrier. V. O.'s longing for identification actually refers to the animus which she would like to possess in you, but she mixes it up with you personally and then of course is deeply disappointed. This disappointment will be repeated, always and everywhere, until man has learnt to distinguish his soul from the other person. Then his soul can return to him. This lesson is a hellish torture for both, but extremely useful, *the* experience one would have wished for you, and assuredly the most fitting torture of all for V. O., who is still possessed by her earth demons. Perhaps she prefers to be torn to pieces by the titans, as happens to many such anima figures. Hence you should always remember, with reverence and devotion, what has been revealed to you in the human shell of V. O., so that your soul may remain inalienably with you, and your access to the earth may never be blocked. Let us hope the same for her, that besides

---

4 ETH Bibliothek identifiers: HS 1056: 488/HS 1056: 29 881

tigers and serpents and eternal spirit there is still a human being in her who can remember with gratitude the revelation of her own spirit in you. But it is only too easy to make a personal tragedy out of what was ultimately a *"Divina Commedia,"* and then a spark of the eternal fire hisses out in a puddle. With best regards,

Ever sincerely yours,

C. G. Jung

P.S. Please excuse the spot of paraffin on the paper. My lamp suddenly seems to have got symptoms of incontinence.

Darmstadt, 30th December 1929[5]

My dear Doctor,

Your letter concerning V.O. did me a lot of good. Especially since I know very well that it is indeed in your power to help V. O. – if she can be helped at all. She is now definitely arriving in Paris in about a week. I am curious to see if she will find her way to you.

The question of a meeting in Zürich on the 12th or 13th has in the meantime also been settled for my part, since I won't get there at all. *Between the two of us*: Mrs. von Martini wrote me an outlandish letter in the style of the "Berner Bund" in which she told me such indiscreet things about the Zürichers as a collective that I can't see Mrs. Martini again for a long time and that I, therefore, had to cancel the Zürich Schauspielhaus *for this time*, since the connection was established by her. Far be it from me, of course, to think that the Zürich audience is as bad as this lady makes it out to be, but for the moment the situation is nevertheless "generally" muddled, for after all I have seen most of them at her place, and I cannot enter her house again. It would have been a pleasure for me to see you at Frau von Schnitzler's. But I am now invited to St. Moritz from January 15th to 20th by Spanish friends, who want to prepare with me my spring lecture tour on the Iberian Peninsula, and I can no longer change these dates. I have asked Mrs. von Schnitzler to discuss verbally with you on the 16th whether a reunion will be possible on my way from St. Moritz to Les Diablerets, where I will spend roughly a month.

With best New Year wishes from house to house,

Yours,

Hermann Keyserling

---

5 ETH Bibliothek identifiers: HS 1056: 403/ HS 1056: 29 882.

Darmstadt, 14th June 1930[6]

Confidential

My dear doctor,

Since it is still possible that Victoria Ocampo will someday come to you, which I hope so much, I am already sharing the following further material with you – if she really does appear at your house, perhaps you will have a cursory look through it first.

I had just disappeared from her sight the previous fall when V.O. transferred her enthusiasm to Waldo Frank; she has now followed him from Paris to New York. In Paris, she had several adventures, *which all ended badly*. But the strangest thing was that from there on she followed a movie star (Mann) to Berlin, where she stayed alone for four weeks – she never met the man in person but always dined at tables near him and wrote him glowing letters. Mutual Argentinean friends who want to bring us back together, tried to persuade me that V.O. was still a 15-year-old girl, a crazy teenager. I think what you said about her as being an "Anima-Nature" is *true*. And one more thing is interesting: said friends deny that V.O. actually suffers at all. From her 15th year on, she has always experienced the same thing, several times every year, and truth be told she just needed the sensation …

I've had a fabulous time in Portugal, Spain, and most recently even Paris. It must be that I am changed because I now meet the same kind of generous sympathy everywhere. In small towns in Spain, *sometimes almost 10% of the population listened to my lectures* – I have never experienced that before. And Paris was also very beautiful. In Spain, I spoke mainly on the rebirth of the Hispanic spiritual kingdom. In a few weeks, I will send you the next "Path to Perfection": there you will find some things that may interest you: an essay of mine "On the Essence of Passion" and a short report on the last conference where I spoke about South America as a symbol.

Yours sincerely,

Hermann Keyserling

---

6   ETH Bibliothek identifiers: HS 1056: 604/ HS 1056: 29 885.

9 September 1930[7]

Dear Count,

I still owe you many thanks for your new book on America. However, I have not got down to reading it yet as I myself have some writing to do. But I shall set about it soon.

When you write about South America, the continent of your inferior function, and at the same time your body forces itself unpleasantly upon your attention, this may well be because body and earth somehow feel irritated by your writing. Your nausea bears this out. Why don't you let your bowels say something too in your new book?

With best greetings and again heartiest thanks,

Jung

Pollensa-Mallorca, Islas Baleares, Formentor, 31st March 1931[8]

My dear doctor,

You surely do not have a lot of time to write, but since I don't know when I will see you again, I would like to ask you something; *peut-être que le coeur vous en dira de répondre* [perhaps your heart will tell you to respond]. I would like to know whether you are familiar with the wish to die. The last time we saw each other, and also before that, you gave me a resigned impression that went beyond all possible external causes. Once you wrote to me about a great inner sacrifice. But have you reached the limit, as I have so often?

From my 20th year on, nothing touches me so deeply – and every time it comes to mind, tears come to my eyes – as Wotan's cry of longing in *"Die Walküre"* (or any other part of the trilogy), "The end!" Especially in the glorious sixth modulation of the double repetition ... I have often been near death, and each time I have been wonderfully peaceful, almost saintly. Recently it was worse than ever. You have probably heard how badly I was in January and February: pneumonia with alarming heart failure. Not nearly recovered, I had to go to Paris, after three days a relapse came, which I prevented from breaking out; if I managed to fill and spellbind the giant hall of the Trocadéro for three days in one week, especially in the final lecture *"La Vie et la Destinée"*, where

---

7 Jung, 09 09 1920, *Letters*, Vol. 1, pp. 75–76.
8 ETH Bibliothek identifiers: HS 1056: 945/ HS 1056: 29 899.

I spoke a lot about death, it was probably mainly because an almost incorporeal spirit spoke through me – or better: a spirit spoke out of my physical shell. I collapsed immediately after. On the train from Paris to Barcelona, I thought I was dying of complete heart failure. The organ soon recovered to some extent – I am not supposed to lack anything directly in the heart – but something new, permanent has remained in my lungs, the slightest movement makes me feverish, I cannot and must not do anything of my own accord. And I had to continue working until the day before yesterday. Twice I had to get out of bed, as a real "revenant", in Barcelona for lectures. Here I spent a real Darmstadt week in Spanish, under the pine trees by the sea, which was one of the most beautiful of my experience. And I was completely different than usual: almost without physical vitality, but completely serene, unable to get angry, and everyone's love just flooded towards me. The wave is also coming back from South America. Friends of Victoria Ocampo keep coming to me one after another, several Madrileneans visited me on their way to Buenos Aires. Victoria has also asked me for an article for her new magazine, which I wrote during the worst pneumonia, about which she was so happy that she telegraphed to all the world about it (not to me; we no longer have a personal relationship).

What is this all about? Am I at the end? There really seems to be no art to being a saint. A lack of salt may bring you close to it, heavy illness makes the thing perfect. But I am not really up to it. If I am healthy I always think of death, full of fear – the thought of the cessation of my radiant life force is dreadful to me. I have been in this state for several months now, and I would welcome a brother in death.

Meanwhile I *do not believe* that I am really already at the end – I look very well, and what I have achieved in overcoming illness during the last week (when I went to Paris, I was just at the beginning of convalescence, which explains my relapses!) proves that I still have great strength. *On the other hand*, I have not had any dreams of death or execution for a long time, everything takes place in my daytime consciousness, which is probably a worrying sign considering my nature. There is only one thing that *depresses* me: that I have not been able to *write* for more than a year. Count Hardenberg insists that Victoria Ocampo must have poisoned or rather "bewitched" me. The experience must have given me a deep shock, although I feel little of it directly. Certainly, I am no longer the same.

If you can think of something to say about all this, please write to me. You can reach me here (Hôtel Formentor, Pallensa, Mallorca, Spain – takes 5 days for letters) until April 27th, then again in Darmstadt. The hotel is quite wonderful – a wonderful house by the sea, 70 kilometres from any railroad connection; originally the love nest of an Argentine. With real Spanish magnificence, the Catalonians have invited me to stay as *their guest* and rest as long as I want. All this human warmth does me good.

By the way, the Conferencia Club in Barcelona wants to invite you to give lectures. If they approach you, *I urge you to accept* – it is a most interesting milieu and the [radio] coverage from Barcelona is very good. I have already spoken there twice and will probably come again in 1932. You do speak French?

By the way, I also had a good time in France. I was impressed by the openness of the widest circles to the most profoundly spiritual things: *Ce n'est pas de l'Esprit, c'est du* pain *que vous nous donnez* [It's not of the spirit, it's bread that you give us]. But also the "spiritual types" were so wonderfully different from the German ones. The French have the *probité intellectuelle* [intellectual integrity] ahead of our spiritual countrymen.

Happy Easter and warm greetings to you all from

Hermann Keyserling

---

23 April 1931[9]

Dear Count,

From your description I have the impression that your South American experience, especially the encounter with V.O., has constellated contents in your unconscious that are the source of continued disturbances. For better or worse we must (in collaboration with the South American earth) take V.O. as the anima, who (like South America) stands for the whole unconscious. The unconscious has a different rhythm from consciousness and different goals. Until now you have been accustomed, by means of intuition and literary work, to subordinate everything the psyche offered you to the aims of your conscious mind, or to create out of it a conscious view of the world. You have made South America out of V.O. Now it is a question of expressing those contents which can be located neither in V.O. nor in S.A. (and which seem to you still completely unknown), not by moulding them into a picture of the external world or incorporating them in such a picture, but, on the contrary, by subordinating your philosophical skill and descriptive powers to

---

9   ETH Bibliothek identifiers: HS 1056: 1166/ HS 1056: 29 900.

those unknown contents. Then those contents will be able to mould an inner picture of the world without your guidance or intention. The initial question to be directed to the invisible world would be: "Who or what has come alive in S.A.? Who or what has entered my psychic life and created disturbances and wants to be heard?" To this you should add: "Let it speak!" Then switch off your noisy consciousness and listen quietly inwards and look at the images that appear before your inner eye, or hearken to the words which the muscles of your speech apparatus are trying to form. Write down what then comes without criticism. Images should be drawn or painted assiduously no matter whether you can do it or not.

Once you have got at least fragments of these contents, then you may meditate on them *afterwards*. Don't criticize anything away! If any questions arise, put them to the unconscious again the next day. Don't be content with your own explanations no matter how intelligent they are. Remember that your health is seriously at stake, and that the unconscious has an unknown and far-reaching control over it.

Treat any drawing the same way. Meditate on them afterwards and every day go on developing what is unsatisfactory about them. The important thing is to let the unconscious take the lead. You must always be convinced that you have mere after-knowledge and nothing else. In this case the unconscious really does know better.

Forgive me for delaying my answer so long. With best wishes,

Yours sincerely,

C. G. Jung

---

13 August 1931[10]

Dear Count,

First I must ask you to forgive me for not reacting earlier to your interesting MS [part of *South American Meditations*]. It is rich and significant in content. You are inaugurating a new and contemporary style of "sentimental journey", though it is considerably bloodier than its predecessors. South America has also brought you face to face, plainly and honestly, with the dark underworld, the chthonic unconscious. It is a classic case of the collective unconscious being constellated by the

10   ETH Bibliothek identifiers: HS 1056: 29 903/ HS 1056: 1167

activation of the inferior function, which because of its contamination with the contents of the collective unconscious always drags this up with it. Simultaneously the anima emerges in exemplary fashion from the primeval slime, laden with all the pulpy and monstrous appendages of the deep. And outside, conjured up by her appearance inside, Victoria Ocampo is forced into your magic circle – a meaningful adventure whose continuation arouses my curiosity! That was an encounter with the daemonism[11] of the earth, and it has never yet been described better.

I wish you all luck with the continuation, but would advise you to cut down on "cultural speculation" as much as possible, otherwise you will blur what is most impressive about your work – the personal experience with its exemplary subjectivity.

I hope you are all right in health. With best regards,

Yours sincerely,

C. G. Jung

Darmstadt, 14th December 1931[12]

My dear doctor,

What could it mean that last night, after months of not dreaming of Victoria Ocampo at all – and up until then solely of her, and very often of her as a she-devil – I dreamed a wonderfully pleasant dream with her as the central figure? I was at a seaside resort. But there were *various* pools, which were carefully filled by the tide. I was striving for the open sea, which was not always easy in the bathing costume since I had to pass through a crowd of people. But I was afraid that if I went dressed, my clothes would be stolen. V.O. was also at this bathing place. Touchingly soft, quite aloof, only a "good friend" and eagerly willing to help me translate my *Südamerikanische Meditationen* into Spanish!

Please do not bother to answer in writing – I write only quickly because I forget dreams too easily. I will see you in January. On January 8th, I will give the first lecture of my Swiss tour in Zürich, then I have

---

11   Elsewhere Jung writes, "The more clearly the archetype is constellated, the more powerful will be its fascination, and the resultant religious statements will formulate it accordingly, as something 'daemonic' or 'divine'. Such statements indicate possession by an archetype." "A Psychological Approach to the Dogma of the Trinity", §223.
12   ETH Bibliothek identifier: HS 1056: 29 906/ HS 1056: 949a

to move on immediately, but I will be back around January 20 for about 8 days of dental treatment in your capital.

My great work is 5/6 finished. It will be something completely different from everything I created before. Not a modern "Sentimental Journey" like you said, but a modern *Divina Commedia*. I have never been so moved and delighted.

Warm Christmas wishes and New Year greetings from house to house.

Yours,

Hermann Keyserling

---

24 December 1931[13]

Dear Count,

Your dream eludes my understanding as I don't know what conscious situation it is compensating. Academically speaking, "bath" always signifies "change", "rebirth", "renewal". "Sea" = the collective unconscious. V.O. is undoubtedly the anima, representing the coll. unc. In the psychological sense your South America book corresponds to a "night sea journey", i.e., another rebirth ritual. Could this dream be connected with the fact that you have as good as finished the book? As a rule a book or work of art amounts to an external ritual action, which does not by itself produce a change in the subject since it merely deputizes for him. Often the (ritual) work can grip the author retroactively and afterwards bring about a psychic change in him if he has not gone through the initial experience or has not done so sufficiently. This is a fateful question I cannot decide. But if it should be your destiny to go through further changes in order to arrive at an illumination and detachment of consciousness you have not yet attained, then this dream would be a message and a warning that you are again confronted with the collective unconscious and the anima just as you were in South America.

I have regretted very much not having seen you in the summer. Unfortunately you were within reachable distance just at the time when I had shut myself away from the world for a month. These retreats are so important to me that nothing can interrupt them. Please forgive me. I am at home in January, from the 15th on. If you came on the 20th, I would be most happy to see you again.

---

13   ETH Bibliothek identifier: HS 1056: 29 907.

I need hardly say how much I am looking forward to your *Divina Commedia*. I hope you have been sent my new book. It is only a collection of essays. With best wishes for the New Year.

Yours sincerely,

C. G. Jung

Darmstadt, 9th October 1932[14]

My dear doctor,

It will interest you that my *Meditationen* have already stirred Victoria Ocampo up to a certain degree of manifestation. The day before yesterday I was surprised by a telegram from Buenos Aires: *Votre livre est plein de pages géniales, je vous félicite* [Your book is full of brilliant pages. I congratulate you].

Frau von Schnitzler told me the other day that you had intended to write about my book in the *Neue Züricher Zeitung*, but that an unknown editor has beaten you to it. You can imagine how sorry I am about that. Will you perhaps consider writing a psychological study about this book, similar to the one about Joyce's "Ulysses" (which, by the way, I hardly understood, his mindset is alien to me) perhaps in the *Neue Züricher Zeitung*, after all? Or in the *Europäische Revue* where Rohan's[15] unconsciousness has played a nasty trick on me? Rohan's (as he claims) well-intended article is a school example of vented resentment, since he is known to be my student. He really does harm by allowing himself this – in the worst sense of the Jewish word, *schnoddrige*,[16] – act of disrespect. Otherwise, I certainly cannot complain. Of those who have spoken, only the Russian Orthodox Berdjajeff[17] and some French women have understood me deeply. But the purely positive reaction of Argentina was a great joy for me, which, despite its otherwise tremendous national vanity, does not even notice the negative aspects mixed

---

14   ETH Bibliothek identifiers: HS 1056: 1408/ HS 1056: 29 912.
15   Karl Anton Prinz Rohan (1898–1975), an Austrian writer who edited the *Europäische Revue* from 1925 to 1936.
16   The translator notes, "*Schnoddrige*: perhaps a Yiddish word or a German word of unknown origin, meaning: 'disrespectful, lacking respect' but not because the critic has a better knowledge of things, but to the contrary: being disrespectful without caring to check facts, admitting that one's criticism could be wrong."
17   Nikolai Berdyaev (1874–1948), a Russian philosopher exiled first to Berlin and then to France.

into the positive. It goes without saying that the typical German, whom the Russian defines as soulless (*besduschnyi*), understands only the rational in the book, or the artistic.

Please convey a much belated thanks to your wife for her beautiful letter.

With many greetings from house to house,

Yours,

Hermann Keyserling

Part Four

Ocampo and Jung, 1934–1943

In her first letter to Jung in June 1934, Ocampo thanks him for his analytical psychology and praises Psychological Types and Modern Man in Search of a Soul, which she intends to publish in Spanish. She travels to Zürich and meets him at his home in Küsnacht briefly, between patients. On her way into that meeting, she depotentiates her inferiority complex by connecting to Jung through his collection of detective novels; on her way out, they refer lightly to one of his two dogs as introverted, the other extroverted. (All this she relates later in her memoir; see Part Six). Later she writes to him from her Zürich hotel, having waited for a second, longer meeting. Years later, during wartime, she writes again to ask for an essay for her literary review, Sur. This book presents these letters for the first time, and this section also includes Jung's preface composed especially for Ocampo's Spanish-language edition of Psychological Types. These documents are housed in Special Collections, ETH Bibliothek. Some of Ocampo's letters in the Jung archives there bear the handwritten classifying heading "Keyserling" rather than "Ocampo".[1]

SS Cap Arcona,[2]

Atlantic Ocean

June 12, 1934

Dear Dr Jung:

Since my friend Ortega y Gasset published *The Psychology of the Unconscious* and since I read the English translation of *Psychological Types* I have been wanting to meet you, to know you. Your books have been a great help to me. I admire them and I am grateful to them, to you, for all I have found in them. I feel I owe you half of my actual

---

1 Letters translated from the French by Craig Stephenson. Jung's foreword to the Argentine edition of *Psychological Types* translated by R. F. C. Hull.
2 ETH Bibliothek identifier: HS 1056: 2863; Ocampo, V.

DOI: 10.4324/9781003266099-4

serenity … perhaps more than half! And I shall always be indebted to you for it. Unfortunately, or fortunately, this serenity is not complete, nor continuous! But I suppose few human beings know such uninterrupted and unimpaired bliss … Few or none? We will talk about that when we meet. Because I hope we will meet, soon.

I am South American (Argentine). We have common friends, I believe, and maybe you heard my name, maybe not. I am quite certain you never saw my review, *SUR*. South America is so terribly far from you, Europeans … though we, Americans, are so terribly near and suffer so much of the Atlantic Ocean. The Atlantic Ocean is like a mental disease in some of us. DISTANCE. Exile! We are always exiled. Exiled in America! Exiled in Europe! We can't do without Europe, but neither can we do without America. We stifle in America, and we stifle – for other reasons – in Europe. Perhaps, sometime, something will be born of it. In the meantime our anguish is intense.[3]

SUR has been publishing some English books translated in Spanish (Huxley's *Pointcounterpoint*, Lawrence's *Kangaroo*, etc. Unfortunately the crisis is making everything rather difficult. Nevertheless I hope the Spanish translation and publication of *Psychological Types* will be an *affaire conclue* when I get to Paris. I wrote to my agent in Madrid about it.

I am reading now *Modern Man in Search of a Soul*. I should very much like to have that book translated too. Before I started reading it, I wrote an article for *LA NACION* (Buenos Aires) on Huxley's last book, *Beyond the Bay of Mexique*[4] [sic]. I should like you to read that article (if you have some spare time) because it will help you to understand how deeply moved I must have been by *Modern Man in Search of a Soul* and how I must treasure those pages. You don't read Spanish, I suppose. Can I send you my article in French? Can I write to you in French? I don't feel quite at home in English but I do in French.

Are you staying in Zürich for a while? Where shall I go to see you? Where will it be more convenient to you and when?

3 In her 1931 essay, "Palabras francesas", Ocampo writes, "If I hadn't been American, after all, I probably wouldn't have felt this thirst to explain, to explain us and to explain myself. In Europe when something is produced, you could say it is explained beforehand; each event gives the impression of carrying an identity tag from the time it occurs and is appropriately shelved. Here, on the other hand, each thing, each event is suspicious and suspected of being something without precedent. We have to examine it from top to bottom to try to identify it, and sometimes when we try to apply the explanations that analogous cases would receive in Europe, we find that they don't fit. Then here we are, obliged to close our eyes and to advance, gropingly and hazardously, toward ourselves …" Quoted in Gabriela Mistral and Victoria Ocampo, *This America of Ours*, 9.

4 Aldous Huxley's travel book, *Beyond the Mexique Bay*, was published by Chatto and Windus in 1934.

If some lectures could be arranged for you in Argentina, next year, would you feel tempted?

Please let me have an answer as quickly as possible, because all my other plans will wait till this most important business of having a talk with you is fixed. Can you, will you arrange it? Anyhow I thank you for all you have already given to me.

Victoria Ocampo
27 avenue Malakaff
Paris

I shall be in Paris the 21 of June.

June 26, 1934[5]
Mme Victoria Ocampo,
27 Avenue Malakoff,
Paris

Dear Madam,

Unfortunately I don't read Spanish, but you can write to me in French, just as well if you don't like the English.

If you want to meet me it ought to be in Zürich, because next week I shall begin my vacations which I usually spend not altogether too far from Zürich. Not knowing your program I don't know when an interview would suit you. I could see you in July but I should prefer it to be between the first and the 18th of August. As far as the 13th of July I'm coming down every Friday to my place at the above address, which is a sort of suburb of Zürich. Thus I could see you on any of those Fridays if you let me know in time, i.e., about a week ahead.

I can't say that I feel particularly tempted to lecture in Argentine [sic], because as a whole I don't like lecturing. There is too kuch [sic] talk in the world anyhow.

I have been surprised by your remark that Ortega y Gasset has published the *Psychology of the Unconscious*. I had no idea that he had a hand in it. It is nice to know that what one has written has meant something to somebody.

Sincerely yours,

C. G. Jung

5   ETH Bibliothek identifier: HS 1056: 3277; Keyserling.

27 Avenue Malakoff[6]
Passy 25–93
28 June 1934

Dear Dr Jung:

Everything that has something to do with the "Revista de Occidente" has something to do with Ortega. And I doubt if he had not a hand in the publication of your book. Of course there is too much talk in the world, but your kind of talk is not quite the same as everyone else's, I believe. Sorry you are not tempted.

I shall try to go to Zürich in August, as you prefer it.

Yes! Your books have meant and mean very much to me.

Sincerely yours,

Victoria Ocampo

Hotel Baur au Lac[7]
Zürich
16 October

Dr Jung,

I leave Zurich, where I came especially to see you, with the bitter regret that I could not really speak with you as I would have liked. I needed very much to do so. But since you had no time to spare, I won't insist. Just imagine that I had almost given up coming to see you because of your letter! That letter was like a bucket of cold water. I had, thanks to that letter, the impression that you, who understand everything (at least everything that, in my opinion, is essential in life) had not understood the tone of my letter. That is to say, the degree to which I was sincere and the degree to which your books meant something deeply important in my life.

It would be necessary, Dr Jung, for me to go and consult you as a sick person, without really being sick. Indeed, my moral sickness consists in being tormented by a variety of attitudes that are in appearance contradictory.

You could help me see more clearly (and I believe that only by speaking with you this miracle would come into effect), and I would

---

6   ETH Bibliothek identifier: HS 1056: 2864; Ocampo, V.
7   ETH Bibliothek identifier: HS 1056: 2865; Ocampo, V. Translated from the French.

be as grateful to you as if you had cured me of a torment, a physical ailment. If you could only classify me in the same way you classify your dogs, that would amount to the same thing as winning a battle against the enemy ...

What do you think of this?

For my part, I believe that, at this moment, you are the only person whose help can be effective for me. As I familiarize myself with your thinking, and I apologize if I appear presumptuous, it seems to me that I'll arrive at a relative peace of mind. This would allow me to work better than I do now, and especially to disperse myself less.

As far as I'm concerned, that's the situation.

As for your lectures in Argentina, I want to repeat that this trip might be of some interest to you, and would be enormously interesting to us.

As soon as I arrive in Paris, I will send you the last issue of my magazine where your book is already announced, as well as two of the volumes published by us, so that you can see what they look like.

I hope (and if I didn't hope this, I would feel truly despondent) that *Psychological Types* will find in all of Latin America (that cannot be accused of lacking vastness) as well as in Spain ... at least ten readers! You can see that I am neither very ambitious nor very optimistic. But I am stubborn. If there is anyone in our Americas that this book should reach, then it's necessary that that someone be indeed reached. And I will make every effort to achieve this.

I'm leaving Zurich this evening. If I don't call you, it's because I've nothing more to say.

When you have time for a client who wishes to consult you, you'll let me know.

With fondest memories, and with the assurance of my sincere admiration.

Victoria Ocampo

P.S.: I'm sending you a short commentary on the *Commedia* published twelve years ago in a Buenos Aires newspaper for the sixth centenary of Dante. It has no value other than to reveal my thirst for order, an order that I admire in Dante ... an order that I cannot enter except by my own means, or at least enter in the same way. The Catholic Church horrifies me. The *church*, you understand.

I'm sorry I can't send you my more recent writings (that are of greater value, a fact that pleases me) but they have only been published in Spanish.

October 25, 1934[8]

Madame Victoria Ocampo
Banque Espagnole du Rio de la Plata
8 Av de l'Opéra
Paris

Dear Madam,

You will find here the preface for the Spanish edition of *Psychologische Typen.*

I very much regretted, on telephoning you the other day, not to find you at your hotel, and I would like to rethank you again for your efforts to publish this translation. I would be obliged if you would also convey my thanks to Monsieur de la Serna.[9]

Yours faithfully,

C. G. Jung

Foreword to the Argentine Edition, *Psychological Types.*

No book that makes an essentially new contribution to knowledge enjoys the privilege of being thoroughly understood. Perhaps it is most difficult of all for new psychological insights to make any headway. A psychology that is grounded on experience always touches upon personal and intimate matters and thus arouses everything that is contradictory and unclarified in the human psyche. If one is plunged, as I am for professional reasons, into the chaos of psychological opinions, prejudices, and susceptibilities, one gets a profound and indelible impression of the diversity of individual psychic dispositions, tendencies, and convictions, while on the other hand one increasingly feels the need for some kind of order among the chaotic multiplicity of points of view. This need calls for a critical orientation and for general principles and criteria, not too specific in their formulation, which may serve as *points de repère* in sorting out the empirical material. What I have attempted in this book is essentially a critical psychology.

This fundamental tendency in my work has often been overlooked, and far too many readers have succumbed to the error of thinking that Chapter X ("General Descriptions of the Types") represents the essential content and purpose of the book, in the sense that it provides a system of classification and a practical guide to a good judgment of human character. Indeed, even in medical circles the opinion has got about that my method of treatment

---

8   ETH Bibliothek identifier: HS 1056: 9278; Keyserling.
9   Ramón Gómez de la Serna (1888–1963), an important Spanish writer, translated the book.

consists in fitting patients into this system and giving them corresponding "advice". This regrettable misunderstanding completely ignores the fact that this kind of classification is nothing but a childish parlour game, every bit as futile as the division of mankind into brachycephalics and dolichocephalics. My typology is far rather a critical apparatus serving to sort out and organize the welter of empirical material, but not in any sense to stick labels on people at first sight. It is not a physiognomy and not an anthropological system, but a critical psychology dealing with the organization and delimitation of psychic processes that can be shown to be typical. For this reason I have placed the general typology and the definitions at the end of the book, after having described, in Chapters I to IX, the processes in question with the help of various examples. I would therefore recommend the reader who really wants to understand my book to immerse himself first of all in Chapters II and V. He will gain more from them than from any typological terminology superficially picked up, since this serves no other purpose than a totally useless desire to stick on labels.

It is now my pleasant duty to express my sincerest thanks to Madame Victoria Ocampo for her great help in securing the publication of this book, and to Señor Ramón de la Serna for his work of translation.

Küsnacht/Zürich
October 1934
C. G. Jung

March 17, 1943[10]

Mar del Plata,
San Martin 689
Buenos Aires

Dear Dr Jung:

I don't know if you still remember my visit, on a very rainy day. Through me your *Tipos psicológicos* were translated in Spanish.

I should very much like to publish in my revue *SUR* (a monthly magazine) something lately written by you (and if possible, written for us).

Will you please let me know if you get this letter? Letters travel with some difficulty nowadays.

Yours sincerely,

Victoria Ocampo

---

10   ETH Bibliothek identifier: HS 1056: 10539; Ocampo, V.

Küsnacht-Zch[11]

July 3rd 1943
Mrs Victoria Ocampo
San Martin, 689
Buenos Aires
Argentina

Dear Mrs. Ocampo,

Your letter of March 17th reached me a few days ago. I certainly remember your visit to Zürich and your proposition to get my book about types published. I should like to live up to your expectations as to have an article of my pen for your magazine. Unfortunately we have to be content if letters go through in these times. I'm afraid that it would be absolutely useless to try to send manuscripts.

   Hoping you are always in good health, I remain

Yours sincerely

C. G. Jung

11   ETH Bibliothek identifier: HS 1056: 10792; Keyserling.

Part Five

Ocampo and Jung Meet, 1934

Ocampo's memoir of her meeting with Jung was published in 1936 in La Nación (Buenos Aires) and later collected in her Domingos en Hyde Park. She first describes a disagreement with a Parisian magazine editor over her use of Jung's word "introversion". In the second half of this memory piece she describes her brief encounter with Jung. While Ocampo's memoir was excerpted in C.G. Jung Speaking: Interviews and Encounters, editors William McGuire and R. F. C. Hull cut her account, included here, of why Jung's critical psychology was so important to her experience as a South American.[1]

Ways of Being: A Visit to Jung

Grasset, the Parisian publisher, has brought out a series of volumes grouped under the title, "Pour mon plaisir". I have had many occasions to congratulate myself that my own pleasure contributed to this. And when I'm asked about translations to be published by the press I direct, when they insist on the need to draw up a plan and follow it, when they become impatient and complain, "Why that book and not this other one?", I feel that the only truthful answer is, "For my pleasure". Grasset is a hundred times right.

Let's be clear about this notion of my pleasure. I personally don't need translations to read English and French texts. I read with greater enjoyment in both these languages than in my own. But there are those who, for one reason or another, have not been able to venture beyond Spanish. I have friends who have remained prisoners within its boundaries, and surely many unknown friends who find themselves in the same circumstances. It is of them that I think, because the compulsion to share with the largest number of people possible the readings that thrill me, has always been very forceful in me (a vice indeed unpunished because books belong to that species of

1 Translated from the Spanish by Alberto Manguel; excerpted in *C. G. Jung Speaking,* edited by McGuire and Hull.

DOI: 10.4324/9781003266099-5

authentic treasures that don't diminish when they are shared but, on the contrary, increase).

This brief preamble in which "the hateful I" occupies so much space (concealed or not, it is the space that belongs to it always in all writings, and I smile at those who pretend the contrary) was indispensable to arrive at this: to my friends known and unknown I offer "for my pleasure" the Spanish translation of Jung's most important work [*Psychological Types*].

The profane can be interested in this work, as well as the specialists. For those who enjoy novels, I can say that it is as gripping as a novel. For those who don't enjoy them (let's lower our voices, the novelists might hear me), I will say that it is as gripping as those novels that fascinate us precisely because they read like scientific works, like essays (which makes knowledgeable critics say that they are failed novels). Everyone can therefore find in it one's pleasure, one's thing.

The irrefutable fact of the existence of two essential types, antagonistic (that divide and branch out in turn) and the mutual miscomprehensions, the discords that derive from this, not only in the field of analytical psychology and other areas of science, but very particularly in the personal relationships between people, is the core of this extraordinary book.

For centuries, a handful of insightful beings, that at all times has constituted the salt of the earth, has realized the existence of two types of human beings. They were given different names according to the styles of the time. Jung, following his, calls them today "introverted" and "extraverted".

The peculiar characteristic of the mental activity of the extravert is that it is sparked by the object, by the outside world. From this are borne for him ideas, feelings, intuitions, and sensations. Contrariwise, the introvert retreats from the object, from the exterior world. He retreats to/quarters in his interior world, and what he thinks or feels about the object has more reality for him than the object itself. In a word, the extravert reaches herself only through the exterior world, while the introvert only reaches the exterior world through herself alone. Each of these ways of being has its advantages and disadvantages. According to the degree to which individuals are extraverted or introverted, the incomprehension between them varies in intensity. Sometimes it is absolute and leads to a mutual despising. Extraverts and introverts look at each other with malevolent reproach, they insult each other courteously or rudely, according to their temperament and upbringing.

I insist a little on the definition of the terms "introvert" and "extravert" – though I persist in believing that people of a certain culture are familiar with them as much as I am – because in this regard a singular adventure happened to me.

A brilliant woman, a poet, who occupied in Paris a splendid situation, asked me six years ago to allow her to read one of my articles, with the intention of publishing it – if judged worthy – in an important Parisian magazine. Among the articles I had written, I carefully chose the pages that seemed to me the least bad, and sent them to her. The answer was not long in arriving. She phoned me, congratulated me, but added that she needed to see me to speak about the article, in which she advised me to eliminate certain paragraphs. It took me less than five minutes to grab my hat, jump into a taxi, and arrive at her place. She began with some praise – "Ah, what poetry in all those childhood memories!" – and she ended with a reproach: "What does this 'introversion' mean? Do you mean 'introspection'? *The fact is that 'introversion' is not in the Littré Dictionary*.[2] And also, in a literary article/essay, these pseudo-scientific terms, that is to say pedantic terms, are inadmissible. If at least they were everyday terms!" In other words: If I wanted to appear in a magazine whose doors had been opened to me with such generosity, I had to eliminate from my article the offensive passage, the passage in which, I believed, the terms invented by Jung were *indispensable*.

This ultimatum left me puzzled. I felt absolutely that this was not a pretext: that Madame X believed what she was saying to me, and that it would be enough for me to give in for my article to be accepted. But the more I probed, the less I found in my mind the pre-eminence of an absolute respect for the *Littré* that every well-constituted head should possess. From that I inferred that this lack was due to my origin in the Americas and that I had to resign myself to it. A matter of dharma.

The words "introversion" and "extraversion" remained in my article, and the doors of the magazine were closed to me.

I confess that these words were indispensable to me. I was willing to sacrifice for them, not daily bread but daily vanity, that stupid vanity that we all know but that means so little and vanishes so easily when we become possessed by a passion.

In "Varieties of Intelligence", an essay that circles constantly around *Psychological Types*, Huxley has this to say:

> Few things are more disquieting than to discover, on the evidence of some casual remark, that you are speaking to a person whose mind is radically alien to your own. Between one easy chair in front of the fire and another a gulf suddenly yawns; you must have a strong head to be able to look into it without feeling giddy.[3]

Who amongst us has not felt this disagreeable and anguishing sensation? And for how many among us has it not been repeated to the point of suffering?

Jung's book clarifies many of the aspects of this problem, one of the most painful that exists. And at least regarding our intelligence, does one not heal

2 Émile Littré's *Dictionnaire de la Langue Française* was completed in 1873 and the *Supplément* in 1877.

3 Aldous Huxley (1894–1963), "Varieties of Intelligence", *Proper Studies* (London: Chatto and Windus, 1933, p. 75.

oneself by the very fact of understanding? (Even if only understanding why we do not understand.)

The heart has other ways, is less easy to heal, and, anyway, much slower. Perhaps because it lies in regions of human nature that escape all governance.

If we descend into these regions – not exactly those of the heart, but those that lie at the antipodes of the angel – there we discover that even abstract terms, frigid terms like "extraverted" and "introverted", acquire warmth. Insensibly when sitting next to the hearth we bounce them from one armchair to another, these terms – that are pleasing to our intelligence because they are associated with the cleaning up of certain obscure mechanisms – become altered into unforeseen and secret reproaches, indeed, into dissimulated insults. When a man who believes himself to be extraverted calls you an introvert, you lady, be on your guard. And you should be on your guard, sir, when a woman who believes herself to be introverted calls you an extravert. In the depths of their subconsciouses, these words are implicitly proceeded by the adjective "BIG".

And yet, in any case we emerge benefitting from this, it is to our gain. Before, they would simply have called us idiots.

However, let us always remember that Jung, precisely in the foreword written for the Argentine edition, warns us: "My typology is far rather a critical apparatus serving to sort out and organize the welter of empirical material, but not in any sense to stick labels on people at first sight" (Part Four).

Someone who is capable of understanding needs few words. This is proverbial. A word to the wise.

In October of 1934, I took a small detour as I was returning from Rome to Paris. I stopped in Zürich to meet the author of *Psychological Types*. It was pouring with rain that afternoon when my taxi crossed in Küsnacht a garden that smelt of wet earth and left me armed with an umbrella and disarmed by contradictory emotions, in front of the door of Dr Jung. Was it because of the long train ride, the sudden change in the weather, the rain, the proximity to a great man? I don't know. I felt growing and spreading in me one of those inferiority complexes that make us feel and wonderfully perform the role of an idiot. Under these sorry conditions I, my umbrella, and my emotions entered the house of the famous Swiss psychiatrist. But my umbrella, whose luck I envied at the moment, remained in the hall while we (my emotions and I) were forced to climb the stairs. We were asked to wait in a small room lined with books. That wait was providential. On the shelf I suddenly saw, lined up in a tight row, a regiment of detective novels. The arrival of the dove with the olive branch must not have produced in the heart of Noah a greater joy than this discovery produced in mine. It announced: "Land!"

"*Homo sum*", I thought. In the house of Dr Jung, he or his family read these solidly silly stories that were also read in mine, that you also read and that are as relaxing as a yawn. Instantly I recovered my poise. Certainly I knew from experience the weakness that certain princes of the mind felt for detective novels; my own library, rich in this kind of work, has been on many occasions sacked for its greed. But in spite of this, I had not expected to meet Edgar Wallace[4] in the house of the most eminent professor of Zürich University. I felt in ecstasy.

Utterly reassured, I entered Dr Jung's study a few minutes later.

I immediately I realized that he is tall, very tall. But curiously my eyes, that I raise up to him, don't recognize in that face more than an expression of power, or of an intelligence in which it is bathed; an intelligence that advances towards me like an enormous elephant, hiding all the rest. An elephantine intelligence! I have the impression that that colossal intelligence that sees everything, does not see me; I have the impression that it will step on me and squash me. Instinctively I feel that I should step out of its way and throw things at it. It grabs them, one by one, delicately, with that incredible ability of elephants … (whether to rip up a tree trunk or pick up a lump of sugar). And in this way we talk.

But suddenly he tells me something that I am still pondering, and which I believe from that interview is the observation worth repeating. When I asked him, would he not like to give lectures in Argentina, he answered: "What for? They would not interest anyone. The audience would not understand …" Because they are Latinos? Because they are Catholic?[5]

I would have wanted at that point that he give me a long explanatory lecture on the subject, but his clients were waiting for him with who knows what heavy load of complexes.

Jung accompanied me to the entrance hall, in which I took again my umbrella, no longer envied. His two dogs did not want to leave him and, stumbling over them, we went down the stairs together. One of the dogs was jumping around, the other, taciturn, moved unwillingly. Extraverted the one, introverted the other, my host said, laughing. I did not need to ask which was which.

Soon we will know if Jung was or wasn't right when he said that he would not be of interest to the Argentinian public. The enthusiasm that his book will produce will tell.

According to his own confession, *Psychological Types*, which I offer to my friends known and unknown, is the fruit of almost twenty years of work in the field of practical psychology.

Huxley says that when we read Jung's books, we feel that his intuitive knowledge of the human is as deep as that of Dostoevsky. As far as I am concerned, I confess that a book such as *Psychological Types* has moved me as much as *The Brothers Karamazov*.

March 1936.

4   (1875–1932), a prolific British writer of thrillers.
5   In *C. G. Jung Speaking*, edited by McGuire and Hull, the translation of these questions is punctuated incorrectly.

Part Six

Ocampo and Keyserling Meet Again, 1939

Ocampo and Keyserling begin exchanging letters again in February 1939 after Ocampo travels by car from Paris to Darmstadt to visit him. Words added in square brackets are the translator's speculations from Keyserling's notoriously unclear handwriting; ellipsis in square brackets means some text is left out because it appeared undecipherable; ellipsis with no square brackets means text has been deliberately omitted. Keyserling's side of the correspondence is housed at the Keyserling Archives, Fundación Sur Archives.[1]

Priz Christianweg 4, Darmstadt[2]

February 15, 1939

I am still so very much moved, dear, by the deep joy that your visit has given me, having suffered horribly from the ugliness of certain memories – the only memory of such an evening's end in my entire life – I am utterly grateful to you for a gesture that made the torrent of our relationship, so full of cataracts, overflow like a conversion in extremis "into Beauty". For me, everything is fine and good now, and nothing prevents us from being profound friends, hemisphere to hemisphere in a perpetual constellation, until death. There is only one thing that torments me: whether there lingers in you remnants of old resentments, or if this last meeting created in you any new "revulsions". Since you cannot speak and your face is almost always a cipher, I cannot read your soul.

Well, you promised to repress nothing and write to me frankly if you have still – or again – something weighing on your heart. I noticed that the verbal answer I gave to your letter surprised you in many ways. So I'm not sure you understand me or even that you believe that every word I told you corresponds to my truth, which is indeed the case. I have

1 Translated from the French by Craig Stephenson.
2 Fundación Sur Archives identifier: CORR-KEY2-020-W, 186 11-22/48

DOI: 10.4324/9781003266099-6

my points of view, I have nothing to add, but it came to my mind this morning that I did not respond at all to some of your statements, including the one that seems most important to you, since it was also the earliest part of your farewell letter from Buenos Aires: well, I cannot answer it directly, because of your pure spiritual fervour, close to idolatry, which, as you expressed yourself in 1929, I "poisoned". I see this fervour from a completely different angle than you do, and it is out of delicacy that so far I have not picked up on your words regarding this line of thought. But I must, so that at least there will be no longer any misunderstanding through my fault. If what I say to you is unpleasant, please forgive me, I do it out of confidence in your desire to progress, but here it is for me to be absolutely certain [that] I am objectively right. Well, it is the worst injustice, a million times worse in my eyes than that which you suffered by my fault, to idealize someone as you have idealized me, because no man could be as you conceived me, and such an idealization amounts in practice to a denigration and a defilement of the true man.

Unconsciously you demanded that I be as I could not be, and everything that has happened since is due to a psychological process, by means of which – unconsciously, of course – you made me pay for the fact of this reality, but nobody who was in love with my work, neither before nor after you, ever felt repulsed by my person: the fact that such a repulsion occurred is against nature, because normally admiration for a spirit or a work makes one love even the worst flaws of people. That you immediately felt, when you saw me, "a physical distance as strong as the spiritual attraction that made me come to you" (I quote verbatim from your farewell letter, the cruellest I've ever read, which I afterwards burned, but which remains engraved in my memory), was not at all due to what you think, but it was the inevitable psychological consequence of a false vision [practically speaking] of a human being. In such a case, as [compensation] for the exaggeration in one direction, another necessarily occurs on another level. An exaggerated repulsion [must] confuse you and compensate for the idealization, so that you don't fall into a schizophrenic madness. However, your vision of me remained schizophrenic after you met me, and that is the root of all, or at least almost all of this evil. Since then, you have clearly separated the spirit from the man, which is always wrong, and in my case so wrong that, until very recently, no one I had ever met understood me as badly as you did at the beginning of our meeting. You speak, for example, of my "talent" that you [held] in admiration. This sentence constitutes such a wounding misunderstanding for a man like me, that I saw in this choice of words only a pure expression of meanness.

Because I have no "talent", or, to speak more precisely, nothing in my work is due to what talents I have: anyone who [understands] the first thing about my work knows that I am a substantial spirit who incarnates in everything, each one of my gestures being as important as a book. If many of these gestures are not lovely, it is due to the fact that this incarnation is far from over. I'll gladly agree that in 1929, of course, I was [a sort of] embryo, horrible in many ways, but I hope you noticed that in 1939 I am already less embryonic. It is only you who ever thought (let alone put into print) that I have [the mouth of a baboon].[3]

Because, for anyone other than a butcher, my mouth, beautiful or ugly, is the expression of my spirit. That you could have felt that I was so "fruitily fleshly" (and obnoxious to you) was due to this horrible and cruel and execrable idealization of which I was the victim. Later, in Buenos Aires, you did everything to hurt the human being in me; with the ingenuity of the Sphex wasp (that paralyzes caterpillars to feed its young), you were mean; I had every reason in the world to see you as an Indian who shoots poisoned arrows … I could not find a way to rise above my own sensitivity and did not understand the deep meaning of this double and false vision that you hid in Versailles but showed [so frankly] when I saw you again in Buenos Aires. As soon as I understood this, and this already happened in December 1929, the wounds inflicted on my person and on the human and male being in me could heal at last. Furthermore I have always felt ashamed; a human being of good breeding does not have the right of allowing himself to remain feeling injured!

A grudge is always an odious thing. Suffering is there to help man surpass himself. I am at least as capable of suffering as you, but from the outset, at the very moment that it affects me I see in it a path, and I am incapable of stopping myself at the bare fact, neither in others nor in my own case, that's why I told you the rest without any bad feelings towards you …, but as soon as I lived the horrible experience of Buenos Aires (as horrible for me as Versailles was for you) it helped me to grow. And as soon as *South American Meditations* began to take form in me I blessed you for all the harm you had done to me and I will bless you all my life, and everyone knows that I have a gratitude without bounds for you and a deep feeling. Everyone also knows that I see you as one of the female figures of our time (which no one else among your friends that I know does).

3   On Ocampo's characterization of Keyserling's mouth, see Part Eight.

I wrote to Guy de Pourtalès[4] to send you *La Pêche miraculeuse*, one of the great masterpieces of this half century. If he asks to see you, I'll be very happy if you receive him. He is an exquisite man, much better than all the intellectuals at the [...]

But this, I say incidentally, "The main thing is that this schizophrenic split between the invented ideal and the lived reality has inevitably distorted your whole vision." You have since seen in a completely false light or falsely viewed the relationship of my spirit with my flesh, of the man and the work, you misunderstood me to the point of speaking of my talent (more stupid than nature, I quote you); you even doubted (this time it was one of your sisters who told me, not Moner[5]) my sincerity of my spirit and the elevation of my spirit; this complete ignorance on the part of a woman as intelligent as you (and who had for a while been understanding) can only be explained by the pathology that I have diagnosed. And I'm not sure yet that you are completely healed: I have the clear impression that you have not read and in any case do not understand what I do in the most humanly deep way, in the book you have just published (I am much more human than you, the [cumulative] suffering in the last instance is *ganic*, therefore animal). If my spirit no longer speaks to you as it did before our meeting, it can only be due to the survival in your unconscious of the distorted vision of 1929; there is only one other alternative: that in you *gana* absolutely takes precedence over spirit.

Here I come to an injustice that I really did to you: from the beginning of our meeting, I saw in you a *ganic* being who aspired desperately, exclusively, to spirit, like the plumed serpent. But why did I get to see only a boa, an anaconda? It was due to the same schizophrenic split from which you suffered and which had repercussions in me. Because your mind was living in a completely unreal and whimsical region, detached from your truth, and I saw only the other side.

[It really presented itself to my inner eye in an almost pure state]. This *ganic* side is really stronger in you than in any other being I have met in my life, it is also stronger still than ten years ago, because you have gained in force on all fronts. But [what] I only perceived and saw in 1929 is that the *ganic* being was due to the special "correspondence" that our polarization created or established. It is because of this that I attached such an insane importance to the telluric side [...]

I have had more platonic friendships than anyone in the world, since I don't fundamentally feel my flesh as "mine", and I've never started by wanting a woman whom I loved with spirit and soul – it has always been

4 (1881–1941), a Swiss writer.
5 Dr Gabriel Moner.

the women who did what was necessary to arrive as quickly as possible to an integral [consummation]. But for my part, I am happy that everything happened as it did, because if I had not met you in this strange situation, I would not have had the revelation of earth and spirit. It found expression in the *Meditations*. And quite frankly, I am incapable of understanding, I am fundamentally slow ... horrified by the idea that you do not seem able to succeed in blessing the sufferings that I inflicted on you, as I bless those that I owe to you. And they have been immense, not only [personal] like yours. Because being open to the world, to all others and affected by everything, given completely to this imperiousness that Ortega called your most striking characteristic (that you, and you alone in the world, have judged me and may still judge me as deaf to others) is yet an expression of the pathology of the survivor of 1929. I suffered cosmically, I might have said, that's why I was able to evoke Hell. What you did to me was [really] then of the same order as what the Bolsheviks did to me. You inspired my meditations: by this work which surely is situated and will be placed later by humanity on the same level as a *Divine Comedy* [...] for the 20th century, you have become, thanks to this role of muse, a great figure in history. You already are for many. And please don't tell me that you don't care: it would be so unworthy of you, demonstrating absolutely that your "spiritual fervour" of yesteryear was only *ganic* whim as Moner said and as I also believed for a few months, so that I do not even consider the possibility that you do not absolutely admit I was right for what was said there. A person is only worth what she means spiritually, and the fact that you take your moral and personal well-being so seriously, I see only as an embryonic state that you'll surely overcome and about which I refuse to concern myself. Your fervour for my spirit from 1926 to 1929 is, in my eyes, one of those anticipations of which I have spoken to you and that surely, after our new meeting, will increasingly give way to its realization. Your worthwhile life – apart from your contribution to the *Meditations* – has only just begun. If you truly yearn for spirit, you must wait for your peak – after your sixties, probably much later. I hope you have felt all the joy that your visit gave me and all the deep affection that I tried to radiate towards you. This letter does not require an answer: there is never anything to discuss (when it comes to interior and subjective things), it is of no importance whatsoever whether one is right or wrong in everything (Note: My wife had a long conversation with the Chancellor.[6] But I don't yet know the results.)

---

6 As the granddaughter of Bismarck, his wife pleaded to Hitler on Keyserling's behalf for the return of his passport.

I know that what I wrote to you is the ultimate truth to me and if you hold on to the contrary conviction, that is your business. The [bad] past is [amortized] objectively by your visit, whether you understand it or not. If you seriously meditate on this letter, you will quickly come to consider yourself from a point of view and at a level higher than you [seem] to do now.

But I hasten to add: if you feel the inner need, talk to me about it, in the name of God! [...] this letter constitutes an attempt at a psycho-analysis, and it will necessarily evoke counter-movements that should not be repressed. I am so happy now that the ugliness of 1929 has been wiped out of our lives that I am ready for all intellectual sacrifices to satisfy the needs of your soul, as far as I can.

With a strong Spanish hug and for always,

H.K.

I have written this with the gold pen you gave me in 1928.

Prinz Christianweg 4, Darmstadt[7]

February 16, 1939

How awful! You have had a narrow escape,[8] and I sympathize with you with all my being. I don't find it the same at all: physical suffering is absolutely [denied] meaning, there is no way to "conquer the destiny" of a toothache and nothing worse than [...] of a damaged throat. God (or whoever it is: the Void) will want you to recover quickly: boas have, in general, a limitless capacity for regeneration.

Did this accident happen by chance between 10 p.m. and midnight? I believe not – but if so, it would have been another coincidence. Between those hours, I suddenly slipped back, as if a cannon ball [had] taken out my legs, and I fell stiffly with my 120 kilos onto my back on a very hard floor. But I don't even have a bruise! – The mutual coincidence of which I'm thinking and this one, absolutely all those that are [p...] have either succumbed to disasters or were damaged or finally had narrow escapes, between 1937 and 1939. Your [case] has [...] my friends, about fifty [parallels], so much so that I am still working on them. If indeed you have had this narrow escape, this means to me that your stars [begin

---

7 Fundación Sur Archives identifier: CORR-KEY2-021; 186 23-26/48.
8 Ocampo suffered a car accident while driving back at night from Darmstadt to Paris.

again] to rise, in number [one hundred ...] with mine. I will tell you an astrological secret that has increased the emotion that your [arrival] produces in me. This January I entered "the house behind the house" (or country, homeland, family). For a long time now I have lived only an intimate life. But now, on the same day you [...] me, my wife returned after many years to her birthplace to act on my behalf.

I regret that my psychoanalytic letter finds you in such a bad state. If it wounds you in any way, please forgive me. For me everything is alright now, but I know that happy new relationships can only be established [on] the basis of full knowledge and acceptance of each other's views and feelings.

(I noticed that you didn't know everything about everyone I met when I answered verbally your letter from Traube).

[Yet] there is no need to agree; I believe, on the contrary, that our motto [should] be forever and ever: let's agree [to differ ...], our reactions and our intimate needs are completely different. And yet [can] we not be friends, celestial body to celestial body, through empty space?

Do you treat your throat pain with ice packs? It's still the best treatment.

My wife just got back, exhausted, but I think she did everything she could. In her person survives most of the manoeuvring and diplomatic arts of her grandfather. She chatted for [long] hours with the gentleman in question, who promised to take care personally of everything that concerned her. But the result is unpredictable, of course. I am sure there will be no war.

Good and speedy recovery! My wife [sends you] a thousand [...], she deeply regrets not having been able to see you this time and thanks you for coming and for sheathing me [so preciously during] these days that [were] most difficult to bear alone.

With all my most affectionate thoughts.

H.K.

P.S. Do not write to me by airmail, please, because such letters always take longer. An ordinary letter rarely takes more than 14 to 16 hours, yours took more.

Do I write clearly enough? To write, it's necessary for me to make an acrobatic effort like that of a circus cyclist who has to perform 3 minutes to the hour without falling.

Send me your news soon, one could give little [...] who cares for you.

Do me the pleasure of sending me a recent portrait of yourself without a hat and with your hair not too straight! What horrors, the hats of my friend, they would make any woman who was not born [Harlequin] [look ugly].

Prinz Christianweg 4, Darmstadt[9]

February 21, 1939

Many thanks for the truly superb photos. My wife also likes them and wishes me to convey, along with her most cordial regards and all her good wishes for a rapid recovery, that she finds you now infinitely, but infinitely more beautiful than you were, judging from your portraits of 1926 to 1929.

I was afraid your pain would last a long time. [...] happily you are so taciturn by nature: in this sense, perhaps you suffer less than others [from] this handicap. Since you are being cared for by Marañón[10] (whom you could greet on my behalf): what is the basis for his immense reputation, [this] doctor? *In España, hasta la gente adinerada insistía en que él presenciara el momento de sus fallecimientos* [In Spain, the wealthy even insist that he be present at the moment of their deaths]. Does he have an outstanding bedside manner? I see him as a great diagnostician. But the treatment that heals is another matter entirely. Is he a miracle worker? A euthanasia specialist? Perhaps Marañón would be interested in my article "On the Idea of the Healer", which has just appeared in Number 4 (February 1939) of the *International Journal of World Medical Sciences and Medicine*, 2 rue Goethe, XVIth arrondisement, so close to your place.

I could not write to you earlier because these last days I was overwhelmed (from the point of view of my [need for] solitude) by the representatives [of] a new group in formation, for whom my doctrine, especially in its latest version, represents the Gospel of the Aquarian Age. And if anyone really needs me, I am completely available, listening to everything. One of these visitors, a very profound Englishwoman, helped me to find the right designation for this intense assertion of self that characterizes any authentic representation of spirit and that is almost never understood by [the living].

Spirit, being purely personal and subjective, can assert itself [only] in a way that causes it to be superficially mistaken as the worst "egotism" in the English sense of the word. And yet, it is the opposite. (It is precisely in order to strip everything that belongs to the region of the empirical ego that the self attains such absolute certainty that the

---

9   Fundación Sur Archives identifier: CORR-KEY2-022-W; 186 27-30/48.
10   Gregorio Marañón (1887–1960), a famous Spanish physician and monarchist who lived in exile from 1937 to 1943.

question of finding, of obeying a logical sequence, [...] does not arise [...]), whatever the name of the out-of-self, of which faith in God is an expression of a lower order.[11] The spiritual ego is originally unforgiving since it is formed only as a function of stripping. But you are right: the Doctrine [...] that has been transformed, transubstantiated into Pure Compassion represents a stage higher than that of him whose influence is impersonal to the rest. By receiving all these visits, I saw once again how much each individual has his "natural radius of action" (see "The Natural Reach of Personality" in *The Recovery of Truth*) that can be surpassed. Each sun has its system of planets. You certainly do not belong to mine, and I know that I must fight against my natural inclination to attract everyone and everything into my orbit, in order to be able to maintain and cultivate friendly relations [with] a being like you. In fact on the telluric level, our meeting looked a lot like that of a Boa with a Tiger. Fortunately, neither managed to defeat the other.[12] Since you evoke the image of the bull of Altamira[13]: would that have been the result of a successful cross between Tiger and Python? I believe that this monster would have exceeded the limits of all human imagination ...

You know that the [Greek] term *Paradeisos* (Paradise) originally means Garden (Zoological). It is within the framework of such a symbolic Paradise, managed perhaps by a discreetly invisible Orpheus, that I best understand future relationships between you and me.

You did very well to write me this long letter. It helped me get the point right. If there is [friendship] between the Tiger and the Serpent, whose instincts [cannot] match, the two must see very clearly, I mean, they must [know] what they would never guess.

Affectionate thoughts,

H.K.

---

11   Keyserling notes, "Can you write to me as soon as possible about the exact place, day, and time, as exact as possible, of your birth? I have an extraordinary [Dutch] astrologer here who is interested in it."

12   Keyserling notes, "I will [have] framed your three portraits together, and I will hang them in my study below the canvas depicting Orpheus with his lyre moving the animals, including the Tiger and the Serpent."

13   In the cave complex of Altamira, located near the Spanish town of Santillana del Mar in Cantabria, are the famous prehistoric paintings discovered in 1868.

Prinz Christianweg 4, Darmstadt,[14]

Tel. 2042

February 28, 1939

I was afraid that you might not be able to come but if, [impossibly] a possibility [should arise], then please telegraph me immediately. Because if nobody comes here, it's we who will go, so as not to spend a painfully not-too-sad holiday; because we both enjoy celebrating. Manfred, alas, cannot come: he is away with his shooting regiment. He feels frustrated about this, he enjoys so much seeing interesting people, but there is nothing to be done, not even coming to Paris: thank you but his service will last in any case until November 1940.

I showed the hand-writing of your letter written immediately after your "accident" to the best graphologist I know, a true clairvoyant, who had already seen your writing of 1929. Here is what she writes to me today (I translate): "Amazing to be able to write like this after such an accident! What wealth, what abundance of life, what energy, what inner balance! If I compare her writing to that from ten years ago, it seems to me that she has gained considerably in warmth and capacity for faith. On the other hand, she is even less passionate about her desire for power. Oh yes, she is generous, intelligent. She is infinitely less depressed in her soul than she used to be".

This visionary helped me more than anyone in the world. Over a year ago, when I didn't know how to stop myself, she told me that my misfortune was the greatest "blessing in disguise" she had seen, that I had to start an absolutely new life, stripping myself of everything to which I was attached so far, but that this new life would become my real life, the only one that would ultimately count. I immediately understood that she was right, and by means of the desperate and contained effects of finding excruciating pain, I worked to change direction. Now it's done.

As for the rest, how little one knows oneself!

Until 6 months ago, I sincerely believed only in myself, in my own intuition, in making my will strong at all costs. And now I see that precisely in my case, most of it was not done "by me", but "happened" to me. And in fact, I have the wrong will, as others have the wrong mind. For example: I never wanted to get married, and now all those who know us intimately call us "the holy family". I never wanted to have children, being completely devoid of the usual fatherly feelings, and

14   Fundación Sur Archives identifier: CORR-KEY2-023-W; 187 23-29/34.

now my relationship with my sons is what impresses everyone the most. It is ideal; complete independence in every way. And the boys prefer my company to everything that generally makes young people happy.

And now, since you are discreet, I will transcribe for you, to amuse you as a patient, what my dear friend Delamain writes me about this lady who, for love of the grandiose, allowed [to] be published, without even consulting me, fragments of short letters [...] in the article in the *Revue Française* that you probably saw. I was a little scared of her (I never saw her) and wrote to her as little as possible (and God knows how she took advantage!). She wrote to me that Delamain must be seriously, even dangerously, ill. Anxiously, I asked him about her. Here's what he says (but this stays [...] between us): "It seems to me that your concern for me comes out of what Madame B. suggested to you. There is an explanation I must give to you. Even in her feeling aspect, her erotomania would tire a saint. So I write to her more and more depressing letters in order to stop the correspondence in a courteous way. My intention has never been, as it was for her, to use graphology as a mediator of 'repressed' passions." Isn't this amusing?

Heal quickly, dear friend. And do try to come again. If I cannot go to Italy after Easter and nothing yet suggests the possibility of such a trip that would do us great good, we will not move from here, at least not for a long time, not before July.

Have you read Bertrand Russell's latest book on democracy in politics? I saw a review in *La Nación* but there the title is not indicated: If you think this book could make its way to me without getting lost, I would like to have it in Spanish or English.

Affectionate memories,

H.K.

If by any chance you have Spanish reviews of the book you published, it [would please me...] very much if you sent them to me.

Prinz Christianweg 4, Darmstadt[15]

February 29, 1939

Yes, I remember now: I believe you were born in the afternoon. From what I can see, you are Capricorn + Ram = two Boas = *un tesón de primer orden!* [stubbornness of the first order]

---

15   Fundación Sur Archives identifier: CORR-KEY2-024-W; 187 30-31/34.

But of course, I understand nothing about the language of the stars, and what I'm telling you may be completely wrong.

It is only too natural for the shock to be felt after the fact. Do you think you might recuperate by March 4? It will be my wife's birthday. Traditionally, that evening we give a small dinner, for 6-8 people only but always interesting. Unfortunately all of our intelligent friends here are dead or [banished] – absolutely all of my former collaborators at the School of Wisdom are dead, with the sole exception of Jung. But if you can come, perhaps bringing with you a [noteworthy] and intelligent French friend (Drieu? Malraux?) or Spanish (but in this latter case, he must agree to speak in a language other than Castilian) or Argentinian – we would probably have a very [...] little party! And you would make (my wife) immensely happy by coming, and me as well. So far, only men will attend [...]

We invited an extremely intelligent woman, Princess Margaret of Hohenzollern[16] (from the Romanian branch of the family) born Princess of Saxony, but we don't know if she can come, she moves around a lot.

Do you still have a car? [...] are difficult to repair. If you think you will decide a bit in advance, please wire to this address: "Graf Keyserling Darmstadt".

Since photos amuse you, I send you those taken at [...] In the one in the middle, the lady seated at the back [repainted in range], to the right of her is Sta. Belle-coeur, usually very beautiful, but badly portrayed this time. In the same photo on the left, there are two of her brothers, the two men with glasses. After all, this meeting remained purely worldly/ mundane; at least, I didn't note anything else.

You can't imagine how sad my son Manfred was, coming here on the Tuesday after you left! He will be here, of course, on March 4 and would have tremendous joy in getting to know you. He is, moreover, a very good conversationalist.

Affectionate thoughts and good convalescence and prompt recovery.

H.K.

---

16 Princess Margaret Beatrice Feodora of Prussia (1872–1954).

Hotel Waldeck[17]
Freudenstadt (Schwartzwald)
Besitzer Lutz & Bässler
March 6, 1939

I finished my 25 kilometres on foot, in skis in deep snow, [in] a perpetual ascent. In [...], I ache more this morning. Postal [...] such are the immense advantages of advancing in age: if the machine can stop itself without perceptible notice and if the damage is repaired differently – [...] that it (the machine) is solid, much more solid than before.

You have a very good memory. Nonetheless, so that there may be no further misunderstandings from certain passages of my last letter, I remind you of the end of what I was reading to you from a certain manuscript that Monday. The saviour of our age is no longer the Son of the Light who illuminates the Serpent, but the Serpent itself who becomes the Son of the Light. In the same sense, in my *Meditations*, the Tiger at the very moment of its stunning [...] suddenly transforms itself into Buddha, without losing a single one of its [pristine[18]] qualities. So I have passed the stage where I give myself the right to fight nature and I know that if I live long enough[19] all my argumentativeness will turn into immense compassion.

I reflected again on your reflection that I too must participate in the 3rd day of creation, that is to say I reflected on the reason for your question: in fact, despite a fundamental incompatibility between our two ways of life, there is a kinship, the same effusive vitality due to a rooting in elementary life much deeper than that of most, and the same tension between this life and spiritual aspiration, but as for the rest, there is no affinity. But that doesn't matter anymore.

I saw in your review a list of works defended by [...]. There was Unamuno, Baroja, Marañón[20] (in part). Is it me? Would our friend José de España also be struck? If you can inform me of this without criticism and without making value judgments (please don't), I would be much obliged.

---

17   Fundación Sur Archives identifier: CORR-KEY2-025; 186 3–4/ 482.
18   Keyserling notes, "From l'espagnol «pristino», faux ami par primitives, originelles. [from the Spanish for 'pristine', false synonym for primitives, originals]"
19   Keyserling notes, "On the occasion in which you knew [G] had the courage to speak with complete frankness in a way until [this] day..., to speak with the said gentleman about his difficulties. All those who filed them were ... so calm and brave. He listened to them with great attention. But, as I already said, he is convinced [...] any consequence. (Just) that if you know something, it will happen at an unexpected moment, or perhaps from lightning."
20   Miguel de Unamuno (1864–1936), Spanish writer and philosopher; Pío Baroja (1872–1956), Spanish novelist; Dr Gregorio Marañón (1887–1960), Spanish physician and philosopher.

The bad thing is that in Spain there are almost no middling or regular spirits: they are exuberant, superlative (the greatest symbol: Lope de Vega) or they do not exist as spirits. Therefore, cutting off heads could annihilate everything, something that would not produce the same result in France or Germany. This problem worries me very much. Before you see me again, do find out about all this, so that we can understand each other. I regret more than ever that almost no one will follow my advice to start a new life in South America: from there, perhaps after a few years they could return unscathed. On the other hand, after a neutral European exile, they would have enormous difficulties regaining their much-needed authority.

I am very interested to know if you will give the lectures that I have asked O. Why not [watch over] the possible destinies of your continent, the new way of life that is outlined there, instead of commenting on it, European destinies and values among other interpreters? In this cosmic moment, your continent will be able to play a huge role. But only if you consolidate your uniqueness and are not so exclusively South American, so completely non-European, so that [you include] yourself (as the daughter of the Société) instead of watching from behind, as in confession, you could play the role of a Juana Bautista in a new cycle. What is Ortega doing in Portugal? Have you [sic] been hired by Salazar[21]? I wonder if I might come home tomorrow night.

Affectionately,

H.K.

March 12, 1939[22]

I saw a wonderful movie last night in which the main roles were played by Slavs. I was seized by an immense nostalgia for the vast, the infinite, the all "encompassing" of the Russian soul with legends in which I participate more than any other collective soul.

And then I clearly understood how your vitality and your violence are incompatible with mine. All our European, Greek, Slavic, Germanic, and especially Caucasian traditions embody vitality in the form of the Dionysiac. It is yet true today [in] the Caucasus whose tribes live in the backlands of the Black Sea, still preserving the tradition of Iphigenia,

---

21   António de Oliveira Salazar (1889–1970), economist and dictatorial prime minister of Portugal.

22   Fundación Sur Archives identifier: CORR-KEY2-027; 186 33–34/48.

in which every festival is a Bacchanal, all violence of which the immolation [of] the Warm-Blooded, of the Bull of Minos [is the culmination].

You, on the other hand, vital and more realistic than me, have nothing of the Dionysian. In the beginning ... wine, orgy, violence, clamour, writing, the two forms of vitality relate well ... Going from cold-blooded to warm-blooded.

You don't understand any of these metaphors; since for you faults are faults and not (not as for me in the first place) symbols since you do not know – cannot know – that all matter is originally [the] materialization of an immaterial image and that this image is the true reality. So, if I see myself as Tiger, it's to such a point that I recognize myself in every tiger – it is infinitely more true than anything superficial, "fijé" [(sic)fixed] in meta-reality and you cannot perceive this from the outside. [You believe me to be] a Nordic animal ... But it's not this superficial aspect that matters. And the same can be said, mutatis mundi, of the vision that I have of you. I have to resign myself to the fact that where I start to get serious, you start to laugh, that where the European begins to see the beginning of a revelation of spirit, *las macanas*[23] appear to the South American, putting an end to any attempt at profundity. Your continent is indeed the anti-metaphysical continent. That is precisely why it means so much to me. You belong to the world of the Antipodes. Above all I think of this when I visualize you in the company of Gabriela Mistral.[24] Whatever her soul might be (I'm ignorant of her work, and if I did know it, it would probably tell me little). As a type she is essentially Serrana Indian, an *alma de bronce* [a soul of bronze]. A magnificent creature. I could draw her true to life, I think, although I've only seen her once.

Socrates was Russian at heart (his mother was Thracian = [sl .] = Russian). I [affirm the ancient coin and] Russia is huge, despite the sense of [immense firm] of the first, and the total lack of the same sense among the Russians ... But the fact is that they both had an [essentially] Dionysian soul. Greek ecstasy is the "exiting of oneself" in a state of drunkenness, the desire for communion with the entire world in a rapture, the nostalgia to lose oneself in the infinite, while the Indian accepts everything, except coming out from behind the mask of his impassable flesh.

I just write this down without insisting or checking – perhaps it suggests to you something lively for your lectures.

Affectionately,

H.K.

---

23 Made-up stories, cock-and-bull stories.
24 (1889–1957) Chilean poet and diplomat, close epistolary friend of Ocampo.

March 15, 1939[25]
calligraphic study
Work of [...] now filled
with resentment
Oh woman of ill will

Confucius said, "He who does not aspire with all his soul [to go for the opinion], I do not help him to progress. Who doesn't desperately search for the right phrase himself, I don't help him find it. To him to whom I show an angle of a triangle and who does not know how to discriminate exactly and immediately by himself the other two, I turn my back forever".

In the case of the superior man, it is always possible, if you can read two words of a sentence, to reconstruct all the others correctly. By embracing three sentences at a time, exact reconstruction of each word is inevitable. Anyone who tries to decipher a single word of my handwriting is obviously wasting time.

Anyone who has enough [good] will, always learns to read me – my little Argentine secretary (so intellectual but [who knows] Spanish) whom I just hired, already reads everything I write at full speed. So you don't want to bother – so it's not worth the effort for me to trouble you with this again ...

I have already told you with a clarity to blind the Good Lord everything that can be said or almost said, about my travel possibilities. My children understood everything from when they were an embryo. If you don't want to, then let's leave off ... but please don't come back and ask more questions in your really impossible writing.

A superior woman does not have the right to have handwriting as conventional as your[s]. You have a lack in you, a makeup that should in the end be abandoned; if you were to do that, you truly would be an Indian with poisoned arrows.

Try to understand for once and not to laugh precisely where it pays to be serious.

My question concerning Ortega is this: is he also, yes or no, among the unfortunate people of whom you speak? I can – and more importantly I probably could [...] for him, so it is in his best interest that I am fully informed.

25   Fundación Sur Archives identifier: CORR-KEY2-028-W; 186 36-38/48.

No, I don't know Trarieux[26] personally, but I did know a lot about him and I would like you to get to know him and tell me about him. I wrote to him saying that I would like you to see him.

If you go to Italy by car, you can very well come and see me at the most beautiful place of the Riviera di Levante. I think I would be there roughly (from) April 20 to May 30, Piccolo Hotel, Portofino Mare (Génova). But for Semiramis, there is also a luxury hotel in … (end)

Piccolo Hotel,[27]
Portofino – Mare, Génova
May 2, 1939

Dear friend,

Here are two suggestions that may benefit Argentina's intellectual and spiritual progress.

1) The day before yesterday I gave your card to Doctor Roberto Assagioli[28] of Rome (address: via Eufemio 9 Aventino) who is spending a few days here with me. For a long time he has been considered the best psychotherapist in Italy. During the last decade, he has made immense progress. He has gone well beyond Jung on many theoretical points, but above all he himself has gone very, very far on the path of spiritualization. I advised him to send you articles proving what I have just said: that would be of great [...] in the life for A. If *Sur* would like to publish something of his, [it would be splendid] because thanks to these laws here that hinder the possibilities for so many people, especially at home, we can't do much anymore. He [...] now publishes in English, but then I advised him to publish in Spanish: there are not, as far as I know, any important psychologists in Argentina. I believe he would even come, if he were offered what I was offered there.

2) The former professor Heinrich Zimmer[29] had to leave Heidelberg and emigrate because he had married the daughter of the great poet Hugo von Hofmannsthal (Austria). Within a year, Balliol College at Oxford offered him its hospitality, but only a chair, alas. However [...], as [an] indologist, he is an absolutely unique being. He has a particular

---

26   Camille-Ludovic-Gabriel Trarieux (1870–1940), a French poet, playwright, and novelist.
27   Fundación Sur Archives identifier: CORR-KEY2-031-W; 186 41-44/48.
28   (1888–1974), an Italian psychiatrist and founder of transpersonal psychology and psychosynthesis.
29   (1890–1943) German indologist and linguist.

gift for spontaneously dreaming Hindu myths, I mean, waking dreams. They occur to him spontaneously, when he gives his lectures, and in this way he connects within his person our modern psychological era with the highest Hindu antiquity. His books on India and its mythology are the most beautiful (also the most poetic) that I know, but I don't think they've been translated yet. Now, since South America has no noted indologists (that I know of), why not offer him a chair in Buenos Aires or elsewhere? He would surely accept, and he is good enough – although at the moment [...] he only speaks English, apart from German – he could learn Spanish in a few months, if it seems worthwhile. Since you often go to England, wouldn't you look him up? In any case, could you please write to him c / o Balliol College, Oxford, [...] He is someone who could write you some incredibly interesting things for *Sur*.

If you are going to Rome, I hope you'll see Assagioli. His Jewish sensibility has rendered him a little too shy – [under] the blows from the [deities], but he is a very valuable man.

And now I beg you once again to give me news of future possibilities [...]. You know that – as I wrote to you as early as 1936 from Avignon – I had done my best to make the émigré intellectuals understand what they were missing by not going to America, or by not taking sides – neutrality [was seen as] anti-Spanish. Unfortunately, no one seems to have understood – indeed, what Eugenio d'Ors[30] did, his deep motive was pure opportunism, and this is the time to keep high intelligence alive. And the complaint reigning outside today is such that one can only side (within reason) with what is ultimately constructive (whatever that might be like at the present moment) compared to what is ultimately destructive. And Soviet-Russia stands now for what is destructive. Nothing good will come of it – and besides once Stalin is dead, Russia will surely become national-socialist. I know the Russian mind [mentality][in English]. What will happen to Ortega, Marañón, Baroja, Madariaga, etc.? Please inform me. It is absolutely clear now that if they do not return to Spain soon, only America will remain open to them. But perhaps repatriation is forbidden to them? I would love to do what I can to help these poor people, but given the anti-talent for corresponding [that these Spaniards show] it is very difficult to stay informed. Perhaps you [...] now play the great role of transplanter and thus can effect [a new] intellectual *cosecha*/harvest in your country? Please write to me here, where I will stay until the end of the month. In fact, I have to stay here at least until the end of the month. But I did not know that [...]

---

30   (1882–1954) Spanish writer, art critic; in 1938 he became General Director of Fine Arts in the Francoist government in Burgos.

[that we dispose of] the equivalent of two hundred marks per person per month (if I stay two months) and that is too little – we cannot recover [...] However, I cannot tell you how much we enjoy the peace of this paradisiacal site. [...] After so many years the first nights = deep sleep, no heart palpitations and no nightmares. It is only now we feel the fatigue resulting from too much stress. I don't read at all, I swim, I go for a walk, and for the rest I lead a life of pure meditation.

Affectionate thoughts.

H.K.

Part Seven

Keyserling on Jung (1944) and Ocampo (1936, 1941)

In his 1936 letter to Marco Victoria, Keyserling assesses Ocampo's import-ance as "the most telluric woman alive". The chapters on Jung and Ocampo in Keyserling's posthumously published memoir Reise durch die Zeit [Travel through Time, Vol. 2] function as his final takes on them. Keyserling reviews and evaluates his relationship to the pioneers of psychoanalysis, Freud, Adler, Groddeck, and Jung. As a philosopher and practitioner of a spiritual healing or wisdom tradition, he differentiates himself from psychoanalysts and characterologists. He gives his final assessment of Jung and acknowledges that he sometimes fell victim to his cruel invective and coldness. In the later chapters on Ocampo, he recounts the events leading to the failed meetings in Versailles and the subsequent tour of South America, his suffering, and the transformation he underwent as a result in writing South American Meditations. He praises Ocampo as telluric muse but describes himself as having failed to transform or heal spiritually her split psyche.[1]

Letter from Count Keyserling to Marco Victoria, *A Colloquium on Victoria Ocampo.*

Prinz Christianweg 4, Darmstadt

22 July 1936

I've read your colloquium on Victoria with great interest. The general situation you depict is admirably sketched and much of its minutiae – features and details – are proof of very fine observations and a keen judgment. But what interests me most is what is *purely Argentine* in said colloquium. There's much in it of traditional *macana* [sham], much of the *je m'en fiche* [I don't care] of Buenos Aires, much, very much of the extraordinary feeling of inferiority that all Argentinians – without any reason – suffer from.

1 Translated from the German by Gottwalt Pankow.

DOI: 10.4324/9781003266099-7

All in all, your judgment is *sound*. But there lack – in my opinion – the characteristics that define the citizen of the world that, as you your-self say, your compatriot is so earnestly. Perhaps I can render you a service if I *complete* somewhat your dialogue. Because of her personal knowledge of most of the important writers of our time, Victoria truly belongs more to the world than to Argentina. And I believe that she has opened herself more to several European writers than to those closest to her in the southernmost part of the world. (This is another indica-tion of her essential shyness that you define so well.) And because of all this, I believe that what will *remain* of Victoria is something much more important than what South American friends and admirers believe. Of the great initiators of movements – political, social, and religious – it is known that their true graceful influence is utterly different from what they intend and from what their contemporaries see. The same is true with women of great import. In the end, it does not matter what they are or believe themselves to be or what they seem or even do – what matters is their *evocative* power. And I believe that there does not exist, in this moment of History, a more *evocative* woman than Victoria. She is not inspiring – she can't be that because she is too self-absorbed. But there is no doubt that this woman has evoked more – without the majority of her objects being aware of it – than almost all of the women that are spoken of. That is because Victoria is the most powerfully telluric woman alive. Because what matters in her is the telluric root that looks or pulls towards the earth – and that is also true of her very keen intelligence. Her spontaneity – also genuine – is in service of her tellurism. I believe that it is precisely for that reason that she has *evoked* in others so many spiritual forces. I don't believe there exists a *single* man of genius who has heard her and is not indebted to her in this sense. Without her, I would *never* have found the truths and visions that would result in *South-American Meditations*; without her, I would neither have been able to write *Of the Art of Life,* because Victoria (contrary to what you say) is the one who least masters this art; when all is said and done, she is a *grande gâcheuse* [killjoy] as are all independent women with great telluric force. Without her, I would not have arrived to the final synthesis of myself. I believe that this fact alone is more important than everything that Victoria has written and expressed in Argentina. But this concerns not only myself: Ortega also owes much to her, and Drieu la Rochelle, and many, many others she met in Paris. Few realize this, and it is possible that Victoria herself does not know this or does not want to admit it, because this influence has nothing to do with her con-scious aspirations and whatever can satisfy her superficial vanity – but there is no doubt that in this and in nothing else lies Victoria Ocampo's immortal value. And that is much.

Wishing you much success,

Hermann von Keyserling

Travel through Time
C. G. Jung – Psychoanalysis

The summer that in memory appears as the most unpleasant of my life was that of 1921, spent in Vorarlberg, in Laterns and Tschengla, which is why I still associate the region with loss and damnation to this day. In October 1920 we had moved without joy to Darmstadt – my wife, no less than I, was torn from her familiar wide surroundings to settle in a small town (or so we felt) – materially almost penniless, the richer in worries for the future; I had to take up teaching, which was not in my nature at all, within the framework of a School of Wisdom whose name I had invented much earlier than I knew exactly how I should work in it. At the time it had all been difficult for me so that, after the first three lectures of the opening conference, which probably everyone else present experienced as a triumph, I had to go to bed, seriously ill for several weeks for purely psychological reasons. Soon I did enjoy the first students, many really interesting and seriously interested people; on the other hand, the close and frequent contact with people in my consciousness, which I had avoided all my former life, evoked sides of my nature that I liked least. All in all, I lived this first winter in a state of half-dreaming, half-frenetic wakefulness. I often found myself lashing about like a fish thrown on dry land. This often manifested itself to the outside world as a tantrum. In fact, I have hardly ever been annoyed in my life as others are. At the time – and in all situations later when the indications were the same – I sought, seemingly by flapping my wings, to scare away the hostile ideas that were assailing me. As I originally had no firm foothold in the telluric, I know neither the obstinate determination nor the feeling of being in the right, and therefore cannot wish for something in a primitive taken-for-granted way, nor stand up for my wishes or defend myself, I've had to replace with movement (out of my free-floating psyche which in itself is not able to deflect any blow) what others achieve by being still and resilient. This must be so for all disembodied souls … In the spring of 1921, during Rabindranath Tagore's visit to Darmstadt, I placed myself entirely at the service of this personality deeply revered by me at the time; not only did I organize a special session for him, I also took upon myself the task of being his translator, and did everything I could for him. My devotion made me happy; in part, perhaps, from a psychological point of view, because it was a pleasure for me to reflect onto a worthier object the often exaggerated and misinterpreted veneration paid to me at the time as author of the *Travel Diary*. As a result of this session, I encountered the first truly odious resistance and hostility in Germany; it was precisely when I engaged myself most selflessly that the ugliest motives were publicly attributed to me, which I, not at all used to such churlish acts, found an outrageous affront. However, it was then that I realized how, in many respects, I was quite different from what I had imagined myself to be: I had almost ignored the crannies and the sharp and rough edges of my nature; in my previous life, I had been able not to give them the opportunity to manifest themselves; then I only identified completely with the man of the *Travel Diary*. So it was that in the summer after the weeks with Tagore, I felt torn and unsatisfied as never before. In the depths of my nature I felt the direct onslaught of demons, all the more eerie to me as nothing of this was articulated, visually or otherwise. I only felt a rumbling in me all the time or a dull pressure like an inflammation in my gums.

That summer, in Laterns, I read Jung's recently published *Psychological Types*, which had been brought to my attention in a conversation shortly before I left Darmstadt. It was the first psychoanalytical book I ever read, believe it or not, because of course not only the *Travel Diary* but also *Unsterblichkeit [Immortality, 1907]* and even the epilogue of *Das Gefüge der Welt [The Structure of the Universe, 1906]* contain a lot of things that were generally regarded as the exclusive ideas of Freud and his followers. I read Jung's book with great difficulty, firstly because of my chaotic situation at the time, but also because Jung, unlike Freud, had great difficulty in conceptualizing his intuitions in his early writings; that is to say, as much as Jung probably used clear-sounding terms, they rarely corresponded exactly to what he actually meant, in the sense that conception and expression should correlate, and I understood that from the beginning. Nevertheless, *Psychological Types* soon appeared to me as a real eye-opener: I not only learned to understand better and more deeply my nature but also my own insights, which in my opinion were already ahead of psychoanalysis.[2] I felt like Molière's Monsieur Jourdain who was amazed to learn that he had always written prose.[3] Beyond that, however, Jung taught me, as Chamberlain did formerly, to understand my type as a special expression of a more general one, since he made my sensitivity and emotiveness acceptable to me for the first time by showing me that there is such a thing for impressionable artistic natures as an embodiment of real values. But Jung encouraged me, even more than through his *Types*, through his great early work *Symbols of Transformation*,[4] which I read during

2 Keyserling notes, "As an illustration and proof of what is said here, I recommend reading the lecture 'What We Want' from the Weisheitstagung (Wisdom Conference) given in the autumn of the same year (printed in *Schoepferische Erkenntnis / Creative Understanding*)."

3 In *Le Bourgeois Gentilhomme*, Molière has Monsieur Jourdain say "spoken" prose, not "written prose": "*Par ma foi, il y a plus de quarante ans que je dis de la prose sans que j'en susse rien.*"

4 Jung, *Symbols of Transformation, Collected Works*, Vol. 5.

the following winter. For from this book I saw with pleasure that my way of experiencing primarily symbols and not facts is the primordial way of all spiritual experience; this way expressed itself most powerfully and convincingly in the time when the great myths arose, with the whole elementary power of the first breakthrough of the self.

Ever since Vienna, it has been my consciously chosen habit to get to know personally, if at all possible, the authors of books that moved me. When I succeeded in doing so, I usually became immediately aware of what was *behind* the work, of what was underlying it as *Logos spermatikós* or fertile maternal womb; in other words, I internally observed as a simultaneous synopsis, the totality of the possibilities of the minds in question and was often able to save myself from the trouble of reading their writings afterwards. Thus, soon after my encounter with *Psychological Types*, I met not only Jung, but also Freud and Adler, Georg Groddeck, Alphonse Maeder, Pfister, Hattingberg, Heinrich Meng,[5] and in later years, most of the others who are known in vaster circles. In 1923, when I organized an analytical interlude in Darmstadt, I allowed Oscar A. H. Schmitz[6] to analyse me up to a certain point.[7]

In this chapter I would like to tell, first and foremost, about other acquaintances who, even as I write, will no longer be personally known to most of my potential readers, and this I will do in the style of the originally planned "Contemporaries", because what I will have to say here about myself and everything, going beyond individual problems, will have the most concrete effect if I put the emphasis on the personal psychology of the prominent personalities I intend to describe. Undoubtedly the most intellectually significant among the analysts was Freud. The most sympathetic, from the point of view of an average fellow human being (I deliberately say "fellow human being" because this was his favourite expression), was Alfred Adler, an otherwise uncomplicated, one-sided and intellectually even rather meagre mind; his whole theory, spanning and interpreting all human destinies, was in truth an assessment, put forward not without resentment, of the private psychology of his master Sigmund Freud. Personally, the latter was not an eroticist, nor was he in any way a servant of the pleasure principle, and I doubt that love, let alone lust, played any significant role in his life. His was a strict mind, in the true sense of the untranslatable Romanesque word *austere*,

---

5 Georg Groddeck (1886–1934) German physician specializing in psychosomatic medicine; Alphonse Maeder (1882–1971) Swiss physician and psychiatrist; Oskar Pfister (1873–1956) Swiss Lutheran minister and psychoanalyst; Hans von Hattingberg (1879–1944) German neurologist and psychiatrist; Heinrich Meng (1887–1972) German physician and psychoanalyst.

6 Oscar Adolf Hermann Schmitz (1873–1931) German psychoanalyst.

7 Keyserling notes, "The medical and therapeutic insights I came upon at that time are laid down in several essays of *Wiedergeburt* (1927) and in the chapter on 'Health' in *Das Buch vom persönlichen Leben* (1936)."

of the coolest objectivity and pronounced harshness towards himself, which had on the other hand nothing puritanical about it, that is to say, nothing born of the spirit of condemnation. It seemed to me that he had inwardly accepted the position of the Jew as a man of inferior rights in a similar sense to Aesop. Towards the outside world (in the broadest sense) Freud was so defined by the restraint of someone who lives completely devoted to his inner task, that he hardly allowed himself to judge anything outside his mission and, in spite of all his sensitivity and willingness to assert himself, he bore the condemnation of others with the self-sufficiency and ataraxy of the ancient Stoic. This restraint was only seemingly contradicted by the choice of his mostly unattractive, even often obscene *termini technici* [technical terms], which apparently sprang from the spirit to challenge. It was an incorruptibility towards the zeitgeist into which he was born and a sense of prophetic duty that led him to provoke – a psychology that is particularly familiar to me personally. And it is not a very attractive sign of the intellectual righteousness of others that they still cling to this offensive Freudianism and see its essence in pansexualism. As I was able to convince myself in 1940 while rereading the most important of Freud's writings, sexuality does not play nearly as much of a role in Freud's system as even experts attribute to it. Of course, Freud attributed a great deal to original sexuality in which he saw the origin of everything that serves the growth and increase of life: this was in line with his conviction as a scientist, and in many respects it is still shared today by most of those who denigrate Freud. But as I reread, I was deeply moved by the intellectual honesty with which Freud avoided applying or retaining the explanation closest to his nature and history there where his conscience as a researcher had to acknowledge that it was not applicable. Not only Jung, but already Freud recognized the symbolic and ambiguous nature of all psychological realities; already he correctly diagnosed drives other than the erotic, and Freud, with his theory of the superego – regardless of whether it is to be regarded as ultimately successful or not – demonstrated more understanding of the essence of the moral than any later analyst. Freud was, once again, not at all an eroticist but a man of power; he was *par excellence* the case exemplified by Adler, inasmuch as he was substantially inhibited both by his nature and by his conscience as a scientist and doctor, and never overcame his very great inner insecurity. In this context he must have had very traumatic childhood experiences from which he suffered throughout his life. As a man of power, Freud was generally loveless or at least devoid of love.

With Alfred Adler the situation was quite different. He was undoubtedly inspired by a genuine and deep love for his fellow humans; best and most essential was his social conscience, so that if everywhere he went he was popular and understood by everyone this was thanks to his effusive warm-heartedness; his theory, which attributed anything and everything to feelings of inferiority and power complexes, no matter how questionable, is really the best working hypothesis for treating the oppressed, with whom almost all proletarians identify, especially neglected children. And so Adler has prob-ably done the most good of all analysts, quantitatively speaking. Of course, many of the *dei minorum gentium* [gods of the second order] among those I met were of a completely different nature. I often compared their features to the chimeras that adorn or rather spoil the exterior of Gothic cathedrals, and at one point I even felt tempted to say in *Der Weg zur Vollendung [The Path to Perfection*, 1920] the supposition, meant as an allegory, that if the souls of medieval torturers were to have been embodied in someone, it would be in today's psychoanalysts. In fact, not only the prurient, the indiscreet, and the seducers feel attracted to this activity, but particularly sadists, far more so than [those] who choose the profession of surgeon, examining judge, or Chekist.[8] For what makes a born torturer is the personal pleasure of rum-maging in the intimate sphere; objectively, the most refined tortures can hardly be justified, since only eye and ear can differentiate as sharply as the idea of torture demands for its rational justification. In addition, however, the following more general comments should be made in this context. It is no coincidence that psychoanalysis was invented precisely at the turn of the century, as an expression, among others, from within that Naturalism that found only the ugly to be true, from the commonly understood Darwinism that rejoiced that man did not descend from God but from the ape, as well as from the least beautiful tendency of the attitude that became conscious with Nietzsche, whose most generalized motto condenses and symbolizes the Latin word so often quoted by Nietzsche himself: "*o pudenda origo*" ("O shameful origin").[9] Psychoanalysis grew and flourished as a response, among others, to the reality-ignoring idealism of the Age of Education. To that extent, however, it had and has fulfilled a positive task, quite apart from its merits as a discoverer of truth and as a remedy. But after centuries of oppression, repression, and the mendacious masking of everything that was considered ugly and sinful in man, it was only natural that its adepts sprang from among those primarily malicious in nature, and that malicious features gained the upper hand even in those whose overall structure did not really correspond to such emphasis. The world really loves "to blacken the radiant"; nothing pleases the average man more than when the high is explained to him from lower motives. And if, moreover, such a reduction of the positive to the negative is regarded as a sign of deeper insight, then only the evil inten-tion in man – always standing by – will gain the upper hand. This is what I meant when, even before the First World War, knowing Freud only from hearsay but having met several victims of analysis, I once remarked in Paris in response to a question about the truth of Freudianism: "*Cela n'est jamais vrai au début, mais cela finit fort souvent par être vrai*" [This is never true in

8 The word "Chekist" derives from the name given by Lenin to the force he set up to secure and protect Bolshevik power.
9 Friedrich Nietzsche, *Daybreak*, Book II – Aphorism # 102.

the beginning, but it very often ends up being true]. No one will ever see psychoanalysis properly in the context of cultural history who does not see it together with Marxism and Bolshevism and the rebellious resentment of the long oppressed. So I was not at all surprised to learn that Soviet Russia was for a time thinking of replacing religious education with psychoanalysis. This is an integral feature of the advancement of the Fourth Estate, only that it reflects the mentality of the skilled craftsman rather than that of the worker. For there is nothing more characteristic of the basic attitude of all analysts, whether they want to admit it or not, than their combining of the physical and the mental, of the material and the spiritual, on a level which is fundamentally that of the materializing and elaborating craftsman. (I am well aware that what I call here craftsmanship many therapists regard as high art; they believe that through their treatment they can work out the prim-ordial image of a person as he should be, just as Michelangelo chiselled his ideal figures out of marble blocks. But this view speaks not only of hubris but of forthright megalomania. No physician who is not far superior to his patients mentally and spiritually and who is moreover not a true magician of high spirituality, is able to achieve what so many of these ordinary people claim for themselves today. However, it should also be taken into consider-ation that the medical attitude is aimed at normalizing and thus, in the case of being spiritually gifted, at levelling down. Also, that no one can see beyond his own horizon. If every great artist is also a good craftsman, it does not mean that every daring craftsman is a great artist.) Accordingly, most of the psychic healing methods of our time correspond to the spirit of the craftsman and are therefore rarely applicable to, or are on good terms with, essentially spirit-determined types, not to mention domineering natures. I say "on good terms", for the overcoming of the lower by the higher happens precisely if one does not dwell on the latter. But it is among the latter in particular that some excellent small-scale and precision workers, who continue the legacy of the great pioneers, see their main task. Judging from my personal psychology, I don't know how a man like Gustav Heyer[10] whose whole way of working lies in insisting on and taking seriously and teaching what to ignore and what to learn to ignore – instilling new impulses into the patient from a higher level, lifting him up to this level and thus overcoming evil with good – it is simply incomprehensible to me how Heyer can heal at all. And yet, in fact, he achieves excellent healing results.

Most of those who go to analysts partake of craftsman natures themselves and, moreover, are not receptive to purely spiritual impulses. In their cases,

---

10   Gustav Richard Heyer (1890–1967) trained as a Jungian analyst. Jung reviewed favourably two of Heyer's books, *Der Organismus der Seele (translated as The Organism of the Mind)*, 1932, and *Praktische Seelenheilkuunde*, 1935 (see Jung, *Collected Works*, Vol. 18, §§1774–1779). However, Heyer joined the Nazi party in 1937, remaining a member until 1944, and attacked Jung for his criticism of totalitarianism. Jung refused to meet him after the war.

readiness for the latter can only be awakened, if at all, by the most careful detailed work, and in this respect the analytical craftsmen really have, occasionally, been pioneers of the spirit under today's psychological circumstances. Nevertheless, the following applies almost without exception: in the epigones of the pioneers, analysis has become a fundamentally unspiritual, even antispiritual matter, and I do not believe that this is out of any misunderstanding on their part. That analysis does not go beyond the earth-nature of man, as we will see later, is particularly evident in Jung's efforts to explain metaphysical depth psychology. The general tendency towards levelling down did not sprout its ugliest blossoms in psychoanalysis but in characterology.[11] The fact that it did this less and less from decade to decade was due to the medical goals; whoever wants to heal cannot ultimately want to addle, and, by and large, it became clear to most doctors how much the initial reductive procedure did indeed addle. For an enormous number of characterologists, on the other hand, who were not inhibited by any healing purpose, the malicious wilfulness to be ugly and condescending had the most horrible effects. My experience is so general that I assume the predominance of lower motives in a person who takes characterology as his profession, until proven otherwise. After all, "character" is never the last resort but only a means of expression of substantial spirit. There are no "driving forces" which would be spiritually and morally qualified in a certain way by themselves. They are all nothing but means of self-realization, and whoever puts the accent on mere disposition, and judges and condemns from there has a corrupting effect on his victims under all circumstances.

Though I am not able to exclude the more famous characterologists (as far as my knowledge of them is sufficient) from my overall judgement of characterology I would like to state explicitly once again that I do not include the three great founders of psychoanalysis in this context. Freud was above all a disinterested researcher, so much so that one day, when a colleague spoke to him of the healings he had achieved through psychoanalysis, he is said to have said, looking up almost in astonishment: "Oh yes, one can also heal through analysis." To a large extent, as with so many doctors, his medical work was the secondary result of a semi-random choice of profession. Alfred Adler was above all a social worker, with an innate preference for the overworked and the afflicted. Jung was a miner, a pioneer who drilled shafts into the earth with brute force, unlocking and throwing up blocks. I once described his attitude, which corresponds most closely to his nature, as that of a palaeontologist of

---

11   Characterology was the academic study of character associated with the German philosopher Julius Bahnsen (*Contributions to Characterology*, 1867) and prominent in German-speaking countries until the end of the Second World War. Ernst Kretschmer (1888–1964) correlated physique and character types, while Ludwig Klages (1872–1956) connected graphology and neurology. Keyserling expressed his rejection of characterology even before the Nazis co-opted it to describe "natural racial inequalities".

the soul. Jung was no more a born healer than Freud, although he seems to have been a very good psychiatrist, especially in his younger years. On the other hand, he is, beyond his research, a pioneer of the rebirth of the understanding of religious mysteries within the consciousness of modern man. One may characterize sufficiently sharply the mutual relationship of these three pioneers of depth psychology for the purposes of this description with the following. Freud sought to trace all mental complexes back to primal drives that belong to the physiological level. Adler recognized that every person has a guideline according to which he must live if he does not want to fall prey to a "life lie". But it was in this guideline, as Adler understood it, the purpose was not to advance mankind: following Adler's method, all that was achieved was to normalize and therefore, if the level was originally high, it was necessary to level it down. The older Jung became, the more he strove to bring into the centre of consciousness the *prospective* tendency, that is to say, the upwards tendency of the soul that looks towards the future, and thus, not fundamentally different from what the hierophants once did, placing the instinctive in service of what in history is typically regarded as a religious uplift. Here, however, Jung's peculiarly paradoxical position finds its expression. Being himself an utterly telluric man, he sought to trace spiritual development back to telluric motives. In his libido-book (*Symbols of Transformation*), he referred all the sensory connections back to telluric relations (phallus, mother), just as much later (1938) he associated the fate of the soul after the loss of its physicality as described in *The Tibetan Book of the Dead* to Freud's regressive tendencies (incest, the Oedipus complex), in what I consider to be a fanciful way. However, Jung was probably never quite comfortable with such interpretations. Not only psychologically, mythologically, and theologically, but humanistically Jung was probably the most educated man of his time; I say educated and not taught, because I want to stress that his knowledge was always at his disposal as an instrument for creative action. He knew early on what their experiences meant to the religious contemplatives, and the psychologist in him knew of course that in the life of the soul it is meaning that determines reality. But as essentialist as he was as a psychologist, Jung was also a comparative researcher, especially in the field of religion, and anyone who expects something essential from comparisons, as long as he is bound to this idea, must be blinded to the sense of what is absolutely unique, the only exponent of the absolutely universal here on earth. To expect insight from comparisons is one of the greatest of obstacles on the way to knowledge of the essence for whosoever strives to achieve it. Comparisons are possible only on the level of the external, and there they are certainly meaningful; for example, all individual human beings are without doubt "people in general". But what is gained by such a question for the realization of the reality of the soul, which is in any case, from the first to the last, unique? For decades I have been preaching to apparently deaf ears that the empirical exponent of the universal is a "singular" and not the "general" thing. And almost as misleading as the question of similarity or comparability is the question of cause. If the latter is understood to mean the raison d'être, the *ratio essendi*, then the question of cause may stand, even if it is always more insightful to first renounce each and every causal question and simply assimilate the essence, the *haecceitas* of the Scholastics.[12] But most people look for empirical causes when they ask "why", and this question is futile under all circumstances, since no particular phenomenon has fewer than a billion causes, which all together determine its being in this particular way and not in a different one, and therefore it is always an arbitrary act to emphasize one single cause exclusively. Jung has never been released from these two professional failings of the researcher, and therefore never got beyond wavering with regard to the final interpretation. Where he in fact seemed most secure was with the libido, since, to a great degree, he still believed in his first teacher. In *Types* he secured himself, so to speak, by focusing on what epistemology means in relation to assertive metaphysics; in the same way, Kant also rescued himself. In Jung's later writings, he pushed himself towards taking up a basic attitude similar to one I have methodically represented from *Creative Understanding* onwards, and with this it became possible for him to recognize the autonomy of the soul and to gain insights into the metaphysically real. But also here he never really felt quite at ease; he therefore emphasized the impossibility of knowing anything exactly, and devoted himself more and more exclusively to his research. But in fact he was striving for something else, something that cannot be seen and judged from the outside, something that can only be realized inwardly. In his most recent works, which concern arcana such as alchemy, Kabbalistic studies, Paracelsianism and the like, and which pretend to be purely historical, I have long seen the camouflage of a deep relationship to the mysterious, which Jung, as critic and researcher of knowledge, does not want to admit. In this respect, I do not completely rule out what many whisper among themselves, that Jung had secretly prayed for years to the god Abraxas, that peculiar hermaphroditic figure of the Gnostic age. His last book, *Psychology and Alchemy*[13] (which I acquired only after the completion of this chapter) attests to the correctness of my diagnosis. Here Jung proves to be a contemporary reincarnation of the ancient alchemist who experienced soul processes in the material world, while in fact sublimating his soul on a higher plane. These alchemists were also strict empiricists. But through their empirical research they aspired to reach God. By their projection onto matter, they experienced mystical processes of transformation – whereby I, unlike Jung, do not want to exclude the possibility that, in addition, interactions and polarizations took place between the souls of the alchemists and the substances they treated, which made them more "open to substances" so to

12   The irreducible thisness of a thing that makes it particular.
13   Jung, *Psychology and Alchemy, Collected Works*, Vol. 13.

speak; perhaps this explains the high flight of chemistry after its crawling out of the egg of alchemy. I do not want to quote extensively here, but I would like to point out Jung's particularly enlightening accounts on pages 314 and 336 of his book. From these it is clear to me that the man of that time, I mean the man who was inwardly prepared for the efforts and methods of alchemy, whose psychology was very different from ours, experienced directly the soul in the matter, which he handled like a modern chemist, hardly noticing the mere material; the peculiarities of matter, about which we modern people know so much, were completely unknown to him and for internal reasons even inaccessible. Something happened to him when he experimented chemically, similar to what happened to the mystic who meditated with the highest concentration on the unknown, the emptiness or the void: that emptiness was filled from within by spiritual realities, the inner light projected onto the outer darkness that functioned as a background.

In exactly the same way, Jung searches for the metaphysical by concentrating on purely empirical-psychological processes, which in themselves have nothing metaphysical about them. This seems to me to be the key to the mystery of Jung's personal position, which towards the end of his life has caused more and more pure doctors to move away from him. Jung is much more than a mere doctor. He can live on in posterity as the modern naturist's guide to metaphysical reality, even though he himself, only seemingly paradoxically, misunderstands the latter in a naturist way. One only has to hope that Jung's successors do not suffer the same fate as the successors of the great alchemists. After all, they didn't get any further in the intended direction. So alchemy became chemistry, the science of the transformations of matter itself. And of course there is the danger that Jung's school, if it continues on the path he longed for, will suffer the same fate, because from psychology there is no direct path to religion, just as there is no direct path from pure chemistry to God. What the latter sentence means, I have explained in more detail in "Reflections".[14]

Thus, all in all, thanks to a mixture of the archaic and the modern in him and thanks to a peculiar uncouthness paired with a very great sensitivity and intuition, Jung appears as a paradoxically moving intellectual figure. This found a rarely faithful embodiment in his physique. Jung as a body was a bear, plump, strong, and agile, and at the same time without grace; his movements corresponded to his strangely unkempt, even uncouth expression; but he had a head with one of the finest noses I had seen, and the small eyes had an expression that was not only sharp but refined. Translated into the mythical and figurative, Jung as a psychophysical figure was originally, as already mentioned, a miner who blew up quarries and, at first, extracted only roughly hewn blocks. However, from one block or another, he chiselled out a

---

14   Keyserling, "Reflections", *Considerations of Silence and Contemplation.*

promising, sometimes even finely executed torso, and he did this in different styles which were in fact mutually exclusive; he never succeeded in a unifying synthesis of these styles. Thus Jung was a practical diagnostician, a physician, a natural scientist in a nineteenth-century sense, an epistemologist, a humanities scholar, a comparative mythology scholar, a mystagogue in the context of alchemy, a pure historian, the pioneer of a new science of the soul and an aspirant to his own religious experience. Judged by his abilities, not by his longing, Jung was predominantly the empiricist and the comparative scholar. But above all, the chthonic dominated. Recognizing this, I gave Jung the theme "Die Erdbedingtheit der Psyche" ("The Earth-bound Psyche") as part of an overall orchestration at the great wisdom conference "Mensch und Erde" ("Man and Earth") in 1927, and his lecture[15] seems more genuine and therefore more significant than most of what Jung has proclaimed, because this very attitude corresponds exactly to his own nature. Hence Jung's almost complex aversion to the word *Geist* (spirit) and his mistrust of those who live by the spirit. In his introduction to Heinrich Zimmer's posthumous work on Sri Rāmana Maharshi, Jung praises a humble disciple of the great sage who "had surpassed his master because, notwithstanding his cleverness and holiness, he had 'eaten' the world," and then Jung continues: "The man who is only wise and only holy, interests me about as much as the skeleton of a rare saurian, which would not move me to tears ... The experience of holiness may be the most painful of all."[16] If Jung was challenged by anyone, he would immediately profess an extreme chthonicism, a pure earth religion (e.g. his "Wotan") but he did not really mean it. That's why he was extremely annoyed when he was reproached for having certain affinities, for instance, with Alfred Rosenberg.[17] Let us also remember his invective against me, which I quoted to a considerable extent in the chapter on freedom in the *Das Buch vom persönlichen Leben* (*Book of Personal Life*), and about which Heinrich Zimmer once remarked to me with humour: "Jung looks on you as the fox disapprovingly follows the flight of the bird from its den." Later I realized that the depth psychologist must be unspiritual, even anti-spiritual and spirit-blind, in order to do his job. He must linger and emphasize precisely that which must be pierced and penetrated by sight or experience, and in this respect be

15 Jung's original 1927 paper "Die Erdbedingtheit der Psyche," edited by Keyserling, was translated as "Mind and Earth" and published in *Contributions to Analytical Psychology* (1928). That essay was divided and rewritten as two essays: "Die Struktur der Seele" ("The Structure of the Psyche", *Collected Works*, Vol. 8) and "Seele und Erde" ("Mind and Earth", *Collected Works*, Vol. 10).

16 C. G. Jung, "The Holy Men of India", *Collected Works*, Vol. 11, §953. The essay first appeared as an introduction to Heinrich Zimmer, *Der Weg zum Selbst: Lehre und Leben des indischen Heiligen Shri Ramana Maharshi aus Tiruvannamalai* (1944). Zimmer died in 1943 in New Rochelle, New York.

17 (1893–1946), a German Nazi theorist and ideologue, executed at Nuremberg for war crimes and crimes against humanity.

disregarded, so that the substantial spirit becomes conscious of itself. Hence the fateful failure of any psychotherapist who wants to play the saviour rather than the healer – he can only restore a lost normal balance. Whereas the one in whom substantial spirit dominates, without medical technique and without any consideration of empirical conditions, can immediately elevate the one who surrenders to his influence above his early level and thus, as a mostly unintended consequence, where necessary, of course, heal him. Hence the absurdity of all analysts' attempts from the perspective of depth psychology to understand or explain Indian or Chinese or Tibetan wisdom whose roots lie in the spiritual. Either substantial spirit exists or it does not. With this question, stands or falls the matter of whether religion and metaphysics are in line with reality. If, however, it does exist, a person needs not have become conscious of it, and many activities require remaining unconscious.

And yet the above does not exhaust all the richness of Jung's possibilities. In general, he wrote very badly. But in his studies of Joyce and Picasso,[18] paradoxically, he was a literary critic of great stature. Probably Jung himself never strived for a firm inner form, which he nevertheless praises as a goal under the name of integration and towards which he tries to help others, because his profession required the structure of the soul to remain loose. Whoever follows the incoherent ideas of others and then guides them by his own incoherent ideas, whoever has to immerse himself completely in dreams, must not be psychologically fixed in any way. Hence the typical human unreliability of analysts, together with their inability to become aware of it. With his invectives of the year 1934, Jung expressed with serious digger-wasp-like certainty exactly (and by the way, completely misleadingly) what was bound to harm me most in the situation at that time, and he never realized what he was doing, so that in the end I simply forgave him with a laugh; for he certainly did not want to harm me on purpose.[19] Ultimately, the typical human unreliability of analysts is of course related to their involuntary interest only in the motives for their actions and not in their effects and consequences. They are satisfied to the best of their consciences if they can diagnose failures in themselves or determine a psychological reason for their failure, whatever misfortune may have arisen from their actions. And in the same way, they are ultimately unscrupulous towards others as well. According to their disposition they are only directly open to psychological reality, not to mental or to physical (reality); this psychic reality is what I would like to call the turning over of the soul, the to and fro and up and down, the fluctuating, which as such has no goals and knows no values. For whoever is now so adjusted, every situation in life becomes an analytical situation – marriage, courtship, war – with the result that the turning over, having become conscious as such, does

---

18   Jung, "Ulysses: A Monologue", *Collected Works*, Vol. 15, §§163–203; "Picasso", *Collected Works*, Vol. 15, §§204–214.
19   See Jung's 1934 letters to Keyserling in Part Three of this book.

not lead to formation but to solution and in extreme cases, to dissolution. This can be seen most clearly in the typical analyst's lack of sense of attitude. Attitude means being formed by the spirit, it corresponds to the artistic form in real life, and it is the primary expression of a spirit-determined life. The analyst involuntarily sees in it repression, strain, or (emotional) numbness; he is itching, so to speak, to dissolve every attitude by peeling away its motives and components. Given his nature he cannot see that he strives to de-spirit man. Blind believers already see such destroyers in those who seek to understand. They are indeed that, but not in a bad sense, because belief in something external is always provisional. Analysts are real destroyers, because they rob people of their own form. This is often healing, namely where it does not correspond to a person itself. But it becomes life-threatening when it endangers the spiritual rootedness of a person. It is here where the well-known resistance to analysis can be completely justified. But back to Jung. The last thing that was said about him does of course contribute to the spiritual values of his work if it is to be judged as completed. But it must not be so. The older Jung becomes, the more he guards himself against it. His work is above all an enormous geological revelation in the science of the soul, probably one of the greatest of all history to date.

C. G. Jung – Analyst and Analysand

If I remember correctly, I became personally acquainted with Jung in 1921 or 1922 and have been in constant direct or indirect contact with him ever since. He spoke several times at Darmstadt conferences; we corresponded many times over the years. In the long run, my circle more or less followed his and vice versa, and so it can be assumed that we, knowing pretty much everything about one another, have mutually enriched or stimulated or corrected one another, as far as this was possible for two contemporaries for whom inhibitions invariably existed. But there was never a human relationship between Jung and me. The telluric man in him remained somehow unsympathetic to the spiritual aviator, the Swiss must have found strange the harmless generosity of the aristocrat. And what Jung did not like, or what the situation of teacher and analyst did not protect him from, bothered him. This outwardly strong, even coarse, uncouth man was, as a soul, supremely sensitive, which is why he lived out everything, as far as possible, from behind the protective walls of his very happy home and his unconditional supporters, or he simply unrealized it for himself in the analytical situation. So he always appeared in Darmstadt with a kind of bodyguard. If Jung was touched personally where he did not want to be, then out of self-protection he could be extraordinarily loveless, even cruel. I remember a conversation in Zermatt with the American child psychologist [Frances] Wickes. She said:

For a time it depressed us that patients who were analysed according to the Jungian method often died or committed suicide. Now we are reassured: only integration in general, we have now realized, is what counts; and it is not said that this must take place just in this life.

Through this fantastical misinterpretation by a factual and humourless American woman speaks an unmistakably genuine grim Jungian humour. The grumpier Jung pretended to be, the deeper he had been touched. Sometimes, whenever I heard something from him in a similar vein, I thought of a bear that an uncle of mine struck in the backbone while it was climbing over a ditch: not quite understanding why it was not getting any further, and feeling dull pain, it bit itself, upset by its own rump. Once, when we met in Frankfurt before the death of Richard Wilhelm, who was very close to him, Jung said rather flippantly that Wilhelm should just die quietly now, having completed [his translation of] *The Secret of the Golden Flower,* his *nec plus ultra* [nothing further beyond]. I have no doubt that those who are humourless have often been harmed by this kind of talk. I even know precisely one such case: that of Oscar A. H. Schmitz. Schmitz allowed himself to be taken in by Jung in an appalling way. After Jung's significance was rightly recognized, the wave of popularity that first lifted and carried Jung in German-speaking lands was due almost entirely to the brave Schmitz, who was an apostle by nature and who had an astonishing gift of making difficult things easy to understand without lowering their level. In 1921 Schmitz wanted to live out his need for admiration through me, which I refused to accept. Jung, to whom he then turned, being accustomed to transference, put up with it, which he made harmless for himself by cracking jokes about his apostle to third parties. But the effect of the situation on Schmitz was anything but harmless: thanks to his analysis with Jung, he believed himself to have matured to world superiority. He saw himself more or less as an *arhat.*[20] When death approached him in the terrible form of bladder cancer, Schmitz realized that integration in Jung's mind, even if it is achieved (which I doubt was the case for Schmitz), does not mean ascending to the *arhat* stage; thus in need of support through faith, he lost all inner support. His death is said to have been horrific, an awful struggle with fate up to the very last moment. I believe that at the time, I saved Schmitz's wife spiritually by explaining to her the fact that her husband had lost his footing because he had misunderstood psychoanalysis to be a religious doctrine of salvation; such a misunderstanding must take its revenge but in no way affects the character image of the person who is deluded in good faith. Of course, Jung was not directly to blame here. But apparently, in his

---

20   In Buddhism, an *arhat* is an individual who has gained insight into the true nature of existence and has achieved nirvana.

fear of too close contact, he had not warned his analysand sufficiently. And that Jung was aware of this is shown by the fact that he wrote Schmitz's wife in an unfriendly manner after his death, and, I know, never mentioned him again afterwards. In the same vein, Jung occasionally said and wrote about people whom he certainly did not intend to harm without quite realizing what he was doing, writing things that damaged them as accurately as a digger-wasp hitting the ganglia of a caterpillar. From the standpoint of Jung's own science, the most interesting thing about what I've briefly suggested here – for which I could give many more examples – is that analysts, in all cases known to me, are unsolved analytical cases, but so it must be.

Only those who do not succeed in resolving the conflicts of their soul within themselves, and yet have the gift of being aware of them in their projection onto others, feel the need to deal with the soul of others as intensely and meticulously as analytic technique demands; and only in this way do the necessary skills grow and mature. Those who feel the urge to materialize their ideas on paper are those who cannot be clearly aware of them in any other way. The latter is to a large extent my case, as my creative urge in general stems from the fact that my deepest point is unconscious and only becomes accessible to me through highlighted creativity. Had I been gifted with visions and the like, I would certainly not have been able to write the most profound of my works, as very few of those who have received revelations have reported them convincingly. Since most analysts today are themselves analysed, it shows how little being analysed must mean. In his last writings, Jung himself arrived to my insight, published as early as 1922, that releasing tensions is not in itself an ideal goal and that only fate and misery perform the miracle; that so many patients nowadays in their awakened primitive life expect the doctor to believe in miracles. Moreover, the true relationship between analyst and analysand offers yet another illustration of the general organic law of correlation: just as bees and clover depend on each other, so do doctors and patients with their respective ailments. And very tellingly in my experience, with regard to others, the most clairvoyant analysts never see through themselves. Here then, in addition to the law of correlation, the law of productivity of the inadequate is applicable. I do not believe that a criticism of Jung's personality (as of all great men in general, and his place is among these) is in the least detrimental to his importance. It is difficult, actually inhuman, to be a pioneer, so much so that special protective devices are almost always required for the soul, devices which are not otherwise wrongly considered pathological, in order to endure the fateful loneliness and at the same time the exposure. From this point of view, if one reads again Jung's invective against me, in which he recommends that I be absorbed into the community, and in doing so thinks of his own immense loneliness, then some things appear in a different light from how Jung prefers to present his persona. When my book *The Spectrum of Europe* came out I was in America. In Chicago, I received a distraught letter from Jung. I cannot find it at this moment, but I think that my memory is not too wrong if I give the meaning of its content as follows: "Are you strong enough to face the world on your own? I'm worried about you. I too was once a heavenly storm. But then it felt too far for me. I bought a country house and erected an altar in the garden, which" – unfortunately I don't remember the Latin text, my quotation may only be thirty percent exact – "bore the inscription: To Baucis, the sacrifice of Philemon."[21]

Let these personal reminiscences close with my last memory of Freud. Like almost all people who are above all hungry for power – had he not been so, he would never have become such a fantastically intolerant church father – Freud was mentally weak by nature, physiologically poorly armed against unpleasant impressions, extremely shy and accordingly reserved, polite, and formal in social exchanges. When he was sixty-eight, an apparently malignant ulcer began to grow in the roof of his mouth, and Freud then had what he thought was cancer operated on so thoroughly that subsequently all of his mouth was more or less prosthetic. In fact, however, it was not cancer – that is why there were no relapses – and Groddeck was probably right when he told me then the following: For decades he had noticed that the number 68 played a special role in Freud's imagination. Groddeck had interpreted this to suggest that Freud intended to retire at that age. In order to achieve his goal, he would have imagined a cancer, which in his case was purely psychogenic. But since his life clock had not really expired, Freud lived on despite the horrific operation. In fact, Freud was very attached to life, especially as he grew old, and the experience I am about to describe is related to this. I visited Freud after many years. I came in through another room at right angles to his room, and I saw behind the protruding wall of his room Freud's legs bobbing over the table. I was astonished, because this display did not look like the shy and correct man at all. When I then saw Freud's face, it looked downright cheeky to me. And he, the otherwise overly polite man, began to lash out at me. I remained silent. I understood that by making up his mind to die he had outwardly overcome his shyness. And when he began to pontificate, saying that he did not fear death, that he was ready to die at any moment, I said calmly to

---

21   Jung's letter reads in part:

> 2 January 1928. Dear Count, You identify with the eternal creative, restless, and ruthless god in yourself therefore you see through everything personal – a tremendous fate which it would be ridiculous either to praise or to censure! I was compelled to respect Nietzsche's *amor fati* until I had my fill of it, then I built a little house way out in the country near the mountains and carved an inscription on the wall: *Philimonis sacrum – Fausti poenitentia* [shrine of Philemon – repentance of Faust] and "dis-identified" myself with the god. I have never regretted this doubtless very unholy act. By temperament I despise the 'personal', any kind of 'togetherness', but it is so strong a force, this whole crushing unspiritual weight of the earth, that I fear it. I can rouse my body to revolt against the spirit, so that before reaching the zenith of my flight I fall lamed to earth. That is the danger you too must reckon with.
>
> Jung, *Letters*, Vol. 1, 49.

him: "That's not true." And then I asked without transition: "Tell me, master, have you ever loved anyone?" The old man became as if paralyzed. "Yes, once, actually only once. That was one of my sons, whom I loved passionately, and he was the one who had to die early." After that Freud was changed. As I stepped out into the cold winter night, he held my hand until the blizzard drove him back into his house.

C. G. Jung – Depth Psychology

You can only do the analysts justice if you see them as pure pioneers. Other revolutionaries and precursors have always been somehow eccentric, and in all of them a spiritual striving had an instinctual basis that, from a medical point of view, was abnormal or hardly normal but for them was the prerequisite for their productivity. So it is certainly correct that, judged from the standpoint of his private life, Alexander the Great had to defeat the great king of the Persians in order to come to terms with his own father who had abused his mother, and to whom he, as a prince, felt responsible but could not intervene because of her wicked life, neither publicly nor in front of his determining ego. With the proper modifications, my own experience of the mother is also susceptible of a correct analytical interpretation. Of course, depth psychology has also conjured up many unpleasant, unproductive, and damaging things, not only personally but also collectively, and the passion for psychoanalysis, in most of those who were seduced by it in its first years when it became fashionable, was based on nothing more than an inclination towards pornography rendered socially acceptable thanks to a new science and healing method. The matter is similar to the invention of the tailcoat or *frac*. Monsieur Frac (that was his real name) once, when he had burned a hole in the front of his frock coat and had to go to a highly official gathering, happened to have the courage to pin his coat together in such a way that it turned into a tailcoat. The enthusiasm it provoked among many of those present, especially among the women, that made the tailcoat immediately became the formal suit for men, needs no further explanation. When I think back to my Victorian youth and then to what has become socially acceptable since analysis became popular, it seems to me that this revolution is more decisive than any other social revolutions I have experienced. Especially in Anglo-Saxon countries, where in my youth not even the word "leg" was allowed to be spoken in public. The analysts are among the protagonists of this revolt of telluric forces, the general meaning of which I defined in my *Révolution Mondiale* in 1933 and which, at the time I am now writing, dominates the entire panorama of the human world. Certainly, the analysts represent the lower organs (in the physical sense) among their elements. They deal, so to speak, with the intestinal functions of current events, whereby inevitably they bring to the surface not only a lot of dirt but also a lot of love for dirt. It is significant that Heyer speaks of an intestinal soul.

Just the same, all the unpleasant things that psychoanalysis signifies and has triggered does nothing to alter the tremendous merit of analysts. This is also part of the fact that, thanks to their new discoveries, many characters who are not in themselves harmless, have found a positive opportunity to act. In the same way, many natures release themselves from predominantly destructive tendencies by taking up the profession of police officers or judges, and some psychopaths save themselves from the madhouse by working as psychiatrists. A great deal of pathos can be converted into ethos, thus getting rid of its compulsive character. At some point, psychoanalysis will be, as one is used to say, an old-fashioned point of view: not, however, in so far as its theory and practice will have been proven erroneous, but after its knowledge and methods have become common property, the self-evident tool of every virile person dealing with other men, as was every genuine woman since Eve who *connait son métier de femme* [knows her job as woman]. To a certain extent, this is already the case today. From year to year it becomes more and more clear to me how transient psychoanalysis is. It is a discipline that must be learned in order to be later forgotten, as is the case with reading and writing. How many illusions of the first decades of the life of depth psychology can already be declared obsolete today! At first it was thought that everything and anything could be traced back to psychological problems. In the end (beginning at the moment I write this) this was true of politics. But then it turned out that the depth psychologists and analysts are, of all men, the ones most apt to judge collective psychological problems wrongheadedly. In collective psychology, it is not at all a question of deep processes, which only take place individually in the soul, but by and large of mutual contagion, which belongs to the field of suggestion, the results of which are vitalized by elementary forces belonging to the region of the subhuman. Here Gustave Le Bon,[22] as simplistic as his personal psychology was, and probably for that very reason, looked more deeply than the most subtle of analysts. Just how completely misleading all explanations of religious and metaphysical experiences by depth psychology are, and must fatally be, I have shown in detail in earlier works (especially in the chapter on religion and psychology in my *Considerations of Silence and Contemplation*). The most tragically touching expression of this became known to me only recently: Freud spent the last years of his life writing a psychoanalysis of the Bible! When you consider that Freud was an Old Testament Jew through and through, the symbol of the snake biting its own tail springs to mind.

What was really epoch-making in psychoanalysis – just as epoch-making as the deeds of Galileo and Copernicus were in their time – is quite different from what it is generally either praised or reviled for: it is that from the

22   (1841–1931) French doctor and polymath, well-known for his psychosociological study of crowds.

standpoint of the condition prevailing in the twentieth century among white people of the old intellectual culture, the autonomous reality of the soul has been rediscovered and cognitively founded or at least started to be substantiated. (The fact that there are still some psychologists who regard the soul as a brain function, such as the well-known Berlin psychotherapist Schultz,[23] is one of those grotesque reaction phenomena that are characteristic of transitional periods. It must be recognized that this same Schultz, with his theory and practice of autogenic training, has gone a considerable way to render the meaning of Indian Hatha Yoga useful for Europeans. Lastly, Christianity did this as long as its tradition, in reaction to the sensualism of late antiquity in whose atmosphere it evolved, still lived on in the unconscious. But in the last officially Christian centuries, the ideal place for the appreciative consciousness of the soul shifted more and more into the sphere of what was transcendent in the Kantian sense; that is, to what transcended possible experience, to that which one could only believe. With that shift, the soul became divested. If Schopenhauer was already of the opinion that one could not speak of the soul as if it were "a well-known and well-accredited person", most thinkers in my youth were sceptical about its existence. There was spirit, yes; idealism demanded that. But soul? It is fantastic how prejudice can make the most evident thing unappreciable. Every age becomes as if hypnotized by some undiscussed prerequisites and only through preventive wars and punitive actions can the new, self-evident truth – because it is a matter of self-evidence – save itself, mostly by a miracle similar to those used in mythology to save heroes. How was it possible that for decades, almost centuries, hardly any keen, deep mind was aware of the quality of the inner life that was immediately given to it? That a Kant could stop at the abstract knowing subject, Hegel at an objective spirit never experienced by anyone, Fichte at an ego that posited the not-ego? That the first scientific psychology only recognized individual sensations as real, and that the imagery of dreams, familiar to everyone, remained outside all serious consideration until after 1900? Conversely, how could Darwinism, which is striking in the face of every unbiased view of life as it really is, and as everyone experiences within and without, ever make sense? For the latter, I can think of no better reason than that causality and the idea of development were modern at the time: every teaching based on these principles had a great chance of success, which, as I believe my grandfather once put it, was both mistaken and plausible.

The only biologist of that period who remained unselfconscious, Karl Ernst von Baer,[24] was considered out of fashion at the time. As a child, I only lived on the level of the psyche, oriented from and towards it, and yet I was so

23   Johannes Schultz (1884–1970), who developed autogenic therapy, a relaxation technique, in the 1920s, as outlined in his 1932 book, *Autogenic Training*. From 1936–1945, Schultz worked as an assistant at the German Institute for Psychological Research in Berlin.

24   (1792–1876), a Baltic German explorer and scientist.

influenced by the zeitgeist that in 1909 I thought it an unheard-of achievement (with "Schopenhauer as model") that I might reach the idea that meaning creates facts and not the other way around. Indeed, many years later, confused by the prejudices of my developmental years awash in the unconscious, I had to swim against the current of my spontaneous sequences of images and ideas, so to speak, in order to describe even with reasonable correctness my psychological experience – that is, the most directly given of all circumstances; my interpretations lagged far behind my images and ideas for a long time, as they still do today. Precisely because I have made progress internally since then, today I can better appreciate what is right about my early offerings more than a quarter of a century ago, when I did not understand their ultimate meaning. It is a very strange thing about a culture whose conscious level of existence is precisely that of the least spontaneous and therefore least alive, namely that of understanding concepts: since the understanding can only determine what its intuitive premises already contain, its supremacy prevents all experience of something new in spirit; it only allows new outside worlds to be assimilated. It is truly a miracle, and only this can explain (taking into account the extremely short period of intellectual predominance, biologically speaking) the fact that this attitude has not rendered superficial, flattened, and dumbfounded the Westerner much more than it did. In any case, this has made spiritual impartiality so difficult that the great spiritual pioneers of our time, i.e., primarily the scientific discoverers of the soul, deserve far more admiration than Galileo and Copernicus. The religious belief in dogma did not prevent the spontaneous creativity of the soul, it only regulated it and made its outbursts seem slightly sinful; it correctly assessed the fundamental reality of mind and soul. Indeed, as paradoxical as it sounds, in the times of the Inquisition the spirit-determined soul was freer than in the nineteenth century, because nothing paralyzed its development from within. What resistance Freud had to overcome in comparison! In the end, he too sought connection with the materialism of his time, as did so many lesser innovators in the Middle Ages with the church; hence its reductive procedure in the spirit of "nothing but". Precisely because of this, Jung's relatively questionable theory of a libido that obeys the law of energy conservation and, like the physical counterpart of this concept, is changeable and finite.

Personally, I am convinced that the substantial spirit, i.e., the meaningful and ultimately creative part of what Jung calls soul, does not obey the law of conservation of energy: at most, the vital earth-born psychic forces obey it, and even here I harbour doubts. The general rule in this field is that the more a person spends, the richer one is; the muscle that grows through exercise is its most concrete expression. But it would be superhuman for the pioneers of the soul to be free from the ideas of the pre-psychological age; rather, they are held in place by them, as by an umbilical cord. Fortunately, although I never intentionally practiced psychology before 1921, I made a very early distinction between intention and intuition on the one hand, and materialization and

expression on the other, as can be seen in my *Unsterblichkeit [Immortality]*.
But I owe this to the fact that, though originally inclined to see with penetrating sight, I never considered concepts and words to be the final instances.
The grammaticality of the Greeks never made sense to me, nor did I infer
real being or non-being from logical necessity, possibility, or impossibility,
nor did I ever start from the word, as most thinkers do. Even as a student,
I was annoyed when I heard a discussion about whether an important man
really was a philosopher or a poet, because the word "poet" or "philosopher" can only be a predicate and never a starting point. Originally I lived
and experienced symbolically, like a primitive; the word was primarily an
image to me and, as an image, the symbol and model of another, more profoundly documented: so in the field of spirit and soul I never believed in original uniqueness. The act of reading between the lines, the immediate sense
of the *sous-entendu* [innuendo], these were my earliest mental faculties, which
I had particularly cultivated during my aestheticizing period, because they
were the basis of all the pampering I have enjoyed since my 21st year in the
circles interested in the spirit, in all the countries that I successively visited. In
this respect, I naively experienced from the start the background that analysts
methodically work out, and that is why, in order to establish an organic relationship between my philosophy of sense apprehension and depth psychology, and to take advantage as far as possible of the authentic knowledge
derived from these for my own specific ends, I only required that my thinking,
directed towards understanding, focus on what I was already doing.

In the lecture "What we want" at the second Wisdom Conference of 1921,
I expressed the bases of this for the first time. But precisely because I was
unconsciously and from the beginning more or less an analyst, insofar as
I involuntarily saw through everything that was obvious, the conscious preoccupation with depth psychology troubled me so much that I can count
this period of my existence among the significant adventures of my soul
(which is why I was able to include the present chapter in this volume: indeed,
had to write this chapter at all). I felt like a girl who is entirely sensual and
unconsciously oriented towards everything, but who has however remained
unenlightened. Indeed, from my experience with depth psychology, I fully
understood why so many girls, even many boys – I was one of them up to my
fifteenth year – do not want to receive explanations at all: it is very different
whether one acts from the unconscious or through what one consciously
knows, expresses, and does. These are such different planes of existence that
becoming what you are, as long as one understands becoming as becoming
conscious, can easily lead to a catastrophe. And it was only from this experience of mine that I understood why, in revolutionary times, people and social
classes who were about to fall almost never noticed that the hour has struck.
As recently as 1917, no responsible Russian statesman was in close contact
with the people, to learn that it was not the democracy led by intellectuals
that endangered tsarism but the grey masses ripe for Bolshevism. In the same

way, the old gentlemen of the Estonian nobility leisurely played cards in the Actienclub while the Reds approached Reval[25] inexorably in 1918 or 1919 and simply denied that there was a risk of death. I like to talk about "a blind spot in the eye of the soul". This metaphor may not be objective, but I've gotten used to it. What one does not want to see, because one's unconscious knows that seeing would destroy his previous equilibrium, one really does not see. So many powerful kings and ministers actually lived in a fool's paradise until the moment they were overthrown.

But back to the factual report on my life. At the time, I read whatever analytical literature came into my hands, corresponded with many analysts, and occasionally worked with several in practice. And in my polarization with these people and their writings, I became aware of many peculiar things that I had not thought of on my own, although they were very close to the surface in me. The greatest magician among analysts – and undoubtedly the most important of all as a human being – was Georg Groddeck.[26] I had met him in Sweden in 1924; I was immediately fascinated by his genuinely diabolical face, as if peeking out from a hell furnace, from whose face at the same time emerged such deep kindness. My heart went out to him, almost in a maternal way, because I felt the endless vulnerability of his soul, which is why he was so fond of stinging and poisonous expressions. All the time he was alive, he kept coming back to Darmstadt, and no more beautiful tribute has ever been paid to me than that of Groddeck, because he once wrote to me shortly before his death: "You're the only person who hasn't hurt me a single time. Thank you." Our closer acquaintance began with Groddeck's promise to cure me, forever and in a single week, of a relapsing phlebitis with ulcers, the full cure of which other doctors doubted. Of course I went to Groddeck in Baden-Baden, and the wounds truly closed, the leg recovered its shape, and up to the time of writing this there has been no relapse. Groddeck healed a little as he appeared: through kindly directed agony. He literally boiled my leg, and his special type of massage, during which he analysed the procedure, guiding himself through my expressions of pain, was, technically judged, torture. However, in the case of the patients with whom he was congenial, Groddeck worked wonders. As an analyst, Groddeck functioned as the most incredible catalyst I could think of. He said next to nothing, but everything that prompted liberation occurred to me spontaneously in his presence. I owe my first insight into the deeper meaning of my experience of the mother to being with Groddeck. What made Groddeck's wu-wei[27]so magical is difficult to

25   Now Tallinn, Estonia.

26   Georg Groddeck (1866–1934). Freud credited Groddeck with coining the term "id", but the two differed in their conceptualizations.

27   Wu-wei is the ancient Chinese practice of taking no action that is not in accord with the Dao, the natural course of the universe, as practised among the philosophers of early Daoism.

determine in detail. On the whole, it was probably based on his own complete ease. Of course, like every analyst I know, he too was an unsolved analytical case, but otherwise non-fixation in the style of Lao Tse[28] was truly his own. So he could not help having a loosening effect on others. I became conscious of image after image in his presence – and yet Groddeck hardly ever asked a question.[29]

Before I got into practical analysis, I had no idea that I was an essentially visual person. Of course, from the age of three, whenever I felt like it, I was able to materialize inner images with the speed of an exhibition painter, but I only saw these images when projected onto paper; I had to draw them to become aware of them. As I analysed with Hattingberg[30] for a few days in the same year that I got to know Groddeck, and before I worked with him, when I tried to make associations, it happened that I never "thought" at all, but simply produced picture after picture, which were then reflected in my upper consciousness in thoughts or broken down into logical chains. So little does one know oneself! So much one must be made aware of even one's own inner life in order to become conscious of it! Now Jung never tried anything with me; we merely talked for a long time about relevant things, and occasionally I wrote to him about interesting dreams that did not immediately escape the grasp of consciousness when I woke up, as is the rule with me. The following memory seems to me to be worth reproducing because it illustrates Jung's ability to look deeply in a particularly charming way. Oscar A. H. Schmitz raved about his beautiful and pioneering dreams so often that I finally got angry. I asked Jung how it came about that I had never had a wonderful dream à la Schmitz – none at all, as far as I could judge, contained things more important than what I was consciously experiencing day-to-day. Jung promptly replied: "You live entirely from day-consciousness and towards this. So you must encounter during the day what others dream at night". Anyone who has read the first volume of these memoirs will be able to judge merely from it alone how perfectly right Jung was. In my case, the people with whom I reacted were what poignant and ground-breaking images mean for others. And in fact, I always met people who were suitable for this role. Of course, the projection mechanism also played a part here, at least insofar as the people concerned meant something different and more to me than they would have meant to someone else; from their point of view, to a certain extent I robbed them of their identity. Nonetheless, for me, the external

---

28   Reputed author of the *Tao Te Ching* and founder of Taoism.
29   Keyserling refers to similar sentiments about Groddeck he published in *Wegs zur Vollendung*, *23* (1934).
30   In addition to his analysis in 1922 with Schmitz, Keyserling also worked with Hans von Hattingberg (1879–1944), the München-based neurologist and psychoanalyst who directed the research department of the Göring Institute, and with Georg Groddeck. In 1925 Freud referred Keyserling to Karl Abraham (1877–1925).

reality did not correspond in an ordinary degree to what otherwise happens only on the level of internal images. The most striking example of this is my experience of my mother. My mother was really lover and beloved on the one hand, and the terrible and destructive one on the other: Kali, which so many origin myths portray in a similar way. Reality mirrored in exactly the same way the image of the soul when I married. If I had been consciously determined to do anything since 1912, it was never to marry and deliberately to fade away. At the first sight of my future wife, children appeared in the picture, and it occurred to me that my life would proceed like that of Bismarck. I was still consciously against it – but this did not prevent me, when I went to Rayküll as landowner for the last time in autumn 1918, from making the first arrangements for accepting a wife. When later I returned to Germany, the idea of marriage continued to obsess me against my will; I tried to escape geographically. Pneumonia kept me, of all places, in the house of my future mother-in-law, and so gracious fate took its course. In the same sense, I have never just encountered something meaningless (but I have often done something that was absurd!). This must obviously be due to that particular psychological structure that Jung detected. I still cannot fully understand the casual connection today. But I am certain that the being of a person as such represents a specific force that fashions its fate through attraction and repulsion stemming from the unconscious. Even during the World War, I thought of Roman Ungern-Sternberg,[31] that given the particular tension in his nature (one pole of which was metaphysical knowledge and holiness, the other the most gruesome cruelty) he belonged to Mongolia, whose human condition is characterized by this tension: by "pure chance" Ungern actually went there and died as their temporary ruler. The admirable things as Alfred Keyserling[32] encountered again and again throughout his life, only he, apparently, could experience. In the same way, I don't know of anyone who, as a matter of course, has come across so many amazing beings of occult or magical disposition in the East as Hans Hasso von Veltheim-Ostrau.[33] But in my experience, this only happens to those in whom real life replaces what inner images signify to others. Outwardly, the pure dreamer and poet rarely experiences a great deal, at least nothing that in itself, as an external matter, means anything as much as that which is evoked in the sphere of the subject. The person whose psychological type I share has probably always known a similar antipathy to poetry as I feel; I simply cannot stand poetry, but my whole life is a poem.

---

31   Nikolai Robert Maximilian Freiherr von Ungern-Sternberg (1886–1921), also referred to as Baron Ungern, an anti-Communist general in the Russian Civil War and a warlord who fought in Mongolia against China. He was Keyserling's cousin.

32   Alfred Graf Keyserling (1857–1929).

33   Hans-Hasso Ludolf Martin Freiherr von Veltheim-Ostrau (1885–1956), a German Indologist, anthroposophist, and spiritualist.

In order to experience the many truly real things that have happened to me and continue to happen, one must live primarily in the region of the senses and not take facts and designs seriously. As soon as one clings to their peculiarities, the relationships "from sense to sense" (as I might express it) are made impossible. So under no circumstances should one adopt a scholarly demeanour, or that of a scholar. Here Jung was very different from me, and this explains most of his merits as well as many of his limitations. To get back to the problem of experiencing the waking life: Jung was actually quite an owl in his own right. His own dream life meant most to him, certainly for many years, and it preoccupied him during the day, just as others dream about daily events at night. Hence Jung's ability to interpret dreams, which appeared more and more stupendous, and from year to year more and more free from prejudices; also, the impartiality of his arbitrary judgements wherever they appeared – he was subjectively certain of the meaningfulness of his ideas. (All analysts generally tend to such arbitrariness, since they have to absorb the ideas from the unconscious of others through their own unconscious, and come up with interpretations as if they were their own ideas.) Hence his disposition to assimilate all daily reality through his unconscious. But precisely from there stem the most important limitations of Jung's talent. In order to be able to work as he did, Jung had to take dream formations, and thus formations in general, seriously. It is precisely because of this that he has become a great scholar of comparative symbolism and a historian of symbolism, or, to put it more generally, a morphologist of the formations of the unconscious just as Frobenius[34] was a cultural morphologist. But on the other hand, this same disposition and attitude made it difficult, even often impossible, for Jung to live directly out of the meaning and to see through the appearances down to their original meaning. He even became progressively more hostile, or hostile to the original spirit. He got stuck, he had to stay stuck, in the realm of comparative imaginology.

C. G. Jung – Psychological Craftsman

I cannot round off this chapter in any conclusive way: the soul grows steadily in transformation as new aspects reveal themselves, and thus also the symbolic centre to which they are referred in observation – in this case Jung – is always gaining new features. Here I will only refer back to my personal experience and to the difficulty to become conceptually aware of it. One never learns to know oneself as one really is merely through introspection, but only by the effect of one's own reality and one's reactions to it, in the same way that only experimentation conveys sure knowledge of the nature outside us. That is exactly why realization as a collective phenomenon proceeds so slowly. The

---

34   Leo Viktor Frobenius (1873–1938), a German ethnologist and archaeologist.

wrong must redeem itself properly before it is revealed. It is especially difficult to let go of one's prejudices, because they condition the view from within and therefore represent "transcendental forms" in the Kantian sense, no matter how low their level. That is why pioneers as such, no matter how much they err, and although they are usually soon outstripped, are a thousand times more admirable than the greatest achievers and perfectionists, because, in their case, incomparably greater originality is required. Nature is conservative through and through. From her point of view, original ideas mean something similar to organic mutations, and one knows how rarely such mutations occur. Tarde, in his wonderfully witty, far too-little-known book *Les lois de l'imitation*,[35] tried to prove that since Adam's time only a few dozen really original ideas extended the possibilities of human thinking and working; almost everything that is considered to be innovative was only imitation or modification of what already existed. In this way, thousands of years passed until the first usable airplane was invented, but as soon as the first one arrived, every month some kind of improvement saw the light of day. The reason for this sad state of affairs is that we humans are not masters of our ideas, since they originate entirely in the unconscious. Only indirectly can we promote their emergence and govern their development, namely by exposing the unconscious to favourable influences. But the main difficulty has not been touched upon yet. It could be that in the end a few gifted individuals will be granted ideas as pure gifts from God, and many others will make use of these without too much trouble. The inventor is given nothing in the end, as the saying goes, in spite of the grace of the idea. He must organically form the new idea into the pre-existing structure of spirit and soul, so that it may become fruitful, for without a firm connection to it, the idea lacks support and cannot have a positive effect. And here the innovator experiences within himself, for a long time, the same resistances which he will later encounter in public. It is tremendously difficult and requires enormous self-discipline not to strip his own novelty of its originality by reducing it to what is already known. Only those who are aware of this from their own experience can appreciate what true originality means and what a powerful ethos its effect presupposes. Buffon's famous words refer to this, and to this alone: "*Le génie, ce n'est qu'une longue patience*" [Genius is only being patient for a long time]. Thus Jung is truly worthy of veneration, however unhewn he has left some blocks blasted out in his drillings: this work is done more and more satisfactorily by much lesser minds than Jung's, little by little and without much mental effort. In doing this better, they should, of course, be wary of pretending that their corrections are even approximately equal in importance and value to the original achievements, however incorrect they may have been in the

---

35   Gabriel Tarde, *Les Lois de l'Imitation*, 1890; *The Laws of Imitation*, trans. Elsie Clews Parson, New York: Henry Holt, 1903.

individual. In this sense, I have always been indignant when I have read the critical remarks of these overdiscriminating and finicky workers who place themselves on a superior plane. For the essential difference between pioneers and epigones is precisely a difference in essence, and therefore immeasurable, and cannot be bridged by anything at all.

But of course, Jung hardly taught anything about the soul itself. His concept of libido is a leftover of the nineteenth century, and the connection of body and soul, which Jung implicitly states, does not exist. Here, however, Jung could not arrive at decisive insights at all – precisely because he is a psychologist and only a psychologist. In order to really grasp one's own soul, as it ultimately is, one must have gained a certain supra-psychic interior stronghold in real terms (and not in theory). And this goal cannot be reached through research, but only by a change of one's condition. Indian wisdom teaches that a man can see God only after he has become God. The analytical psychologist would grasp the same truth in the following way: one can project only what lives in oneself. Jehovah appeared to Moses in the burning bush, and Christ to Saul as a dazzling light in the clouds, only after their gods had seized them inwardly and assimilated them into themselves. Thus Ramakrishna spontaneously saw in every woman the divine mother Kali, because he himself had reached the inner state that corresponded to this image. Now the soul has its depths in the metaphysical and can therefore only be correctly situated by a metaphysically-directed consciousness, not by the psychologist observing from outside. Hence the fateful inadequacy of Jung's attempts to interpret Eastern wisdom analytically: he does not, as he believes, penetrate it; on the contrary, he traces its very being back to its correspondences in the empirical, just as all reductive interpretation fails to grasp the thing itself but only makes conscious its correspondences on other levels. The psychologist as such is just an intermediate being and an inhabitant of the intermediate realm. His science resembles a rudderless barge that is rocked back and forth on the high seas. The barge does not sink in the waves, but overwhelmed by powerful currents it finds no way to the mainland. And landing or sinking, perhaps also flying up into the sky, is what matters in the end.

This chapter has turned out more "objective" than the others, and it is longer than I intended. This is due to the fact that, to a certain extent, I had to disassociate myself in order to look at my innermost self from the outside, so as to deal not only implicitly but explicitly, with the psychology of the unconscious. Like few individuals, I live – I must repeat this again and again, because whoever does not begin here cannot possibly understand me – not only originally but unalterably out of the unconscious, whose essence is that it cannot be made directly conscious at all; by this I particularly mean that I lose my impartiality and my involuntary radiance is impaired if I know exactly what I am doing at the moment of manifesting myself or acting out. Thus, on the one hand, everything belonging to the region of the unconscious is more familiar to me than to most men; in this, my psychology resembles that of women, who quite naturally deal primarily with unconscious impulses. On the other hand, I have to do violence or ravish myself, so to speak, in order to raise what was originally unconscious in me to consciousness, for the resulting shift in the weight of my soul's appearance does not correspond to its actual fate. I am essentially the "blind seer", as I described myself in 1927 in "Mein Glaube" ["My Faith"], and shall remain so until I come to a critical point that I have not yet reached, and perhaps never will. However, precisely for the sake of this violation, the period in which depth psychology was the focus of my interest belongs once again among the most important adventures of my soul. At that time, more directly than ever before or after, I challenged the nocturnal figures and forces that live in me (as in every human being) to emerge into the daylight. I tried, as never before nor after, to replace destinies with artificial interventions, starting from the all-powerful prejudices of the analysts, which I had temporarily adopted as working hypotheses. Today, after almost a quarter of a century, I look back and see that I was only very modestly successful. My basic attitude has remained the original one: very few of the tensions that my analyst friends judged as complexes have been resolved or balanced, and many have even increased. And this is certainly not due to the fact that I have never been "thoroughly analysed", because the example of all thoroughly analysed analysts known to me proves that analysis does not change one's basic structure, and that every particular structure has a complex effect from the point of view of others. My being, however, has been less affected than most by analytic inspection, as much as I gained in knowledge and ability, and this mainly for three reasons. First, because, as I said, I live essentially out of the unconscious. Second, because seeing through is my ability, which is originally directed outwardly and therefore severely affects my inner being. Finally and above all, because psychoanalysis is definitely a matter of the intermediate realm, and I have no original relationship to that realm at all. Whatever is intermediate, in whatever sense, means nothing to me, and I can only master it to some extent merely as an actor. Psychologists of the Adlerian school will, of course, draw from this explanation a short-circuit due to a lack of community feeling, and be contented with this, unless they attempt to "totally" improve me. But, if they did this, they would be completely wrong, both theoretically and practically. The primary and essential feeling of community, which I have tried to determine exactly in the chapter "Commonality" in my *Reflections of Silence and Contemplation*, is missing in me not more but less than in others. I have never seen myself other than as an organ of humanity, never lived merely for private personal interest. What I lack is a direct relationship to the intermediate realm corresponding to this original one. Hence my constantly recurring misunderstandings and conflicts with my fellow men, according to the degree in which these intermediate realm-values were recognized. Here, then, I arrive at the most positive aspect of my preoccupation with depth psychology from the point of view of my life as a whole. Inwardly, without contact with the intermediate realm, I have gradually learned to reckon better with it, thanks to external experience and a steadily increased understanding. Where my consciousness had enough power over my primordial impulses, thanks to a depth psychological education, I consciously shaped my relationships to other people in such a way that they became more bearable than they would otherwise have been. And where I recognized that the self-will of the unconscious was *plus fort que moi* [stronger than me], I restrained myself more and more, and left the mastery of that side of my existence more and more to others. With this, I returned, after long and far-flung detours, admittedly on a higher level, to the life-technique of my youth. On a higher level: because what was then only external technique has since become primordial "life as art". Whereby it has finally become apparent to me how utterly trivial and unimportant what most people would call "character" ultimately is. It may well be that my harsh condemnation of the characterologists has been judged a complex in readers from the circle of analysts; probably complexes are really involved here, just as is my extreme disgruntlement towards anyone who tells me to my face that my handwriting is difficult to read. But if it is really a matter of complexes here, it only proves once more what power little complexes have. Of course, every normal human being reacts with increasing sourness the more often one steps on his foot. Precisely because of my long occupation with problems of depth psychology, guided by a very rich individual as well as collective experience, it has become finally clear to me that character is meaningless from the point of view of the substantial spirit, the human being's essence, and that it depends only on what this spirit does with its innate character.

What I first explained in the Himalaya section of the *Travel Diary* has since become for me a fundamental insight for any future improvement of the human condition. Characterology as well as depth psychology in its most degrading, malignant aspect must completely drain every last festering matter from the organism of communal life. Without strong telluric instincts and impulses, no striving for higher things is possible on earth, and they are all ambivalent and are regarded at first mostly negatively. The latter is especially true of the drives for power, fame, and wealth. Accordingly, most of the later saints were originally questionable fellows. Precisely because this is so, I recognize Nietzsche's call for man to become evil again, a call that has since been followed to a grandiose extent: most of the ugliness that defines the image of mankind today has arisen from the repression of evil; only after becoming aware of what has been repressed, affirming it, and allowing it to vent itself for a time, can the same primordial dispositions take on a positive aspect, and without their cooperation there is no full life. In this respect the good of tomorrow actually depends on the venting of the evil of today. When development has come this far, the psychoanalytic era of cultural history will have been left behind, as so many other contingent circumstances have been overcome forever: its problems will become irrelevant, like the problems of Ibsen's dramas ever since the true emancipation of women. The psychological problems will then be posed once more, as they were in wise times before the

analytic period. Only one example of this to close this chapter: today, people are catalogued according to psychophysical and psychological types, mainly from Kretschmer[36] and Jung, or from their classifications. But judged from the point of view of the substantial spirit it is irrelevant whether one is leptosome or pyknic, schizothymic or cycloid, whether one is extraverted or introverted. It is not indifferent, however, to which primordial state one belongs. I have already indicated that the whole edifice of depth psychology springs almost entirely from the psychology of the craftsman. But the psychology of the craftsman is originally and unalterably different from that of the master-man, of the prophet, priest, merchant, even of the worker, the latter appearing in a new way once more, similarly free and generous and as superior to matter as the conqueror, the ancestor of the nobleman. Whether one is a master or a slave does not depend on the intermediate realm, but on the original being, which no analytical treatment is able to change. No worldview will ever change the fact that one can only enjoy serving the born master, that only he who is fated by the spirit can emit spiritual impulses, only the merchant can mediate, only the craftsman execute. After long detours mankind will find its way back to the idea of original vocation and essential destiny.
Completed at Hohenschäftlarn, April 20, 1944.

Victoria Ocampo – Mother-love

In 1939, when I read the wonderful book of the South African Eugène Marais *The White Ant*,[37] nothing – not even the outbreak of what was then called only the European War – made a deeper impression on me than the author's, in my opinion, successful proof that motherly love in nature is triggered by the pain of childbearing. According to Marais, where childbearing is painless, there is no mother love. The first verifiable example of human-like attachment to the brood (on the Darwinian scale of organisms) is offered by scorpions that possess a mammal-like psyche in spite of their particularly hideously pronounced insect-like nature. Everything else, in greater detail, one can read in Marais. He successfully conducted his *experimentum crucis* [an experiment capable of decisively establishing the superiority of a particular hypothesis] with antelopes: while females of this species are especially tender after consciously giving birth, mothers anesthetized during childbirth did not feel any love at all, and even refused to recognize their little ones as theirs.

Since then I suspect that the loosening of family ties among Europeans and especially Americans is also connected with anaesthesia at the difficult hour. But be that as it may, human life also offers enough further examples which

---

36   Ernst Kretschmer (1888–1964), who wrote *Körperbau und Charakter* (1921), which Routledge published as *Physique and Character* (1931).
37   Eugène Marais, *Die Siel van die Mier*, published in Afrikaans in 1925 and as *The Soul of the White Ant*, translated by Winifred de Kok, in 1937.

seem to be more plausibly explainable in the spirit of the broadly understood Maraisian theory; indeed, it offers so many of them that the connection between birth pangs and maternal love has become for me, since I learned about it, a symbol for the connection between nature and spirit in general. In primitive psychology and monogamic culture, he who deflowers a maiden makes her his almost automatically; the same can be said of the rapist, as Groddeck dared affirm when he said that primitive woman considers rape the only genuine proof of love. It has been proved that even today there are women within the most refined circles of southern races, who, in order to reach the apex, demand to be raped. Who cannot decide to be brutal in this psychological moment, must lose them. Every telluric woman of the normal kind automatically becomes someone else when she reaches maternity; new instincts and abilities become dominant in her. Even the man who does not ignore the deepest reverberations of his soul, something that admittedly many do because the pursuit renders them deaf, feels united to the woman he has possessed; this explains not only so many insane marriages, but above all the special complacent cruelty that many men feel when they abandon the women whom earlier they so ardently desired.

Let us now proceed directly from here to apparently pure soul connections. In general, suffering for another human being creates deepest attachment to that person. And in the depths of human nature there is such a positive accent on suffering that the difference between circumstances so essentially at odds as suffering for another person, for another person or because of another person, become increasingly blurred. That is why harshness in the powerful is seldom criticized; on the contrary, it arouses reverence that in turn inspires love. Even cruelty can bind: this is the only explanation for the apotheosis of Lenin, as well as for the tendency that can be observed again and again to excuse or rehabilitate cruel tyrants. This has similar psychological reasons as the deification of cold and cruel beauties. Let us not spoil the possible experience of uncanny natural summits with labels that explain away, for instance, masochism; such labels never do justice to the subject, let alone to its meaning. What matters for understanding is the connection that undoubtedly exists between what is most positive and what is most negative, between the highest and the very lowest. To fashion suffering is in itself not always something evil nor, most of the time, something ugly. Meister Eckhart says in his most beautiful sermon, the one about confinement: "Nothing is as gall-bitter as suffering, but nothing as honey-sweet as having suffered." This sentence follows: "No one enjoys so much eternal happiness as those who stand with Christ in the most bitter hour." And before that there is the famous phrase: "The swiftest horse that carries you to perfection, is suffering." However, the latter is understood correctly and truly only if one considers it together with the awakening of humanlike mother-love of the scorpion through birth pains. Body, soul, and spirit are of course not one, nor can they ever share a common denominator. And yet, they are lawfully connected, and in ways that have not yet, as far as I know, been recognized. In my *Meditations* and in *The Book of Personal Life* I did nothing else but separate the components of the human being, but I have not yet been able to grasp their connection in terms that satisfy me. Obviously, what would be appropriate here is a theory that would allow one to observe comprehensively from a single point of view protists, siphonophores, termite mounds, and humans.

What lives and works with genuine insight in this extremely difficult area, does so almost exclusively in a body of unchallenged tradition. As examples of such embodiments, according to the principle *pars pro toto* [a part taken as representative of the whole], I will only mention the instinct-secure mother who protects her daughter from premature experience, the army commander for whom his men are willing to die, the ascetic master who shows his believers the way to the overcoming of nature. The mother who wants to preserve her daughter's innocence until marriage embodies the wisdom of nature. This appears as Victorian-minded in all higher animals: there is everywhere a clear-cut distinction between virgin and woman, each living on a distinct level. And the woman who follows nature here not only becomes happier, she attains higher perfection than any being not particularly individualized nor more highly gifted who, out of enlightenment, does not recognize the norm of nature. The first man to whom she gives herself really binds her. The first child creates an indissoluble family connection. And if then natural phases trigger their normal mental correspondences, family life usually develops into a happy beauty. Remember that women secure in their nature do not lose confidence in the future, not even during the most terrible catastrophes; in Alfred Weber's words, they "parley" with the most terrible fate and thus really tame it.[38] On the other hand, the kind and considerate military leader is never deified: it is the just one who is and who demands the greatest sacrifices with natural severity. In this case, it is harshness that, among other things, demands the utmost commitment of the soul, and that doing so binds the men to the leader within a framework of justice. Finally, the ascetic master knows that man, as a spiritual being, wants to grow immaculately and that the world-superior self grows in the function of the overcoming of nature, test to successful test, from a steadfastly borne suffering to a steadfastly borne suffering, from inertia overcome to inertia overcome. Consequently, through the hard treatment of nature, he fosters inner freedom, and this is why the spiritual master, hard as he may be, is the most revered and loved of all models. In the realm in which only "what is free" decides, or on the plane of the truly free man, alas so rare, there is only voluntary progress. Thus the ascetic master does not awaken the sense of the natural norm by means of the example of good manners, as the mother does in the case of her daughters; nor does he sternly subdue nature by means of external coercion, as the commander of an army does by means

---

38   (1868–1958), a German economist, geographer, sociologist, and theoretician of culture.

of iron-cast discipline, but he constantly appeals to free determination held sometimes fast by a vow. For he who does not want to advance, of course, yoga is of no use whatsoever. This is valid for the whole field of "what is free", whose most profound symbol is the other crucified thief, whom the Son of God himself could not redeem because he refused to open the gates of his heart to Him. But even in this field, very seldom has a man reached his goal who was not helped by nature. Very seldom has a master of true vocation achieved decisive transformation without the pressure of severe blows of fate or without struggling with the great difficulties that his own nature set against him. (From the point of view of the "self", which is the subject of "what is free", there is hardly any difference between an unfortunate disposition and adverse external circumstances). This has been so much the rule in all previous history that C. G. Jung could claim that no one wants his own highest achievement who has not been forced towards it as the only conceivable way out of suffering and tribulation. I recall here the moving story of my cousin Alfred Keyserling (in *Count Alfred Keyserling Tells*) from the time of his imprisonment in the Peter and Paul Fortress in 1914, where he could have been executed at any moment: in his moment of greatest despair, he was suddenly granted the grace of being able to have his soul leave his body and to look down on himself without pain, from that corner of the room close to the ceiling where icons are hung in Greek Orthodox houses. Jung exaggerates, of course: no doubt the aspiration of all great spiritual strivers was a primordial one. But it seems to be also true, for most of them, that without strong pressure from within or without they would hardly have gone beyond the critical point, that moment of discontinuity in development, comparable to the moment in which water is transformed into steam, that separates the accomplished achiever from the struggling man. Of course, the same can be said of critical points of a lesser degree. Hence the artificial difficulties that every ascetic practice has to deal with. The scientifically comprehensible cause of why natural pressure necessarily supports the free striving of the spirit is probably that the unconscious is not directly accessible nor offered up to consciousness. The latter reacts only to bodily experience, not to imagined pictures, not to insight, not even to made-up difficulties. With the higher man, nevertheless, even in the case of the greatest hardship from the outside world, which later will prove to be a furthering, the emphasis lies on "what is free": either he himself summons up the real difficulties, or else he makes use of them as no one else would, by placing the emphasis entirely on experience and on the possibility of new sense-realization manifested within it, and not on the possible ways of personally escaping his distress; finally, he suffers from (objectively judged) trifles so deeply and so strenuously that it is evidently his subjectivity on which all emphasis rests. One thinks of the exaggerated consciousness of sin and inadequacy of every genuine saint. Already on the much lower level of existence that I myself have so far reached, the same applies: I have become much more sensitive than I was in my youth, I suffer a hundred times more, but almost no longer from external adversity but from my own inadequacy, especially from the fact that external things can still unbalance me. Quite involuntarily, I ascribe the blame for everything to myself; for obviously nothing external would any longer be able to harm me if it did not correspond to a readiness of the soul. The more a human being is now nature-bound, the more the accent actually rests on the exterior. Of millions of human mothers, even among highly bred ones, it is the same as with animal females. But since even in primitives, who do not, in Jesus's words, "have life in them," in the case of mother-love and the like, as in the case of men in self-sacrificing struggles, undoubtedly the sublime appears. It cannot be denied that at lower stages of life, where no "freedom" can yet direct the development of itself, there is something like a pre-stabilized harmony between nature and spirit. I am not at all interested in the notion of a pre-stabilized harmony, which to me is only a first approximation of something that can be grasped more clearly later. Nor am I interested in any theory, but, on the other hand, I advise that my readers accept the proposed notion as a symbol of truth, and not to brood over it. It is just that purely external fate, which seems senseless in itself, can be the condition for the emergence of the sublime, and that under all circumstances there is a lawful connection between the natural and the spiritual. The same thing does not happen to everyone: not everyone is elevated or harmed by the same thing. Somehow freedom and necessity, chance, merit, and grace, always correspond to each other.

Let us now consider other examples of the same basic relationship. Whether or not one believes in the same teaching of all high religions: the right thing, as grotesque as this law of pure reason may seem, is that man should earn his bread; only the inwardly very high can live from begging, from gifts, or even from his revenues without any kind of counter-service, without his soul being damaged. On the other hand, every normal person, who has received some good from others, feels the urge to show gratitude, precisely by means of material goods. Essentially, gratitude as such does not create a feeling of full satisfaction. The blessing of work, of so-called honest earnings and just remuneration can, in my opinion, only be explained in that there is a primordial connection between the material and the psycho-spiritual. For this very reason, idleness corrupts everyone who is not capable of noble leisure, an ability, of course, much more valuable than the inner compulsion to be constantly busy. The intimate connection between material and spiritual is proven especially in the case of the true spiritual creator. This, of course, flows out freely and purely; in and of itself, it only wants to give. And yet, they all instinctively claim to be able to live from their art; they see it as absurd if they have to live in want. Indeed, basically, every spiritually gifted person expects from the depths of his unconscious – however differently his intellect may judge the question – to receive a material countervalue for the inner wealth that he gives away. At the very least, he expects fame (not recognition: the consciousness of sovereignty of the creative person who is sure of himself judges

outspoken recognition as something almost degrading; in any case, such recognition would not come from his equals). And yet, fame is also the highest
wealth, because to the soul it means the highest possible earthly possession.
Here however, a certain successive order is the only one that makes sense, and
this proves completely that I was justified in presenting the connection of
motherly love and birth pangs as a universal symbol. Material sufferings and
sacrifices must precede spiritual gain; he who has high things to give cannot
first strive for gain. Whoever thinks first of wages when practicing his art,
of fees when healing, of the power to be gained through asceticism, in general whoever thinks first of remuneration, damages his soul, only a shade less
than if he allows himself to be bribed. He prostitutes himself – and from the
point of view of love the whole connection suddenly makes sense. Every soul-
developed woman wants to love first, before she gives herself away; and she is
right, because for the soul, the consequences of the contrary are disastrous;
there is only a small difference between a marriage of convenience and prostitution. In exactly the same way, the artist-teacher-doctor who thinks first
of wages, prostitutes himself. Indeed, prostitution means nothing else than
inversion; the normal order appears as its opposite. And this is objectively
true, as the psychic consequences prove. Consequently, there exists a normal
order, and the deeper the affected level, the more fatal its inversion. Politicians
can afford vices and crime without dire consequences, because politics as such
is an infernal thing. But he who sells his love turns the unsoiled into the soiled;
he who as a writer lies for the sake of gain or position, corrupts himself; he
who selfishly uses the higher forces that spiritualization conjures up, becomes
satanic. Doubtless there are analogous stages and phases in nature similar to
those invented by ascetic practice.

Particularly instructive in this context is the coexistence, only rarely absent,
of higher aspirations, especially ideal ones, and the lust for recognition. The
infamous clan of characterologists has placed particularly cumbersome
obstacles in the path of modern man's understanding, and has sown an evil
seed in the souls of the majority of Germans; for one cannot interpret high as
low without this having an effect on the interpreter. Characterology, at least
as inspired by Klages,[39] has – it does not matter if intentionally or not, since
the primordial being and not the conscious will is the one to decide – tried, in
the spirit of the psychoanalytic "nothing but", to devalue all desire that does
not steer away from this world. But I do not know of any case in the whole of
history in which an intense desire has not had strong telluric roots that are the
instinct for recognition and ambition, together with their correlates of jealousy, lust for power, and the will to succeed; the latter appear separately, every
time, even in the case of a zealous god, as negative. On earth the low impulses

---

39   Friedrich Konrad Eduard Wilhelm Ludwig Klages (1872–1956) was a German philosopher,
     psychologist, graphologist, and writer. See Paul Bishop, *Ludwig Klages and the Philosophy
     of Life: A Vitalist Tool* (London: Routledge, 2019).

are not possible without the corresponding ones on high. Without roots in hell, there is no dynamic; without primeval hunger and fear, no self-assertion. For this very reason, most of those who later became saints were particularly bold sinners – I use the text in reference to Luther's advice to sin boldly.[40] All great artists were born jealous and all great rulers, who were not already born as such, were power-hungry and complete unscrupulous.

Let us now, after we have proved the instinctual expressions of elevated spirituality, with examples from many spheres, turn back to the relationship between nature and spirit in the field of eros and sex. Here, originally, the utmost opposing tension prevails between the sublime and the low. It is of no use to argue that the facts of pure sexual life, from the primordial feelings of the soul and from the spontaneous demand of the spirit, are not ugly, and that the highest expressions of love are not sublime because they are connected with the low, and vice versa. Here, if one truly wants to understand, all the usual masks must fall. I know that, since women identify themselves primordially with their clothed and adorned selves, not with their naked bodies, it is almost impossible for them, by their very nature, not to demand corresponding masks in all intimate questions – if they practice nudism, then nakedness means clothing to them, because this is demanded by the conventions of the prevailing fashion. That is why women, from their point of view, do not lie, no matter how misleadingly they idealize; the naked truth is the business of men. Therefore, the following should be noted in advance to what will be discussed later. The usual sayings about the sanctity of a mother's love are a fraud; C. G. Jung is right when he claims that women would not associate the word love with sanctity if they did not mean something unholy and wanted to make it acceptable to their consciousness. Judged from unbiased knowledge, the pretension of turning something that is in itself natural into something different from what it is, is equivalent to ridiculing the concept of sanctity. As such, the natural is always only natural. However, something else is also true: through certain natural things, it is possible to express purely spiritual things. A true transfiguration of the natural is possible, and indeed such a transfiguration

---

40   Keyserling notes,

Luther's full letter to Melanchthon:

'If you are a preacher of mercy, do not preach an imaginary but the true mercy. If the mercy is true, you must bear the true, not an imaginary sin. God does not save those who are only imaginary sinners. Be a sinner, and let your sins be strong (sin boldly), but let your trust in Christ be stronger, and rejoice in Christ who is the victor over sin, death, and the world. We will commit sins while we are here, for this life is not a place in which justice resides. We, however, says Peter (2 Peter 3:13), are looking forward to a new heaven and a new earth where justice will reign. It suffices that through God's glory we have recognized the Lamb that takes away the sin of the world. No sin can separate us from Him, even if we were to kill or commit adultery a thousand times each day. Do you think such an exalted Lamb paid merely a small price with a meagre sacrifice for our sins? Pray hard for you are truly a sinner'.

is in these certain cases prefigured in nature. Thus all higher communal culture, all deeper love, all disinterested acts, all sacrifice, all mercy, all grace as opposed to right, and ultimately all that we feel to be manifestations of the divine on earth, are expressly preformed in the relationship between husband and wife, and between parents and children.

And yet, the incorporation of what is spiritually and mentally highest into what is natural never need take place. Most people in love are mere instinctive beings, and most human mothers are no more than mother animals; and this always, from the very beginning. But if an embodiment of the spiritual takes place in the natural realm, it rarely lasts. Hence the instinctive rejection of all natural bonds on the part of spiritually striving people. The inspiration of the natural is a process like that of the inspiration of the poet. And what might be said to be a permanent phenomenon, that is to say, independent in talent and mood, is held fast by tradition and convention, that is to say, by psychic and spiritual ties, not by natural ties existing independently of the consent of the spirit. Hence the immediate decay of all custom and morals as soon as certain forms of belief that gave a definite spiritual meaning to the natural perish. Nevertheless, as is evident from what I've been saying, to express this truth in Catholic terms, all creation was and remains subject to God. But from this it can only be concluded that nature and spirit are by no means apart and unrelated as Western Christian philosophy claims. The usual trenchant distinction has its measure of truth and reason in the fact that man is able to create special expressions for purely spiritual and purely mental things, which now live as phenomena of a special kind together with the phenomena of nature. But these phenomena, detached from nature, have little power. Judged from the core of life, they occupy an eccentric place; only referred back to it do they appear alive. This is what it means when an idea or theory only becomes a power through belief in it, or through personal interest. The strongest spiritual powers are always those that manifest themselves through all layers of the human being. Genuine spiritualization therefore does not mean detachment from nature, but a complete compenetration with it.

I am afraid that the intellect will never succeed in grasping this connection conceptually, that is, in a way that is completely comprehensible. But it seems to me that one can come much closer to understanding this than has been successful until now if one looks at the connection between nature and spirit from the point of view of the law of correlation of sense and expression (see *Creative Understanding*[41]), and indeed, looking at it together with the doctrine of the universal alphabet, including universal grammar and syntax, whose letters and norms have always remained the same, and by means of which the most diverse ideas can be expressed. Even in the case of most spiritual love between man and woman, it is the most natural expression of it that fosters a feeling of perfect fulfilment. The same is true, *mutatis mutandis* [with

---

41   *Creative Understanding*, pp. 61–66.

things being changed that have to be changed], of maternal love; it seems impossible to love an adopted child as deeply as one conceived and borne oneself. Of course, there are those highest experiences, very deep and essential, that do not have nor demand correspondences in all strata of the human being. But even here the spiritual suffers from lacking a relationship with nature. Nothing abstract is equal to something concrete. Only knowledge that is related to the empirical and does it justice, and comprehends the entire human being, is real; pure idealism is cut off from life, blind to reality and hopelessly unfruitful; whoever is so easily praised as an idealist in Germany is usually exactly the same person whom the realistic Frenchman succinctly calls an *esprit faux* [a deceitful person]. Without personal interest and adherence to the natural foundations, no unselfish interest can be taken for granted, except in the rare case of a world conqueror. I insist: to rise above the world it is necessary to observe precisely the laws of the world. Even the most sovereign conquering of fate can only be achieved by means of *amor fati* [love of one's fate], whose exemplary representative is not the Stoic, but someone who is deeply connected with nature, someone who accepts unbiasedly everything that falls to him as his. It is no different with placing one's highest trust in God in respect to an unbiased and self-evident surrender to the world process. The doctrine of creative understanding further asserts that essential progress can occur only inwards; every realized sense can become the symbol of a deeper sense which is prefigured in it; one can therefore say that the cosmos extending out in space and time has, in the dimension of pure intensity, a spirit cosmos that can be realized through the universal alphabet. Thus, in borderline cases, natural necessity becomes the appropriate expression of pure freedom, just as the conventional sonnet form, bound by strict rules, does not inhibit the personal inspiration of a great poet but helps it achieve self-realization. Ultimately, the world, to adopt an apt expression by Otto Flake,[42] is a concentric phenomenon. To this extent, every person can realize himself within his proper sphere. The deeper we meditate on a spiritual content that truly concerns us inwardly, the more the deeper meanings will reveal themselves, finally reaching far beyond the person. These uttermost depths not only belong to that person in this precise sense, but in a sense more essential than all superficial feelings and cognitions, and even more than the beloved I. Every realization of a deeper sense, however, gives a new and more essential meaning to the superficial realm that has remained the same. In all cases, however, the fullness of experience and knowledge is the greater and more gratifying – and the power of man appears proportionately greater – the more concentrically he adjusts himself in the sense defined above. Therefore the true mission of man, as I already determined in the very important section of the American chapter of the *Travel Diary*,[43] does not lie in an ever-sharper

42   (1880–1963), a German writer and publisher.
43   Keyserling, *Travel Diary of a Philosopher*, pp. 279–362.

separation between nature and spirit, and an ever-more-differentiated elab-
oration of the various layers and parts of the human being, but conversely,
in an integration that restores to a higher level the wholeness and unity that
existed before the Fall. This possibility, however, as the example of the scorpion mother first made clear to me, is already prefigured in the less spiritual
nature.

Victoria Ocampo – South America

The first draft of what I am still sketching here, but which is clear enough for
the aims of this chapter, can be found with the same focus on the problem of
love in the final chapters of *America*. I wrote those in Versailles in January
1929 in literally the most extraordinary situation of my entire life, under the
spell of the most uncanny woman I have ever met. In her powerful personality, she embodied the keenest divorce between nature and spirit: the most
extreme adherence to nature with the most one-sided and emphatic spiritual striving that I could have ever imagined. As close to the South Pole as
myself to the North Pole, in Argentina, Victoria Ocampo came across my *Die
neuentstehende Welt* (*World in the Making*) in 1927. She felt inflamed by the
spirit in that work with an elemental passion, and afterwards devoured everything I had published. Through a common Spanish friend, she got in touch
with me and invited me to Argentina. At that time, in Zermatt, I was preparing for my trip to North America and replied that I could not leave before
1929, but that I would gladly come then. Victoria Ocampo telegraphed me
back: "I can't wait until 1929". And this was soon followed by an intimate and
intense connection and exchange from far away to far away, from unknown to
unknown, from longing to longing, from image to image, as it only occurs in
fairy tales. At least once a week she sent me a long telegram. She wrote me several letters a day, transported by the feeling of allowing me to share her whole
life. She took long walks to meet the steamers that might bring mail from
me. She was seized by a love for an unknown spirit, like the love only cred-
ibly captured in rare depictions of ecstatic nuns by Spanish painters, among
whom I count El Greco. Victoria Ocampo had her new house in Buenos Aires
actually built for me; she wanted to serve with her whole life that which so
powerfully had attracted her. Later she explained the feeling that animated
her and that she had discovered in me, as idolatry. I knew nothing of such
states of mind, and therefore, from the very start, I misunderstood her in
some respects, taking her at her word. For a long time I had known for myself
only what might be called the experiences of wholeness; I could not live a
manifold or divided life. And it did not occur to me that someone who so
intensely experienced the medieval split between the spirit and the flesh, and
also gathered in her conscious self, like worlds apart, earth, heaven, and hell,
should have come to me, the teacher of the unison of all parts of the human
being, of the new connection of soul and spirit, the herald of the ideal of rising

above the world by affirming everything that was real. In fact, I felt troubled by the thought of meeting this woman, for whom I obviously was not only an ideal but an idol, on the soil of the distant foreign part of the world that was her home, and so I begged her to come to Europe first, so that we could get to know each other better, or rather begin to know each other. She came, invited me to Versailles, and during many weeks, while I was working on *America*, she travelled from Paris to spend many hours every day with me. When she first came to see me, I was dazzled. From the many portraits of her that I had seen, I knew that Victoria Ocampo was beautiful. But I was not prepared for such a fantastical beauty, exotic in the purest sense of the word, as if she belonged to another plane of existence, if only because of the astonishing irregularity of her features, which did not impair the unity of the overall image. Above all, the atmosphere that she radiated, that penetrated my every pore from the very first moment, was not at all that of the pure spirit to which she aspired and which she sought in me, but that of the most elemental telluric nature, of a primitive nature of strength and power. Like no other important person I have ever met, Victoria Ocampo embodied the elemental power of the *gana* world, the deepest subsoil of living creation, indeed down to what I later called the world of the Third Day of Creation. The moment she entered my room I became aware of the same depths and abysses in me as well, although, of course, I first saw them only in her. Since this was something completely unknown to me until then, the experience shook me, stirring my soul just as the *puna* would later stir my body; from day to day, night to night, I was seized by elemental forces and demons. All the images that later found expression in *South American Meditations*, and more, took possession of my consciousness from the unconscious. I found peace from what was going on in my innermost depths only when I was working or when Victoria was with me. But the best remedy against oppressive images is always the reality they are supposed to depict, because they never really depict it. I was not at all in love, nor inflamed with passion; but I was possessed from within my depths, bound by what was unknown to me in my own subconscious, which I projected onto Victoria; and I was also intoxicated by the glory of the experience on the upper-world realm, which soon became a poetic fantasy for me in which I was, at the same time, the poet and world, and in which Victoria was the inspiring centre. However, she played this role for me, not as a spiritual being but as a *femme fatale* in her Kundry[44] aspect, and this I experienced myself not as Parsifal but as someone completely given over to the experience, as an Apollonian and Dionysian enthusiast, affirming all nature and all spirit simultaneously and equally, and demanding their harmony. Admittedly, I sometimes felt as if the tension would tear me apart, but even then I did not fear for a moment

---

44 Kundry is a mysterious creature that appears in Wagner's *Parsifal*. In the legend of the Grail, Kundry is a wild woman who, when she is transported to the magical garden of the wizard Klingsor, becomes a beautiful maiden.

that I would not be able to resist her. Discord and dissonance spurred me
on to fulfil the task of creating harmony in it, as well as in me, on a higher
level, and the enormous abundance of new sights and emotions made me feel
even the most severe suffering as happiness. Especially since I saw everything
in the context of the fact that this extraordinary woman had found her way
to me as in a fairy-tale, and now, through what she evoked in me, had given
me a richer gift than I had ever been given. Moreover, as I firmly believed
what she affirmed, I wanted to live completely according to my mission. And
yet, in this mood, I overlooked what was going on in Victoria herself; I took
my reality as absolute reality. At that time, what Victoria later said of me
was true: "You, like many people of very rich nature, are deaf to others."
Overwhelmed by my personal experience, I completely forgot what she was
looking for in me and what I was supposed to give her; it did not even occur
to me that I could disappoint her.

But more of this later. What I am describing here took place in the realm of
my inner images, which at the time were still unclear to me and not yet ready
to emerge, though at first, but only indirectly and unconsciously, this affected
our personal relationship. At that time, as I said, I was working feverishly
on the completion of *America*. My American publisher wanted the manuscript that spring. The original version of the book was in English, which is
why Victoria, who does not speak German, could participate in its creation.
I stayed in the old-fashioned Hôtel des Réservoirs, where I lived all by myself,
leaving my rooms only for long solitary walks in the park whose neglect within
the strict original layout I felt to be particularly suited to my state of mind
at the time. When Victoria Ocampo visited me she said very little if I did not
read to her from what I had just written, thereby stimulating her to conversation. Like all female pristine temperaments, she was of a quiet nature, and
was often silent. In spite of being tremendously stimulating, she did not provoke but adapted herself plainly to the state of mind and soul of the moment.
Her presence radiated the singular spontaneity that characterized her, and her
special charm lay in a natural manner such as I have otherwise known only in
great ladies of Old Russia, coupled with an unequalled vitality, a great intellectual and aesthetic refinement, and a generosity and magnanimity of heart
and spirit; I have never met a woman of less pettiness. I'll give an example of
what I mean: Once, Victoria Ocampo became enraptured by Rabindranath
Tagore. Tagore, completely unworldly and unpredictable in his decisions, had
been tricked in India by an impostor who claimed to be a representative of
the Peruvian government and who invited him to a commemoration of the
anti-Spanish spirit for the Incas. On the spur of the moment, Tagore decided
to travel, practically with no money, to Buenos Aires, a city the poet imagined
to be a kind of suburb of Lima. He arrived there to find, to his surprise, that
no one was waiting for him. Dismayed, perplexed, and confused, he holed
himself up in a small inn on the harbour. Victoria discovered him there and
at once lodged him in a cottage, which she had specially set up for him in San

Isidro, surrounded by beautiful gardens. But at that time she had little cash. This often happened to her, because she was always so generous that she spent everything she had on others who sparked her affection. As rich as she was, she always got into financial difficulties, from which she was usually rescued in completely incomprehensible ways by her two servants, José and Fanny, who were devoted to her but knew nothing about finances. On that occasion, Victoria did not hesitate to sell her jewellery; with what she got, she was able to look after Tagore for several months. She was as generous, again and again, throughout her life, without thinking anything of it, and usually she soon forgot what she had done. Not only in a material way was Victoria Ocampo, for a woman, incredibly disinterested, despite her ego-centeredness (recall what is written about *ensimismamiento* in the chapter entitled "Sorrow" in the *Meditations*[45]). Without actually being benevolent, because she lacked the imagination of the heart (and what did not touch her directly she did not notice) she was utterly without malice. Often she appeared to me like an unruffled giant snake, that could crush one in a purely absent-minded embrace. Since she exercised an extraordinary charm on men of imagination and since, as a *gana*, she was a pristinely primordial woman, she delighted sometimes in cruel games, and in other love games. And for this, she seldom lacked opportunities. But consciously and deliberately, she lived entirely for intellectual and artistic interests, to which she was receptive to an almost limitless extent, like a farmer practicing crop rotation. From the depths of her being, however, she strove to escape her *gana* fate. Even then, she hoped one day to end up as a saint, and because of this she suffered from her power as a *femme fatale*. She often felt her life to be a burden that she could hardly bear. I truly have not known another soul that could despair so deeply and so fervently strive for liberation from "a state of creature sadness."

But I completely overlooked all this deep striving of hers as soon as we met in person: such a powerful effect her primal nature had on me. This was such a revelation that I completely forgot the end to which she had found her way from the Antipodes to reach me. So I did not even notice what impression my proximity made on her. The same thing has often happened to me. Rarely have I felt directly how I affect others and how they relate to me, and thus I have always been surprised to a greater or lesser degree by most personal experiences. My nature is organized in such a way that it directly intuits only super-personal connections, and personal things only in super-personal connections. That is why I feel the empirical as directly related to me only when it is shown to me unmistakably. This is what Victoria avoided doing during our entire first encounter; instead, she inserted herself in a seemingly casual way into my poetry. In truth, however, she experienced moving experiences

---

45   "In the place of egoism South America has *ensimismamiento*; it is a characteristic fact that among modern languages Spanish alone provides the equivalent; *ensimismamiento* means literally 'immersion in the Self.'" *South American Meditations*, p. 305.

similar to mine, only without positive omens. With the fervour of a praying mantis she had rushed to me – and had found a man who was not only everything other than a god, but moreover who disdained to play any other role than the one appropriate to his real spiritually conditioned life. In my attitude towards her, I affirmed and emphasized just that from which she wanted to free herself. It did not even occur to me to help her solve her own problem in the spirit expected by her, because I inwardly rejected its questioning as wrong. I wanted to lead her from the cleaving to the unity, and to the realization that the spirit must imagine everything telluric, instead of fleeing from it, and that only then can it realize itself. But though Victoria Ocampo strove towards the upper spheres, she nevertheless took her connection to the earth so seriously that she identified herself inwardly with every impulse of the *gana*. Each layer of her being was independent, and she lived out one after the other. Moreover, she perceived my earthiness as incompatible with hers; the refined Indian southerner lacked any sense of the Nordic warrior, of the berserker. She could not understand the natural manner in which I did violence to myself and was therefore also capable of doing violence to others, there where I thought it made sense. She manifested the specifically South American horror of violence that I described in "*Delicadeza*". For weeks, she hardly realized this herself – she was carried away by the spirit-born passion that she felt and nurtured for me from afar, for almost three years. And so, for a long time, despite all impressions to the contrary, I lived on for her as part of her poetry, just as she lived on for me as part of mine.

But Victoria Ocampo was a woman and as such, deeply realistic and *matter of fact*. If a man does not correspond to the ideal transferred to him, a typical woman, if she admits this to herself even once, does not try to hold onto the ideal while acknowledging the inadequacy of empiricism, but gives it up and sees in the man only a failing factuality. Consequently, she bases herself entirely on her empirical character; thus the original field of tension ceases at some point to exist, usually very suddenly. Victoria must have already been very distant from me even after a few weeks, but out of consideration for me and my work, and probably also out of concern not to lose me, she revealed nothing of it to me. I only noticed a growing sadness in her, the cause of which I did not recognize, and so I tried to help her in my own way – which, alas, could no longer be of help to her. Once sunk back into her *gana* – one remembers the image of the feathered snake[46] in the *Meditations* – she did not attempt to strive beyond herself; she rather wanted to be confirmed in her essence. After she had worshipped in a fantastically idealizing way, she now only wanted to be admired as she really was. Once, she confessed the following to me, though I did not understand it at that time: a divergence in her

---

46 "It is the Plumed Serpent. The animal which goes on its belly and eats the dust would take wing. But it can only rise for a short flight" (p. 332).

conception of Christ's redeemability. Christ's greatness would have consisted in the fact that he did not want to change man but felt mercy towards him just as he was, and comforted him and forgave him. This alone was what was meant by Christian love. In this sense, of course, I lack all charity. In this manner, a strange conflict between poetry and truth was brewing. She had come to me as a poet but then gave up on my poetry because she was empirically disappointed. I, on the other hand, held steadfastly to my poetry, which signified my highest reality, and sought to include in that reality everything that did not originally fit in it by continuing to write something different from that which I had originally planned. To her, true life consisted in factuality; to me it consisted solely in what I defined in *Das Buch vom persönlichen Leben* as "Life as Art." And the resistance that Victoria offered to "becoming-a-poem" by me, stimulated me to a particularly emphatic, even sometimes violent kind of poetry. And while I saw in the poet in me my true self, she felt more and more that my seeing through her factuality, and my emphasizing the meaning of her life, was a sort of assassination attempt on her consciousness of her own identity. But as I said, I did not feel at that time how Victoria felt. In retrospect, I must sadly acknowledge that I could have noticed from the very beginning that Victoria Ocampo was far too formidable, self-willed, and sensual a personality to play for long a role that she did not want to play of her own accord. But I just didn't notice it. I left Versailles in the high spirits of past and future fulfilment. And in the same mood, I embarked for Argentina four months later.

With Victoria, everything was different. No sooner was I gone, no sooner did new people enter her daily circle, capturing her first impressions and sensations, than the spell began to fade away. Soon it was completely gone. All *gana* melodies are finite, and between every old and every new one lies oblivion. When I arrived in Buenos Aires, I was received by a person I did not know. There was nothing left of the *donna umile* [humble woman], the *admiratrice fervente* [fervent admirer], the person to whom my spirit had meant everything. An old Argentine of much experience later told me with the humorous cynicism of his race, "You had expected to find a dead canary, but now it was a tigress you met." Outwardly Victoria remained my great friend, introduced me everywhere, did everything for me, picked me up for every lecture, and no outsider could notice the slightest hint of alienation. But she was now from head to foot the sovereign queen, the one woman of her whole continent who, thanks to her involuntary power and her very unusual courage, was able to force recognition for her personal and very unconventional law of life from the entire very conventional society to which she belonged. Although many criticized her or made fun of her, her actual influence was so great that usually even a slight hint from her was enough for everything she wanted to occur immediately. For this queen, I was now merely one man among many, one admirer among many, for whom she showed some interest only as a patron. Not without irony, she now did everything in her power to destroy the poem into which I had completely immersed myself and as part of which I had embarked on my journey to South America. Now she did not want to acknowledge that her interest in me had been different from the one she felt in other writers; now I was supposed to have been just one lover among other lovers. In this process of destruction, she proceeded with such cleverness, with such tact and with such consistency, that I could not maintain my poem for myself. Victoria Ocampo enjoyed her iconoclastic attitude as much as she had enjoyed her idolatry. She felt completely free, and blossomed into a new beauty. Indeed, against the background of the country to which she belonged, and as self-confident sovereign, she seemed much more beautiful than I had ever seen her in Versailles.

And yet, to me, Victoria's breaking out of my poem meant the third great catastrophe of the soul that had befallen me in my life; since I was now 49 years old, it shook me more deeply than a catastrophe could shake a pliable youth. Inwardly I had completely adjusted myself to the fact that Victoria belonged to me on the level of "Life as Art," as a muse of a certain kind. What she later called her idolatry towards me, I accepted as the natural and unshakeable basis of our relationship, and I absolutely affirmed it, since I expected from her the highest exaltation. From the vibration of this basic tone, there resulted for me, as a matter of course, the resonances of all corresponding undertones, middle tones, and overtones. Later, I was to ask myself at times whether I did not do wrong in not only accepting the absence of but also not demanding the original relationship between man and woman which was, from the point of view of a normal relationship, actually quite mad, even more eccentric than that of Beatrice and Dante. And this not only from the point of view of that vanity to which everyone has a right, because it protects one from the loss of faith in oneself, a faith which always affects the image of oneself, and consequently one's "reputation".

Every woman who is loved elicits the self-evident claim to be worshipped by her lover as a higher being; this also applies to every beloved man in the admittedly mostly unacknowledged depths of his telluric nature. And yet such idealizing and being idealized has never harmed a worthy man; it has always been a strong stimulus, even if most often it later led to disillusionment. As a matter of fact, this idealizing and being idealized is the correlate of the birth of one becoming conscious of one's uniqueness, and thus of the superhuman in man. In principle, what some mystics express in this way is valid also here: that in praying it is not the human being who prays, but the god within him: whoever lifts his soul to the divine, dismisses for a time his earth-bound ego. In this respect, the man who worships the object of love as a higher being, emphasizes the highest in himself; that is why the higher development of so many began with a great passion often directed at a person unworthy of it. And in the same way, being worshipped forces one to attune oneself involuntarily to one's own highest level, and allow oneself to be imbued with it. In this sense, every mother who experiences things deeply feels herself to be a goddess for her small children and, in spite of the dangerous omnipotence complex involuntarily constellated in her, she rises to the role of goddess and, at the same time, elevates the child who venerates her. Ramakrishna worshipped as Divine Mother every woman he met, even if she was a whore; insofar as he himself lived on the level of what he envisioned in the image of the Divine Mother, he saw through every woman into what actually exists in her as the highest possibility; Jesus did not behave differently towards Mary Magdalene. The most natural analogy of this is found in the mother who unwaveringly sees the highest possibility in her children, as wicked as they might appear to be, thus preparing the way for its realization. The idolatry of love, therefore, does not mean much more than creative meditation capable of fashioning the image of a god: it draws out one's own highest being. In this lies the most important and positive sense of love; this is what we mean when we say that God is love and praise love as the fastest way to Him. In this respect, Victoria's idolatry of me during what was probably the most promising phase of her life regarding a possible higher development, had been her own path to herself. Here I disappointed her, and in this, not in human incompatibility, lay the root of what was to be for me a catastrophe upon my arrival in South America. From the very first moment of our meeting, I perceived Victoria as a pure *gana* being, taking on at first the appearance of what the man she is charming sees in her, as every woman does involuntarily. And thus I extinguished that which had led her to me. Later, she wrote to me, in a bitter farewell letter, that my attitude towards her had poisoned all that she offered me so fully. This was in relation to my seeing her as the serpent of the Third Day of Creation. Today, of course, I judge the whole situation differently. I admire the tremendous strength she had shown by enduring for months on end the discrepancy between us and expressing, in spite of this, the most tender consideration for me. And it was a fully justified act of self-rescue that she later returned to the safety of her primal nature. But for me, as I have said, the transformation from the idolizing to the degrading, only allowing my spirit to be considered as "talent" and interpreting everything super-personal as a function of the banal and private, was a catastrophe. My actual life moves exclusively on the level of "life as art"; I hardly notice the empirical as such, because from the outset it belongs to me as an element of spiritual relationships. And Victoria has been the one person in my whole life who, thanks to her elementary primal power, succeeded temporarily in misleading me as to my spiritual personality. With this, there began a time of literally hellish tortures. With all the fibres of my being I struggled to defend myself against the destruction of my identity. At the same time, however, I clearly experienced in myself elementary forces that had been working within me but only vaguely until then, and fought for their identity, or rather attempted a real revolt of the masses inside me. The telluric realities which had appeared to me in Versailles only as images, now seized my whole being, and sought to devour me or to tear me apart, like the Plutonic forces with Narcissus; thus I became the battlefield for all manner of battles between body, soul, and spirit. At times, the evil in me gained such power that, in spite of my best will, I looked into the satanic realm as before into the divine. The denial of what had been, had to mean betrayal, the worst possible in my eyes. Of course, I became guilty by intimately saying yes to the feelings and sensations that besieged me and distorted my judgment, making me see at times as perfidious enemy she who inspired my work. In this way, out of the feeling of being betrayed, I transfigured Victoria Ocampo into a she-devil or an Indian who shot poisoned arrows at me at close range. And I had really fallen into a trap, insofar as I was completely cut off from my own world, on a distant, foreign continent. And I could not get away. My whole trip to South America was built on Victoria's protestations and promises, the logistical part of which she faithfully kept; but I knew that my most important work for the foreseeable future, which even then, still unborn, would bear the name "South American Meditations," could only take shape over there, and that, moreover, I had a task to fulfil for the sake of that entire South American continent. Because of this, because of what thousands expected of me, I had to persevere. No one was allowed to notice what and how I suffered: for the world, Victoria and I were and remained closest friends. For a temperament like mine, which lacks any talent for acting, this predicament alone meant hell.

Gradually, however, this began to turn into a purgatory, and to melt me into a new person, for whom what remained the same on the outside no longer signified the same. The poetry died, as part of what I originally experienced through Victoria and her entire continent. But since it regenerated and finally restored unity of my whole organism, whose determining centre was to be from then on the free spirit, the empirical formed itself within a new, purely positively determined spiritual context, precisely the one whose objectified version in the *Meditations* made many compare my South American experience with Dante's journey to Hell and to Heaven. Of course, I continued to write my poetry, overcoming what merely existed in order to achieve a deeper realization of meaning. Thereupon Victoria claimed that the concept of justice had no meaning for me. To this I replied with a reference to Richard Wagner, who, when he was looking through a song by Brahms, came across the word *Gerechtigkeit* (justice) in the text, and muttered to himself: "I would never have found sounds for this word, it does not lend itself to be composed." But now I no longer overcame myself by doing violence to the facts of experience but according to the intrinsic laws of nature and spirit, and so it became possible for me to poetically write my life so that the work of art covered everything: joy and suffering, hell and heaven, defeat and victory, in their true mutual relationships. And so my stay in South America became for me, finally and forever, despite terrible suffering, the most joyful, even the most glorious time of my life. Never did I feel so much like a survivor and victor, never was I so free spiritually, so productive. At the same time, however, I never felt such close contact with fellow human beings, indeed with the whole of creation, and a loving contact at that. My feelings for Victoria were transmitted to the whole continent and its inhabitants, who reflected it back to me with the wonderful speedy reaction of the human species. I understood and was understood, what I created was promptly acknowledged. Thus, what I had expected from a woman whom I pursued, was given to me now by an entire continent whose sensations and feelings I in turn reflected. Even today, as I write this, twelve years later, I cannot help but recall the whole South American landscape with a warmth and a deep and conscious attachment that my native land never inspired in me. When I was to return to Argentina from Chile in order to return home to Europe via Brazil, I thought the moment had come to sever the relationship with the person of this continent who had so attracted me, since on my part it could no longer be sincere, and I wrote Victoria Ocampo a farewell letter.[47] With it I symbolically performed a funeral. But I did not really put an end to it: I have never put an end to anything that has inwardly existed, because it can always resurrect under another guise. This ending had an effect on me like that of the fermata after a basic chord is struck by a powerful organ. And thanks to this fermata – how necessary suffering is as a counterpoint to happiness! – my last three days in Buenos Aires were among the most Dionysian-joyful of my whole life. Celebration followed celebration. The last night before my departure there was a party at the home of another friend to whom I owed much, Dona Elena Sansinena de Elizalde.[48] Sitting at the piano for hours, I improvised a musical expression of the spirit of the pampas, whose melodies, harmonies, and abrupt disharmonies resonated with emotion in everyone present. Thus, for once, over the tropical belt and equator, the spirits of the north and south poles rang together in redemptive harmony.

---

47   In a letter dated Cecil Hotel, Concepción, 15 September 1929, Keyserling wrote to Ocampo: "Understand that under the circumstances, I prefer not to see you when I come to Buenos Aires; but obviously, after all you have done for me, I don't have the possibility of refusing a meeting if you so demand it. In her *Autobiografía*, 6, Ocampo comments about this letter: These few lines would have sufficed to make me take the decision I would later regret. It is bad to keep poison inside the body (material and spiritual). An emetic is preferable to a slow elimination. I should have vomited my disgust and indignation on Keyserling in person, at that very moment, in a meeting as tempestuous as he deserved. I should have spoken with him to cure myself of the state of nausea in which I was living (like certain pregnant women) and in which was to live for months, until the *liberation* through writing. But "if you so demand it" held me back. No. No. I would not demand anything from someone who was saying that he didn't have to possibility of refusal". (*Ocampo, Autobiografía*, 1984, 41–43)

48   (1883–1970) a founder in 1925 and president of the cultural institution, Associación Amigos del Arte in Buenos Aires.

Victoria Ocampo – Looking Through

Shortly before the publication of the *South American Meditations*
I communicated the following to the members of the Society for Free
Philosophy in the twentieth issue of *Weg zur Vollendung* as an introduction to
this work for which I had not written a preface:

Years before I wrote the *Travel Diary*, I said to friends that I expected the
decisive stimulus of my life to be a trip around the world. In a similar sense,
I often said to those close to me, as early as 1920: if any world could still mean
something essential to me, it would be South America. Since then, I had forgotten that prediction. And my journey to that continent came about entirely
on the initiative of its inhabitants. But the prediction proved correct. It was
correct even in a more significant sense than the one concerning the trip
around the world. The latter enabled me to form my special dialectic and to
give it expression in an appropriate framework. The variety of life forms in
the context of like-minded creatures caused my "looking through" [seeing
through to the essence or universal] to lead not only to an examination of
the respective objects but to the determination of a uniform core meaning.
And thus, by means of the world, I ultimately determined myself. Hence the
motto of the book: "The shortest way to oneself leads around the world".
What I have since practiced in Darmstadt was the practical repercussion of
the same attitude, only now not inwardly, but rather radiating outwardly. The
summation of this period lies above all in *Schöpferische Erkenntnis [Creative
Understanding]* and *Wiedergeburt [Rebirth]*. But it also informs *Das Spektrum
Europas [Europe]* and *America*. Like the others, basically, the latter books are
about "giving meaning" and "reconnecting soul and spirit", as applied not to
individuals, but to peoples and continents. In this respect, they introduce the
spirit of the School of Wisdom, which addresses the individual, to that wider
framework of experience within which the writer of the *Travel Diary* moved.
Many will now expect that *South American Meditations* belong to the same
series as *Spectrum* and *America*: it does not. It is at least as new in relation to
these as the *Travel Diary* was compared to my earlier books. As far as I can
judge, only one comparison with earlier work is not mistaken: that is with my
first work, *Das Gefüge der Welt: Versuch einer kritischen Philosophie*. It was
world poetry. This term alone best describes the essence of the *Meditations*.

However, *Meditations* is not the poetry of an independent spirit, but the
poetry of a spirit that has absorbed not only the earth but also hell into itself,
and in this respect may say: *nihil humani a me alienum puto.*[49] I have always
striven for such integration. The young man that I was lacked in himself any
conscious connection with the earth. Until a few years ago, my condition

---

49   The full line from Terence, *Heauton Timorumenos*, reads: "*Homo sum: humani nil a me
alienum puto*": I am a human: I regard nothing human as foreign to me.

was, in many respects, comparable to that of the child who lives in his own world and feels every relationship with others as a conflict. For a while, I tried to establish the connection and the marriage of spirit with the earth through psychoanalytic means: I did not succeed. Then my destiny led me to South America. And behold! I had hardly arrived there, when the telluric began to rise into my consciousness. The years of illness since then were completely filled with the completion of this inner upheaval and recasting triggered by South America. In its initial stages, I could write nothing, so little did I know where I wanted to go. As I approached the completion of my inner transformation, the creative instinct awoke again, and with it my capacity for expression. And from then onwards the inner transformation was completed through writing. I have never struggled with any material nearly as much as I have with the *Meditations*. I have completely rewritten all the chapters three to four times, some up to ten times. For since each was a product of the whole man, the powers of the spirit alone were of no help here: all the components of my being had to work together. Now I have the feeling that what could happen has happened. With this I certainly do not claim that the work is perfect. In the case of experiential works, nothing can be attained beyond a completely truthful expression of the condition to which it owes its origins and, depending on its particular nature, authenticity demands greater or lesser perfection. But what I had to say at the time, what I could say, I have said in a way appropriate to my condition. Accordingly, the two final chapters, which concern the problem of spirit, are not the last word for me, whereas what I said in *"Gana"*, *"Delicadeza"*, and "The Emotional Order" might indeed be last words. I have become young once again with this work created in collaboration with so many spiritual forces that were earlier not only unconsumed but unknown to me. I see many things with fresher eyes now than I did when I was twenty. And so I feel further away than ever from my final word.

How could the encounter with the South American world cause such extraordinary things to happen within me? Perhaps because South America represents exactly, almost mathematically, the antipode of the world. There, the accent does not rest on the spiritual, but on the telluric. However, if I myself were not telluric at all, I would not have been able to find my way in the new world. But of course I am telluric, and that to a very high degree; only that in former times I lacked any conscious connection with this part of me. The connection was created by contact with the Continent of the Third Day of Creation. Like a psychoanalyst, it drew out of me what had been buried or repressed or unformed. No psychiatrist would have been able to do the same.

This personal experience led to fundamental results not only because I had a typical experience: it revealed to me the telluric and the terrestrial in man. And I was able to see many things more sharply than usual because I had come from very far away. The worlds of *"Gana"*, *"Delicadeza"*, and "The Emotional Order" had been completely foreign to my consciousness before.

Completely unknown to me was also the state of the "Sadness in Creation".[50] But when in the end I returned home to my innate spirituality, I could suddenly judge it from outside: precisely from the earth. The meditations entitled "The In-break of Spirit" and *"Divina Commedia"* could not be written by a pure spirit but only by a telluric man who had become spiritually conscious.

At that time, in 1932, I only outlined the connections of my 1929 state of mind with the work in which it finally redeemed itself. In the foregoing, I have lifted the veil from the personal experiences that fashioned or triggered those conditions, as far as this can be meaningful for others. From the point of view of the spirit there is no private life, and there must be none; where personal fate can be ground-breaking, it belongs to the world. But the most significant thing remains to be said: very often the happiness and salvation of a person lies in a different direction from that which he has imagined and wished for. This has been my case to an extraordinary degree. It almost looks as if my deliberate will was hostile to my nature, which is why failing to achieve a goal usually became my salvation. If ever I had a firm plan that I announced forcefully, it was never to marry – and it was in marriage that I found fulfilment like few others. If ever I was certain of one thing, it was that my family would die out with me – and I have promising sons. On the other hand, I have not only never become as rich as I consciously aspired to be, I have only ever achieved a minimum of material security and for short periods. Without ever having striven for power, none of my plans, which presupposed *de facto* a position of power and which stood in the foreground of my consciousness for years, has amounted to anything. And though I would like to do everything myself, so that I inwardly rely on no one and prefer to undertake the meanest tasks myself, even gladly taking part in decisions about matters of which I know nothing, everything decisive has "happened" to me mostly through unforeseeable encounters. The emphasis in my upper consciousness lies on my dynamics, and my urge for activity has always stood in the way of my deepest striving; the more I kept still, the further I got. In exactly this way, I expected from my experience of Victoria, under the sign of the uttermost happiness, the tremendous advancement that would come from my South American experience. Instead, I received an even greater encouragement, far more than I expected, under the sign of agony. Looking back, I can summarize the deepest connections, as far as they concern me, as follows. I was stuck in the attitude of the School of Wisdom; for me, there was no possible further development from it in 1929, any more than there was from that of the critical philosopher in 1911. In the latter case, a very small change, hardly noticeable to myself, led to a decisive re-centring of my whole being, enough to make me productive in unexpected ways. In 1929, a melting down

---

50   "The first stage on the road leading from the Sadness in Creation to the bliss of union
     with creative Spirit is the transformation of the fear of suffering to the courage to suffer"
     (p. 331).

of my entire psychic organism was necessary to achieve a rejuvenation. And such a rejuvenation was possible at my age only under a state of agony. I had to be "broken down", just as a rock is broken down by hydrofluoric acid, in order to achieve the goals for which I was still allowed to strive for in this life. And precisely in order to achieve the harmony of my whole being on a higher level, that restoration of unity which was lost with the Fall, and of which I wrote at the end of the beginning of this chapter, I first had to go through an extreme disintegration of all my component parts, and thus an extreme inner tension. All counterforces of the spirit had to awaken, all temptations had to approach me, my all-too-human nature had to become conscious down to the last sub-soil. I had to experience in myself all the incompatibilities that have led to the great divorces and decisions of history. And this not as witness but as someone who is experiencing them. All this experience was made possible for me through my experience with one woman. But hasn't it been so with every human being? Of course, this applies only to those who have had the courage to be themselves and follow their particular law of life. Whoever does not unwaveringly keep to his personal line and give a purely personal meaning to everything that happens to him, that can happen to anyone in fact, will not experience anything significant, even if he is to witness the creation of the world or the end of civilization. With deepest pity I remember the many who declare at every occasion, with a supercilious smile: "This is nothing special, the same has happened to hundreds of thousands." In fact, everyone is for oneself the core and pole of the world. Only in so far as one sees oneself in this way, one does justice to reality. And if one sees something different from others, if one experiences something deep in superficial people and a higher truth in errors, this does not mean self-deception and exaltation, nor distortion of facts, but self-realization. As a young man, I laughed, just as young men are prone to laugh, at the admittedly naive-sounding passage from Brünnhilde's death song in Wagner's *Götterdämmerung*, meaning that the terrible end of all her loves, of all heroes, and finally of the gods themselves was necessary in order *"that a woman can become wise"*. But Brünnhilde was right. Everyone has the right to feel one's fate as she felt it. Every cosmic event manifests itself through the most insignificant private experience as well. And through the most trivial one can experience the greatest.

Everything depends on persons who see and experience more deeply than what lies in the facts because all those who lack such abilities feed on these elect. They experience vicariously for everyone else. I must ask my readers to remember here the theoretical introduction to this chapter (on "V.O."): is my unique experience not suitable to make clear to everyone the whole problem of the relationship of nature and spirit as a concrete demand? Abstract introduction and concrete description belong together, like a construction plan and a finished edifice. In order to complete the allegory, I have only this to do: to explore the concept of substitution. From this it will become clear to what extent all deep experience is substitutional.

One of the primal phenomena of all life is the correlation (the interrelation, mutual conditionality, and cooperation in the division of labour) of all parts within unified wholes; not only intestine and brain are related to each other, so are the sexes, and all creatures living in symbiosis: bees and clover, caterpillars and digger-wasps, carnivores and herbivores, and, among humans, the professional types. This mutual solidarity can also be understood as representative substitution. And on the level of higher spiritual-mental experience only the latter term does justice to the same primordial phenomenon. In order to understand this, let us first consider the symbolism of every psychic formation. Never, except in the case of a preceding arbitrary restriction of the possibilities of meaning (as occurs in science regarding concepts) does a certain expression mean a certain thing alone. Every expression has – I employ here common terms from the practice of dream interpretation, since they can be transferred to other contexts without difficulty – besides its manifest content, innumerable latent meanings that exist not only as *sous-entendu* [innuendo] but are originally there, and are active, whether acknowledged or not. In primordial languages, this manifests itself naively in the fact that the same word often has different and incompatible meanings; at the height of all language development is the fact that every word expressing inwardness, used in a certain way, acquires a timbre that is based on the resonance of every struck note of certain lower, middle, and upper tones. This timbre distinguishes the violin from the trombone, and a master violin from a lesser one. If we now proceed from language to the "in itself", to that which is revealed through the inner, we find that a certain intended meaning serves deeper meanings that can be perceived by seeing through it, and that every certain meaning can therefore signify more and differently, in its very capacity to correspond to that which it represents as appearance. This is the basis of all symbolic and mythical expression. A totem animal is the clan, the fish or the lamb is Christ, the host is Jesus's flesh. For the spirit-determined man in the most real of worlds, namely the world of meaning, this applies in a very concrete way. In this realm, there is basically no difference between the civilized and the primitive man. Not only in the Middle Ages, but still today, the believer finds passages in the Bible, in the Sutras, in the Koran, that exactly express and firmly prove what he means. The psychology of quotation is for the most part the same: thanks to the fact that all senses stand in some relation of correspondence and mirror each other, a sentence that originally belongs to a completely different context, becomes the means of expression or the confirmation of that which is discovered by oneself. Since the associations necessary for such a connection come about in the same way in innumerable people and nations, it seems to me indisputable that even this constitutes a modification of the correlative law that rules all life. From concrete case to concrete case, it is a matter of representation, seen from the point of view of everyone who experiences it. Whoever has realized this will soon also realize how immense the role of substitution is in the spiritual life, within the whole wide scope of this concept. This role is so great that all life and experience, in all its depth and responsibility, cannot be understood except if judged vicariously.

In order to gain insight quickly, let us start with the most difficult to understand of all sanctioned representations, with the myth of the atoning death of Christ and through it, the redemption of all men. This myth can be experienced as an immediately obvious truth only by those whose state of mind is somewhat similar to that of the original Christians; and since this is true in Europe only of few individuals – only in Russia and perhaps also in the Balkans this is still different – the myth is only still believed blindly, judged from the point of view of consciousness; what feeds the faith from within is that which lives on in the unconscious, in a depth not accessible to consciousness, surviving from long past ages. But if we now decide to take the detour, which every rational European of the twentieth century must take in order to find one's way back to the origins, then we can also see the truth of the primeval myth. What is the meaning of the "right word"? That it makes it possible for others to experience in the transmission what first was thought by someone, what was seen by him for the first time, and also subsequently understood completely only by the few in whom the tradition of the one lives on or was reborn. Once a thought is expressed appropriately, then it is objectively here, if not an actual then nevertheless a possible possession for anyone. Judged from the general concept of the organic correlation, this is connected with the fact that creator and he who understands correspond to each other. More objectively, however, for human concepts we express the essence of this by saying that one person has thought for all, or else: what many vaguely suspect, has been made clear by a single deed and imagined forever by objectifying history. Under these circumstances, the same applies to every word formulated according to the law of the correlation of sense and expression, formally judged, and can also be applied to Jesus's vicarious death. The same applies to every deed that can be perceived from a distance, and also to the will, feeling, and passion of close effect, thanks to the suggestive power they radiate.

Now the predominant part of all life runs in the unconscious, and everything that has been conscious sinks at some point into the unconscious, where it does not cease to live but continues to work underground as a guiding cause and co-determining motive of later events. This explains why an experience once had, a decision once taken, a struggle once fought and a suffering once deeply endured, leave the person affected or concerned differently than he used to be, and in the highest cases, transform him through a kind of mutation. Here, too, strictly speaking, it is a case of representative substitution. By the fact that someone in a certain never-recurring state experienced never-recurring things, that someone will have experienced these things for all present and future states. For man is not only physically but also psychically a multicellular being, more similar to the termite mound than to the uniformly-imagined monad. Not only in succession, but also all at once, many souls live in the same breast, (as realized in the end, only apparently), and for these many, the singular experience is transformative for all. Most people will have noticed that certain thoughts and feelings become as if "due" at a certain time, expressed, at first, in the general readiness for their reception and repro- duction, and later in the fact that the ones who seem capable of just such an expression are actually born and, though leading hidden lives, are discovered, like the infant Jesus was discovered by the kings from the East. For a long time I tried to reassure myself with more or less rationalistic interpretations of these coincidences: today I am sure that the whole great context must be understood with an analogy to what happens in the individual when he is deeply moved by a new experience. From the unconscious or through the unconscious, all people are obviously connected. Only in this way can the uniformity of the spirit of each new generation in relation to the earlier ones be understood at all, beyond all national boundaries and enmities. Now, if someone, on the line of the "due" experiences, feels them much more deeply than others, thinks more sharply, imagines more intensely, or wants something more powerfully, he acts as a dominant of the human community in the same sense that a new directive idea or a shattering experience acts in the individual soul; what he does or suffers, immediately touches all people in the turbulent depths of their unconscious, and it is only a question of time and empir- ical circumstances how early or how late this manifests itself in an historical appearance. Things are not, as the environmental theorists suppose: that the readiness of many provokes the singular phenomenon (an interpretation, by the way, that is not more plausible than the opposite one). Both arise in cor- relation to each other, and therefore simultaneously, but the initiating and determining lies with him who creates and not with him who receives. From this insight the common idea of providence can easily be corrected, but this task does not belong here. The saint in his quiet existence offers the primeval symbol of how strongly the stress falls on the creative person, especially since this type of genius is the only one that has been perceived more or less cor- rectly by all peoples at all times. The saint's experience and work, even if invis- ible and unrevealed, really affects the space of the human soul. And thanks to him, all those who connect with him through veneration and receptivity, even those who are only unconsciously touched by him, participate in a higher life that without him they could not even desire, let alone suspect.

Is not the truth of Christ's vicarious sacrifice already proven to be true, without the need for further words? If Jesus really experienced and worked, even only to some extent, what the Gospels report, then really all have object- ively taken part in it in the same sense as all participate in a truth once objectified. But just as the objective truth becomes fruitful for the one who understands it, so he alone reaps the fruits of Jesus's life and death who realizes its meaning. But now comes the main thing: the only one who reaps the harvest of his own doing and suffering is the one who absorbed its reality with his whole being, grasped its meaning completely and admitted it to him- self. Everything depends on this personal attitude, within the individual soul as within all of humanity. To assimilate one's own highest sphere, one must personally put the whole emphasis on it and allow oneself to be completely seized by it. In exactly the same way that one gains contact with another, one does so in the case of one's God only if one opens oneself to Him believingly. Because the dimension of the spiritual cosmos is not that of extension but of intensity. Thanks to this fervour, one can conjure up in the highest what one is able to imagine directly in the appearance.

At the very beginning of the existence of the School of Wisdom I published in *Politik, Wirtschaft, Weisheit* (1922) an essay, "On the Meaning of the Individual", in which I undertook to prove that on today's level of consciousness everyone can have the same meaning for all, as in the past only the elect could. And later, in my study "On the Symbolic Life" (reprinted in *Das Buch vom persönlichen Leben*), I showed how today everyone not only could but should live his life as pure symbol, as all those who are spiritually great have always done. This brings my line of thought to a certain conclusion. In the context of the whole chapter, however, I make it possible to understand to what extent everyone has the right to regard his or her private life as belonging to everyone else. The poet, the one to whom God gave the authority to say how he suffers, has always been granted this right. And no one would find exultation in the representation of the meaningful fate of another, either in drama or in the novel, unless he experienced his own through the same fate. Under these circumstances, is it not outrageous that most people take into account almost nothing of their own life, because they consider it less seriously than that of the characters in a novel and, under the label of *déjà vu*, deprive themselves of their experience of uniqueness and thus forfeit the possibility of self-realization and fulfilment of meaning? I too could have concealed the immense experience of my later manhood, my Victoria experience, by trivializing it and paying attention to how others looked at it from the outside. I know it well: no one saw Victoria Ocampo as great the way I did. Few of those who knew her well, including perhaps herself, will possibly read my account without shaking their heads. But who is it that has had something from her, they or I? Who has done justice to her in a deeper or higher sense, I, the exaggerator, or the meaningless recorder of facts? A woman has really opened up to me a world unknown to me until then, within me as well as outside of me, and has thus given me the impulse for a decisive transformation. It is idle to claim that I might have fulfilled my destiny in another way: it was fulfilled in this and in no other way. In his short life on earth, only few certain opportunities are offered to anyone; and one has to make use of them. Few things have to mean and to reveal everything to one vicariously. If one misses these few opportunities, which always consist in the confluence of certain external coincidences with a corresponding inner readiness, if one does not "watch and pray", one's life remains impoverished, even if all powers of heaven would join forces to fill it. Whoever reads this book of memories may easily get the impression that I have had an outwardly rich life.

In fact, I have experienced much less externally than many of my untalented acquaintances. I have known closely only a few people, I have attended very few artistic performances. The great contemporary events have touched me less, externally and directly, than they do most other men, and by and large mere "facts" are always so very capable of distracting my intuition that even during my journey around the world I have visited as few things as possible. I have not read Xavier de Maistre's *Voyage autour de ma chambre* [Voyage around my room] (1794) and therefore I don't know whether he accomplished what is suggested by the title. But surely it is possible to experience, even in a single room – where every atom is a reproduction of the solar system – the universe itself, and in the encounter and collision with one woman the whole history of Creation.

Completed at Schönhausen, 19 January 1941

Part Eight

Ocampo Rebuts Keyserling (1951)

Ocampo's El Viajero y Una de sus Sombras [A Traveller and One of His Shadows, 1951] is translated here in its entirety. In it, Ocampo firmly refutes Keyserling's portrayal of Argentina in South American Meditations as the Continent of the Third Day of Creation, in other words, as being an undeveloped backwater. She also rebuts his portrayal of her in his memoirs. In this section, unless specified otherwise, all notes are Ocampo's.[1]

> She turns to me, says that she is Penthesilea ... and that she will send me her answer in the form of arrows.
> — Heinrich von Kleist, *Penthesilea*[2]

> To attack the living can be a vile deed, and it is almost always done with the intent to cause harm. The dead cannot be harmed at all; in regards to them, the only thing possible is truth, because only the truth about the dead can be of help to the living.
> — Hermann Keyserling, *Travel through Time*

Addison, Dryden, Pope, he had said, pointing to the Cocoa Tree, and Addison, Dryden, Pope had chimed in her head like an incantation ever since. Who can credit such folly? but so it was. All her experience with Nick Greene had taught her nothing. Such names still exercised over her the most powerful fascination. Something, perhaps, we must believe in, and as Orlando, we have said, had no belief in the usual divinities she bestowed

---

1 Translated from the Spanish by Alberto Manguel.
2 "Odysseus:

> She then, her mantling cheek, with rage or shame,
> Ruddying her harness even to the waist,
> Confus'dly, proudly, almost wildly, turns
> To me and cries: 'I am Penthesilea,
> Queen of the Amazons, too soon ye shall
> Have wingèd answer from our Scythian bows'".
> [Heinrich von Kleist, "Penthesilea"]

DOI: 10.4324/9781003266099-8

her credulity upon great men – yet with a distinction. Admirals, soldiers, statesmen, moved her not at all. But the very thought of a great writer stirred her to such a pitch of belief that she almost believed him to be invisible.

– Virginia Woolf, *Orlando*

Motive

Count Keyserling had told me, several years before his death, that he was writing his memoirs. In 1937 he sent me a chapter of those memoirs, published in *Visva-Bharati* (a magazine founded by Tagore in Bengal) under the title, "Significant Memories", and later changed; and the following note by the author accompanied or rather preceded the chapter:

> This essay is my contribution, in 1937, to a book of memoirs that will be published in benefit of the Keyserling family ... Most of them [he is referring to the members of that illustrious family] still show some of the characteristic features that are transmitted from father to son almost without exception from 1650 until today. One of the Keyserlings was the protector of the composer Johann Sebastian Bach; originally the famous "Goldberg Variations" were composed as a sleeping drug for Carl Hermann Keyserling who, like myself, suffered from insomnia. While he was tutor for the Keyserling family much interested in philosophy, Kant wrote his *Theory of the Heavens*.[3] Dietrich Keyserling was the most influential and intelligent of Frederick the Great's friends. Of my grandfather, Alexander Bismarck used to say that he was the only man whose judgment he feared.

The chapter carried in its margins numerous corrections. I mention it because Keyserling had written in his own hand over the title: "For V.O. See especially pages 17–18", because those pages dealt with my person (my name there rubbing shoulders with Cosima Wagner and Annie Besant, we three women who, for various reasons, seemed more than others to have attracted his attention). The corrections were quite instructive. It is not that I pretend to deserve the praise that the philosopher dispensed on me (perhaps I deserve others, being pig-headed, for example: I lack all false modesty). But the changes to the adjectives merited consideration. Under the stroke that crossed them out or replaced them by other words with less intensity, you could clearly read words such as "superlative" and "wonderful". Of course, everything on those pages was exaggeratedly flattering for me except the crossing out of the hyperbolic adjectives. The changes seemed to me very just, but it seemed odd

---

3 Editor's note: *Universal Natural History and Theory of the Heavens*, subtitled *Or an Attempt to Account for the Constitutional and Mechanical Origin of the Universe upon Newtonian Principles*, is a work written and published anonymously by Immanuel Kant in 1755.

to me that I was made an ocular witness of the process. There might not have been in this even a shadow of an *arrière pensée* [ulterior motive], but a psycho-analyst would have remarked on the fact. And without being a psychoanalyst myself, I could conclude that Keyserling's mental attitude towards V.O. had suffered changes.

In February of 1937, the Darmstadt philosopher wrote to me again to let me know that his work was progressing. His book, he explained, would be something like a journey through time, memoirs of a special genre: "In fact, I will speak of myself under every possible aspect but pointing in each chapter towards another soul who was meaningful for me. The work will be divided in an indefinite number of volumes, and I will probably work on it until my death." The chapters on Tolstoy, Houston Chamberlain, Rudolf Kassner, Bernard Shaw, Miguel de Unamuno, Tagore, were already finished. He offered me one of them for *Sur*: "On many points we think differently; but I don't suppose that will matter to you." Of course, it did not matter to me. The chapter on Kassner was published in my magazine.

In March 1950, several years after Keyserling's death, I received a very intelligent and friendly letter from his wife (born Bismarck and grand-daughter of the Iron Chancellor), letting me know that an entire chapter of the memoirs (for which the title of *Travel through Time* had been defini-tively adopted) carried my name. Countess Keyserling hoped that I would not feel disappointed or hurt by the contents of the chapter: "It is so difficult to foresee the reaction of someone who reads something about himself."

Knowing Keyserling, his boundless imagination, and his impetuous way of collecting "facts" (he called them his personal enemies) which he boasted of despising as "mere", I began to feel uneasy. What new adjectives would he have crossed out, and with what other ones had he replaced them? My curi-osity was sparked, and I let Countess Keyserling know. At last the chapter, written in German, arrived. It was immediately translated into Spanish and passed from the translator's hands into mine. That is why I find myself in this moment writing on a subject (Count Keyserling and one of his polarizations in *Travel through Time*) that I would not have considered in the way in which I will do so, if the chapter in question did not oblige me.

Sailing Upstream

I must sail back upstream through the years until 1927 to recount the Keyserling chapter in my memoirs. At that time I read him with enthusiasm. That winter, I gave a lecture at Amigos del Arte, presenting briefly as far as it was possible for me (I lack any philosophical training) what I knew of Keyserling's work that had impressed me (*The Travel Diary of a Philosopher, World in the Making,* and *Symbolic Figures*). At that time, the author was practically unknown in Argentina. *Revista de Occidente* [the Spanish lan-guage magazine] had introduced me to his work. The lecture appeared in its entirety in *La Nación* and was voluntarily excluded from the first volume of *Testimonios* (published by Revista de Occidente). From that date onwards, I have not written any commentary on Keyserling, neither good nor bad, unless in passing, save in a note for *God Is My Adventure* by Rom Landau.[4] Regarding the chapter in that book dedicated to the founder of the School of Wisdom, I wrote: "Great drinker, great eater, great conversationalist with boundless vitality, exuberant, egotistic, childish, proud, a man of genius, and arbitrary in his interpretations, the Keyserling depicted by Rom Landau is exactly the same one who has strolled through the streets of Buenos Aires." The book to which I refer had beautiful and interesting photographs of the quasi-prophets, quasi-philosophers, quasi-religious reformers under scrutiny. About Keyserling's, I wrote:

> Keyserling, as photogenic as a Hollywood star, with that extraordinarily aristocratic and slender nose, and that extraordinarily brutal and hungry mouth (like that of certain masks or that of a dog-faced baboon), those high cheek bones, those small eyes alive and slightly slanted, that powerful forehead, that little pointed beard: a mixture of East and West.

My comparison of his mouth to that of a baboon had provoked his indignation. I was surprised by so much indignation because we all resemble an animal (for example, Gide's eyes are very close together, like some monkeys), and he himself had often referred to me as an anaconda. My resemblance to that serpent that often reaches a length of ten meters or more must be purely moral. It is a well-known fact that the boa is not poisonous and never attacks man. But it can cause him much trouble through carelessness. However the similitude between Keyserling's mouth and a baboon's was purely material, like Gide's eyes and therefore of no importance, since *facts* according to his doctrine only exist as far as the *meaning* that is lent to them. I judged and judge still this author as a man full of enlightened insights. The fact that nature had lent him also a mouth reminiscent of this or that animal means nothing from the point of view of his creation as a thinker or a writer. The resemblance that I noticed in him, limited to the material realm, is consequently far less serious than that which he remarked between me and the reptile: a purely moral similitude. I learned this method of reasoning straight from Keyserling and, whatever its worth, I apply it to this case.

But for the moment let us leave the animal kingdom that is, however, my kingdom as a telluric woman, and simply as a woman ... if we follow to their

---

4   Editor's note: Rom Landau, *God Is My Adventure*.

ultimate ends certain "trains of thought" of the Darmstadt philosopher and a fair number of his colleagues spread across the planet.[5]

Some Facts

I want to start explaining that for me *facts* exist, up to a reasonable point, even though for Keyserling they do not, or so little that it's not worth taking them into account. "Facts in themselves don't interest me; all that interests me is the meaning of facts." Facts are only interesting when one discovers their meaning, we agree on this. But, rightly or wrongly, I believe that if we deform facts excessively we end by deforming or changing the meaning.

Here are a few facts: towards 1927, I read with passion *The Travel Diary of a Philosopher* and *World in the Making*. I was and I still am, though to a lesser degree, an impetuous and voracious reader.[6]

---

5   To support what I'm saying, it is enough to quote passages from *South American Meditations,* from after the time of my Keyserlingian enthusiasm, of course:

> "In the beginning it was not Man, but Woman; the latter perpetuates as a differentiated form the primordial qualities of animal life" (p. 49). It's evident that this is a projection (in psychoanalysis, this term, as we know, means the act of attributing to another person a desire, a character trait, or an ideal of the subject himself): man associates woman with the primordial state as far as she evokes it in him.
>
> Primordial Woman is completely unchecked by spiritual or ethical motives. She is entirely rooted in the world of the Third Day of Creation ... This is why woman is originally devoid of moral instinct. This is why the real element of her life is disguise and deceit ... This is why man becomes enmeshed and enslaved by primeval woman, by [Prosper Mérimée's] "Carmen", by [Rider Haggard's] "She", and by her alone (p. 41).
>
> For woman, thraldom means "home", the surrounding natural to her. She desires to be bound, desires to suffer ... Her cruelty never means more than lover's play; with her, murder and suicide never mean more than passing moods ... For man, the laws of whose being belong altogether to the upper world, thraldom always means a fall ... Thus, too, all woman-prophetesses were in their essence women of the Earth (pp. 173–174).
>
> Not the Virgin Mary, but Mary Magdalene is the central figure of Christianity (p. 175).
>
> All true women are creatures of sensibility ... All lack an original sense of spiritual connections, whether intellectual or moral (p. 209).

Editor's note: All quotations from Keyserling, *South American Meditations.*

6   I'll give an example: In 1947 I was returning by ship from London to New York. Two days before arriving, I took from the library of the *Queen Elizabeth War and Peace*, which I still hadn't read. I entered at once into an atmosphere from which I couldn't – nor wished – to escape. As I was travelling alone, I wasn't obliged to speak to anyone and that, I believe, increased my state of enchantment. I had to return the novel long before finishing it because they were closing the ship's library on the day before our arrival. I could not free my thoughts from the book, and I wandered through the *Queen Elizabeth* as I had wandered through the house in San Isidro after my mother punished me (o cruelty, of whose rigor she wasn't aware) taking away from me half-read *The Hound of the Baskervilles*. We docked very early and after the customs formalities I went straight to Brentano's and left the bookstore armed with *War and Peace*. I reached the hotel, closed the door of my room, and without unpacking threw myself on the bed and finished the book. Take into account that this happened to me at a

I went from surprise to enthusiasm. Surprise, because I had never heard [anyone] speak of this author; enthusiasm, because he often expressed what seemed to live in me in an embryonic state. To explain what I felt, I'll quote what Keyserling himself wrote regarding Houston Chamberlain (in *Travel through Time*), the discovery of whom produced in him an analogous exultation.

Keyserling confesses to us, to begin with, that he had always loved certain writers in the same way that people fall in love. That is to say, he had overvalued to the point of adoration this or that writer. I don't know if this is as precise in him as he seems to think. It is for me. I have felt literary passions that equalled in fervour an amorous passion, without being of the same kind. These feelings of adoration were indistinctly for artists, thinkers alive or dead, men or women, and I must add, of very unequal worth.

Keyserling's appearance or the appearance of his thinking, was a revelation that meant for me a symbol of "one's own, not yet born". "I felt I was myself and at the same time I felt in the strongest way the mystery of acting out a role," as Keyserling said about Houston Chamberlain.[7]

As I was reading and abundantly underlining the *Travel Diary* my enthusiasm was growing. I learned by chance that Keyserling and I had common friends in Spain. I immediately thought of inviting him to lecture in Buenos Aires; in all of South America, if necessary and if he could not otherwise be brought over. Here as well, what the author of *World in the Making* wrote about Houston Chamberlain is applicable to my case: "I wasn't thinking

---

time when such passions often cooled down. And Tolstoy was not a discovery for me. In 1927, Keyserling was.

7   A letter by George Eliot, [an] extraordinary woman not much read in Argentina, defines the feeling very much in accordance with what I felt:

> I wish you thoroughly to understand that the writers who have most profoundly influenced me – who have rolled away the waters from their bed, raised new mountains and spread delicious valleys for me – are not in the least oracles to me. It is just possible that I may not embrace one of their opinions; that I may wish my life to be shaped quite differently from theirs. For instance, it would signify nothing to me if a very wise person were to stun me with proofs that Rousseau's view of life, religion, and government were miserably erroneous – that he was guilty of some of the worst *bassesses* [basenesses] that have degraded civilized men. I might admit all this; and it would be not the less true that Rousseau's genius has sent that electric thrill through my intellectual and moral frame which has awakened me to new perceptions; which has made man and nature a fresh world of thought and feeling to me; and this not by teaching me any new belief. It is simply that the rushing mighty wind of his inspiration has so quickened my faculties that I have been able to shape more definitely for myself ideas which had previously dwelt as dim *Abnungen* in my soul; the fire of his genius has so fused together old thoughts and prejudices that I have been ready to make new combinations ... It is thus with George Sand. I should never dream of going to her writings as a moral code or text-book.

Editor's note: George Eliot, *George Eliot's Life as Related in Her Letters and Journals*, Vol. 1, ed. J. W. Cross (New York: Harper and Brothers, 1888, pp. 143–144).

about anything precisely, the only thing was this: you have to meet that man because his influence in the story of your life will be transcendental".[8]

In 1924 Tagore had been my guest in a country house of San Isidro. He was convalescing. His stay remains a luminous point in my memory. He was then sixty-four years old and he was all beauty and intelligence, a poet's intelligence that functioned through antennae of an acute sensibility (if this adjective can apply to someone who radiated the deep sweetness of his soul). I fulfilled for him the functions of secretary-hostess. I made sure that he always had fresh flowers in his room, healthy food on his table, his clothes in order; I welcomed his many visitors, I made them come into his room in turn, I translated their words and his (when they didn't speak English), I hinted that they leave when they exceeded the limits of his resilience and exhausted their beloved idol; I kept Tagore company when he felt like it and kept away, much against my wishes, when I surmised his wish to be alone.

Beyond these domestic functions that I joyfully performed up to the point of believing to have found my true vocation, my relationship with Tagore was somewhat akin to that of certain plants to the sun. Linked to that star by their way of life, it matters little that 150 million kilometres separate them from it. Some, like sunflowers, have the *physique du rôle* [physique suited to the character] of friends of the sun; others like the heliotrope, don't. I belong to the heliotrope type. In the presence of Tagore I would remain most of the time inarticulate, tongue-tied, not at all like a golden sunflower, but very like a daisy and the humbly opaque heliotrope. This heliotropic quality was painful at times, but it did not cloud my enjoyment, and the complete success of this first attempt to be secretary-hostess for great writers (in this case, the result was a tender friendship full of admiration with Tagore that lasted until his death) made me wish to continue that experience.

Thanks, then, to this antecedent that was for me "an elevating excitement of the soul", it seemed to me that my new attempt had a good chance to be successful.

Keyserling, invited to lecture, answered that he was engaged until 1929. I then telegraphed the friend who had served as intermediary: "Impossible to foresee if enthusiasm will last till then". I imagined that she only transmitted to Count Keyserling a text changed *ad usum Delphini*.[9] He could have judged my words to be an impertinence or a naïve confession of frivolity because he had not yet introduced into his vocabulary the term, "*gana*".[10]

---

8   Editor's note: Keyserling writes, "It suddenly became clear to me that if I could meet the man who had written this book, I should soon find out what my purpose in life was; for towards him alone, amongst all whose works I had read, I felt a sense of relationship." Keyserling, "Autobiographical Sketch", *The World in the Making*, 25.

9   Editor's note: *Ad usum Delphini*: for the use of the king.

10 This Keyserlingian theory of "*gana*" had its origin in the following anecdote which I related to Keyserling: my sister Silvina one day had not found a caddie in the golf course of Villa Allende. She had the idea then to call over a poorly dressed boy she discovered on the

The fact is I became very impatient with having to wait.

C'est vous qui l'avez dit, Princesses (sic) *de Racine:*
Je meurs si je vous perds, mais je meurs si j'attends...[11]

Not only in love does this impatience burn. You can be impatient of the months, furious of the weeks in other domains and for other reasons.

Correspondence and Rorschach Test

My correspondence with Keyserling (masses of letters) began in these circumstances. He lived in Darmstadt, apparently free of Nazism (at 4 Prinz Christiansweg). Because of his very busy life he always wished to fix much in advance the dates of his travels and lectures. The first letters concerned the conditions of his tour, the best time for them to be successful, the subjects to discuss, etc. Amigos de Arte, the Faculty of Philosophy and Letters, the cultural Argentinian-German Institution[12] and the Jockey Club booked

---

course. I think he didn't even have shoes. She offered him up to ten pesos to carry the clubs. The boy would always answer, "I can't, I can't". Finally she asked, "But why can't you?" The immutable boy said, "*Porque non me da la gana*" [Because I don't feel like it]. I told Keyserling the story to explain why among us, especially in the countryside, in the provinces, money is not the primordial drive, and that the peasants were not servile, and that the inhabitants of the province of Cordoba (may they forgive me the opinion if it sounds too daring) did not seem always devoured by a need to work. The story amused Keyserling immensely, and he began to ponder it, to knead it in the trough of his imagination, to knead us all with it and myself especially. *Gana* did not become for him *envie*, its French synonym, but rather something specifically South American, like *puna* (a high plateau sickness). In *South American Meditations,* it became: "Blind Urge, as opposed to a life determined or co-determined by Spirit ... It is the strongest of all that is strong, and the weakest of all that is weak at the same time; it is primordial puissance and helplessness in one. It lacks all element of imagination ... South American Gana is [an] intrinsically blind urge to which the mere idea of forethought must mean an offence, since it implies a denial of its very essence" (pp. 160–161). From this we can deduce that life in South America is a life "of complete self-indulgence, lack of discipline, lack of all initiative or forethought, and accordingly of all consistency. All activity in South America is the result of a yielding to inner urge" (p. 177). "The irreducible last resort is and remains undifferentiated massive Gana. Gana, not sex, not the instinct of power and retaliation, and most emphatically no prospective tendency is the original phenomenon" (p. 203).

11   Editor's note:

It is you, princesses of Racine, who said it:
'I die if I lose you, but I die if I wait ... '
Racine, *Andromeda*, Act III, Scene 7 (1667)

12   Editor's note: *Institución Cultural Argentino-Germana* was created in 1922 to counterweight the growing influence of the *Université de Paris* in Argentina's academia. Juan Javier Negri, personal correspondence, 10 April 2022.

several lectures. I spoke with the presidents and directors of these institutions. I offered to put up in the house that I was building the Darmstadt philosopher and his wife (in the beginning he talked about coming with her). I remember perfectly having written to him with the offer and assuring him of the pleasure he would give me in accepting. He complained about the insecurity of his material life (from a financial point of view), and I told him that my house would always be at his disposal, if it were of any use ... At the time, I must add, I was not aware of his explosive character.

The transactions in which I intervened defending Keyserling's interest turned out to be long and wearisome. The institutions showed good will, but Keyserling was demanding and somewhat capricious in these matters. I took on the role of buffer between the institutions and him, with the purpose of softening the blows of his ultimatums. Of course, not everyone was willing to show towards him the plenary indulgence that my state of enthusiasm had sparked in me. If he had asked for the moon, I believe I would not have been that shocked. The imperative and categorical tone that was habitual in him took me aback only when I had to show his letters to others. I personally, in the beginning, found them funny. And the impudence that in someone else I would not have easily tolerated, in him always made me laugh.[13]

At first, as I've said, it was decided that the Countess would accompany her husband, and I managed through my insistence to solve the practical matters in the way that Keyserling desired. However I didn't have time to congratulate myself on the success of my negotiations ... Keyserling wrote that his wife would not come; but that, in spite of not coming, she had to go on living in Darmstadt during his absence, and it was necessary that I make the institutions understand, etc. The institutions that were paying for the philosopher's trip did not look at this approvingly. I deployed all my diplomatic skill, willingly or not, to accept the conditions of the founder of the School of Wisdom. They said that they understood wisdom differently.

I will open a parenthesis here: I have always found it not only natural but legitimate that creative thinkers or artists, lacking funds because they never had them or because they lost them (as in Keyserling's case), demanded the capital contribution of those who have not a creative bone in their bodies but who profit from the creations of thinkers and artists. I have always found that there were not enough Maecenas[14] or that those who existed were not sufficiently generous. I have always found that the "rich" behaved in general in a

---

13   Again, to explain my state of mind, I will reach for what Keyserling felt in his crisis of adoration for Houston Chamberlain: "I lacked completely that which turned Chamberlain into a political-spiritual power, his racial credo, his pan-Germanism, his anti-democratic and anti-liberal feelings – these were things that I excused in Chamberlain, as a friend excuses in a friend that which from his personal point of view he cannot approve." *Travel through Time.*

14   Editor's note: a generous patron of the arts.

particularly sordid manner towards the "creators" and that the "merchants" who dealt with the work born from talent or genius exploited ignominiously and without shame those who painfully give birth to those works.

Of course, there are certain creators who know how to defend themselves. They are absolutely right to do so. But the Maecenas and the institutions who foster the Arts and Letters don't like to be treated with impudence. The least that can be said of Keyserling was that he adopted an utterly impudent tone. The fact of having an ancestor for whom Bach composed a lullaby and another for whom Kant worked as tutor, and another like two peas in a pod with Frederick the Great and another whose opinion troubled Bismarck, made the demands of our contemporary Hermann seem, in his opinion, but trifles. Also for me, until the day when, from one oyster to another he exceeded the limit and my stock of patience.

From several sides, warnings reached me that Keyserling was only bearable in small doses. He himself warned me. "My vitality is such that there are people who cannot bear me for more than three days running." But as long as I hadn't met him personally, none of that made an impression on me. I saw him as he appeared to me in his books (one cannot find in books but that which one is prepared to look for in them) and in some of his letters that, with so much difficulty, I deciphered. Because our correspondence during the years that preceded our encounter was copious.

Ever since my childhood I have been a great letter writer. Ortega is of the opinion that women cannot truly express themselves except in epistolary form. In my youth, as far as I myself am concerned, that seemed true. In a word, I always had affection for this sort of expansiveness, and the opportunity Keyserling was offering me to give free rein to my *vice impuni* [unpunished vice] was marvellous. To write to someone we admire and whom we don't even know! What bliss! Double bliss! My epistolary self bolted like a colt. To be able to converse daily through these small signs scribbled by my hand! To receive pages covered with those small signs from someone whom one considers a genius! That the *tête-à-tête* with oneself becomes a *tête-à-tête* with an inhabitant of our imaginary world! Whoever has never plunged into the euphoria of writing and receiving letters (as in music) cannot truly understand me.

To write? But if at the beginning of my life, that was what writing meant, as it must have been for many others, I would write to my mother because I loved her, to my aunt I. because I found her pretty. I never said in any other way to the one that I loved her, to the other that I found her pretty. To articulate in words was something that lay in a region beyond my reach, and any verbal utterance, whether love or admiration, would have degenerated into tears. Only as the years made me less vulnerable have I learned to speak.

I was, therefore, in my element as far as correspondence was concerned. Not because my style was remarkably polished (I have always been careless in this respect) but because of the inexhaustible pleasure that this type of dialogue gave me. Therefore I poured torrents of ink in the direction of Darmstadt. There, Keyserling with his Baltic eyes and Mongolic ancestry, would read my letters and interpret them in his fashion. While I complained about the indecipherability of his handwriting, he criticized me for my clear handwriting that he found lamentably conventional. But did he really read my letters, or did he examine them almost unconsciously as one looks at the ink blots of a Rorschach?[15] And when he imagined that he was analysing the inkblot that I was for him, he was not doing other than what subjects taking the Rorschach test do, projecting themselves.[16]

What cannot be read into the letters of an unknown woman, a devout reader, a woman from another continent and another race? What cannot be read in a correspondent one admires as an author and of whom one is ignorant as a man? It's enough to loosen the reins of the imagination: here I see a clown, here a butterfly, here a top, here a bat; I tell you, it's a cow-hide; you idiot, it's a rock; no, a serpent. And so on.

I would write to Keyserling about all the subjects that interested me at the time and especially about his books and everything they conjured up in me. Happy and contented because I existed for him to the point that he deigned to respond, I would express my thanks in fervent terms. He was for me, more or less, what Houston Chamberlain had been for him at a time when Uncle Edward Keyserling had compared the young Hermann to a child dazzled by a Christmas tree. I was in turn the child before the tree, and he was the tree full of lights that I stared at with my mouth opened.

You should come to Europe, Keyserling started to write to me. And then: it's necessary that you come to Europe so that we can discuss the tour, so that you can teach me to speak Spanish, so that we can get to know one another. And soon afterwards: it's indispensable that you come. This coincided with my burning desire to return to the Old World. But in spite of my dream of meeting Keyserling at last, I began to feel in the pit of my stomach, faced with the simple idea of the meeting, the unease we feel the day before an exam or before visiting the doctor whose diagnosis troubles us.

15   Editor's note: see Damion Searls, *The Inkblots: Hermann Rorschach, His Iconic Test, and the Power of Seeing* (New York: Crown, 2017).
16   Regarding Houston Chamberlain in *Travel through Time*: "Chamberlain never saw Germany as it really was. Too often he embraced a pipe dream in which he could believe it all the more sincerely because it carried no true relationship to the nature of the German. So, for instance, there is a letter or article in which he prophesized that William the Second would carry the title of William the German, the idea that Chamberlain had of William the Second was totally erroneous because he aggrandized it with undue exaggeration. *Something analogous to what happened to Chamberlain happens most times with a predilection for foreign people and countries; they constitute the surest surface for the projection of one's self.*" Italics mine. *South American Meditations* would be Keyserling's reaction in a Rorschach test confronted with the great ink blot of our continent.

Versailles

The date was set: January 1929. The place: Versailles. I was living in an apartment in Paris, 40 rue d'Artois (I like precise details). Keyserling, invited by me, because I did not want to go to see him in Germany, set up with his whole kit and caboodle in the Hôtel des Réservoirs. The kit: a gold fountain pen and pencils. The caboodle: his almost illegible manuscript of *America Set Free*, on which he was working.

Keyserling had set conditions (I did not yet know him except in his letters) that amused me as his other demands, the explosions, exasperated those who had to answer them directly. Above all, he wished that during the month of his stay in Versailles I visit him as often as possible; that I not lead a mundane life (as if I cared for that), a life that might distract me from our conversations; that I not count on him as a man amenable to social gatherings of any kind; that I invite him to meals in Paris with *select* Argentinian friends, ditto the champagne and oysters; that the women attend in evening gowns and the men in tuxedos. These requisites seemed to me innocent and of a touching *gourmandise* of the palette and the eyes. I have always detested champagne, oysters, dinners for which you have to dress, but I understand that others like them.

I had learned by heart the details of this agreement when I arrived that afternoon at the Hôtel des Réservoirs. Keyserling was waiting for me in the small room that he was going to use as his study. Snow was falling or had fallen on that slumbering wintery Versailles that I find so attractive. The Hôtel de Réservoirs in which I had booked rooms for Keyserling, according to his instructions, was a decrepit hotel of a quintessential French charm. The building was of admirable proportions, and one felt inside it as if in the heart of the country. A fiery giant, the founder of the School of Wisdom (I had underestimated his height) came towards me, his hands outstretched. In merely one of them, he might have crushed my two hands. In the square room whose windows opened onto the *pavé du Roi* [King's setts] he seemed to occupy the entire space. Two names came to my mind: Genghis Khan, Tamerlane[17] ... a Genghis Khan-Tamerlane of literature, this time. These are the names of the scions of telluric forces, if I have understood correctly the roles these men played in history. Unless in their male quality they represented the Holy Spirit. I say this as an afterthought, recalling what Keyserling says in his [*South American*] *Meditations*: "Man absolute is as originally 'seeing' as

17   Editor's note: Genghis Khan (1162–1227) was the first Khangan, the great conqueror and Emperor of the Mongol Empire. Timur (1336–1405) was the fourteenth-century warlord and founder of the Timurid Empire, whose life was fictionalized in English literature by Christopher Marlowe in *Tamburlaine* (1587) and by Edgar Allan Poe in *Tamerlane and Other Poems* (1827). Ocampo would have found Keyserling's references to Genghis Khan and Tamerlane (respectively) in his Travel *Diary*, Vol. 1, pp. 200 and 209.

woman absolute is originally 'blind'. This is why he is the original bearer of Spirit; this is why the word 'history' is instinctively understood by each and all to be man's history" (p. 165). This classification, this attitude concerning the male and female of the species is further reinforced by this passage from *Das Buch vom Ursprung* [*The Book of Origins*, 1947]:

> Woman is the most religious element of humanity, the one who prays. However it is very difficult for her to undergo directly the interior experience of the spirit. Even the interior experiences of the most authentic female saints have an incarnation character definitely pronounced. This explains the primordially female cult of the phallus. Psychology of the unconscious has demonstrated that, contrary to the early theories of psychoanalysis, sexual representations did not refer in most cases to a sexual reality but had a symbolic meaning and were the most obviously adjusted symbols to human nature to represent the primordial. This is precisely in what sense and why the phallus represents, naturally, above all, the spirit.

Now, to admit and even affirm, as Keyserling does, that the man who is primordially viral is primordially a seer, as the primordial woman is primordially blind, is to adhere in a word to the belief that even for us, civilized people, the phallus (a symbol of the masculine) legitimately represents Spirit. It's interesting to consider this declaration of faith in light of a text by Simone de Beauvoir, from *The Second Sex*:

> The grown man regards his organ as a symbol of transcendence and power; it pleases his vanity like a voluntary muscle and at the same time like a magical gift: it is a liberty rich in all the contingency of the fact given yet freely wished; it is under this contradictory aspect that he is enchanted with it, but he is suspicious of deception. That organ by which he thought to assert himself does not obey him; heavy with unsatisfied desires, unexpectedly becoming erect, sometimes relieving itself during sleep, it manifests a suspect and capricious vitality. Man aspires to make Spirit triumph over Life, action over passivity; his consciousness keeps nature at a distance, his will shapes her, but in his sex organ he finds himself again beset with life, nature, and passivity.[18]

Spiritual supremacy in the masculine realm (as if the Spirit had a sexual identity outside the field of grammar) and the fact that man bestows upon himself the title of *representative of the Spirit*, with the simple pretext that he is, in the species, the carrier of spermatozoids has always seemed to me comic

18   Editor's note: Simone de Beauvoir, *The Second Sex*, trans. H. M. Parshley (New York: Vintage Books, 1989), p. 162.

in certain aspects and tragic in others. Because mistakes, consolidated by reason (and the interests) of the strongest, and then transformed into acceptable and accepted prejudices by the masses, are always tragic. But the reason of the strongest cannot be the best except in the animal kingdom, never in the spiritual one, the kingdom of man and woman, those unknowns.

This preceding digression will serve to establish that I have never admitted (even if it were the opinion of all thinkers and prophets) that man as carrier of spermatozoids is the representative of the Holy Spirit on Earth, while woman, as carrier of ovules, is the representative of telluric forces.[19] I repeat, I believe that, on the contrary, if men have seen woman as the representative of telluric forces, it is due to the phenomena of projection. The reaction caused in them by the woman as woman made them attribute to her the impressions they felt regarding her. Because woman made them telluric, they proclaimed her telluric. Because woman awakened in them their emotivity, they proclaimed her emotional. Because women's proximity acted on certain of their glands, they proclaimed her animal. And finally and mainly because they sought consciously or unconsciously to find in the company of woman thrills of a sexual nature, most of the time they left the spirit in the closet like an unnecessary umbrella and ended up believing (or began to believe) that they were the true representatives of the Spirit, the Spirit that naturally they did not find in woman because they lacked the organ to perceive it (that particular organ having remained in the closet).

All these thoughts came to me, of course, much later, and not at the moment in which, seeing Keyserling for the first time in the Hôtel des Réservoirs, I summed up in two famous names, Genghis Khan and Tamerlane, the image that the Baltic giant evoked for me. I have some extremely vague notions about these two characters, but I imagine that if I were to meet them suddenly at the entrance of the Grand Trianon or next to the fountain of Char Embourbé, it would have produced in me the same astonishment that the founder of the School of Wisdom produced in me in a little room of exquisite proportions whose frame seemed to burst, thanks to his uncommon height and his laughter like a Homeric god. He himself said this about himself: "I have always had a temperament that allowed me to find a propitious echo in the legend that said I descended from Genghis Khan, not only spiritually but as if we said, like a bird of prey; he was quick, hot-blooded, violent, irascible, unrestrained, and totally inaesthetic." That was indeed my impression that afternoon of January 3rd. It disoriented me not a little, and I immediately saw that big clouds were gathering on the horizon and that they would not all be rose-coloured. But a sky full of grey clouds, like the ones el Greco painted when depicting Toledo, can also be very beautiful, I thought. Furthermore

---

19   I don't see why a spermatozoid should be more spiritual than an ovule.

these muddled feelings did nothing but pass through me like lightning flashes, precursors to a new lucidity.

We had dinner together that night. I had certainly not expected to meet Parsifal under the guise of the Darmstadt philosopher; rather, thundering Jupiter. But I had not counted on the arrivals of Bacchus and Pantagruel. This cumulative character of his person darkly fed what I would call my Penthesilea complex.[20] Darkly, I say, because I felt very intimidated, very tongue-tied with him. That he might have found some resemblance between myself and Kundry was later a revelation to me.[21] Proof of the power of his imagination. But when I left the Hôtel des Réservoirs that night, I knew as little of the impression I had made on him as that which he had made on me. And this quid pro quo was to prolong itself as in a classical vaudeville. It is true that I never communicated to him in Versailles the vertiginous development that was growing in my interior being, the complex of Penthesilea. But let us not forget that in Versailles there were two people in diametrically opposing situations: one hungry to speak, the other hungry to listen; one gifted with speech, the other tongue-tied; one all assurance, the other all a-tremor. Seven months earlier, from Buenos Aires, I had written to Keyserling: "I ask myself how you will manage to find out my thoughts and my feelings. You give me the impression of going always at full speed. I feel as quickly as you do. But I don't jump to express myself, I don't articulate with your great velocity. When I want to express myself, I am slow; I feel suddenly deprived of the means, deprived of experience, as if I were weighed down by generations and generations of beings who only practiced silence. All my thoughts, my feelings, have the shape of a cry, the shapeless and terrible form of a cry or a moan." On his side Keyserling, like almost all richly endowed thinkers, was in a certain sense deaf to his fellow humans when he became obsessed with an idea (as I found out one afternoon). My thoughts, my true feelings, were not perceived but interpreted by him according to his poetic fantasy.

Presentiments and Divergences

The fact is that I returned to Paris the night of our first meeting full of apprehensions. I remember the snow in the night on the road, and the English word "misgivings" came to my mind, perhaps because it consists of the word "miss" (not to hit the bull's eye) and "giving".

20 Editor's note: Penthesilea, daughter of Mars, was one of the queens of the Amazons. In the legend, Penthesilea ran to the rescue of Priam at Troy and died at the hands of Achilles who later bemoaned her death. In his famous tragedy, Kleist inverts the facts: Penthesilea kills Achilles. See Kleist, "Penthesilea," pp. 313–420. Goethe wrote after reading the play: "I cannot yet familiarize myself with *Penthesilea*. It belongs to a race so fabulous, and it moves in a realm so strange that I need a certain time to acclimatize myself to both."

21 Editor's note: Keyserling takes up Kundry, the cursed messenger of the Grail knights in Wagner's *Parsifal*, to describe Ocampo. See Part Seven.

From then onwards, I became determined not to allow myself to be perturbed by the instinctive rebelliousness that the very presence of Keyserling sparked in me. We belonged surely to different animal species, I thought. But it was important that the clear awareness of such difference not cloud our relationship in the only realm that was important in the present case: the intellectual, spiritual realm.

In 1928 Dr Gabriel Moner, a great Keyserling reader like myself, would frequently come to speak with me about the writer. Fully fluent in German, he would translate passages of the books that had not appeared in other languages. I recall speaking at length with him about *Wiedergeburt*, in the preface to which Keyserling writes: "In *Symbolic Figures* I lay the roots of my conviction that no one can do any more than incite, that there are no ethics superior to fecundity, etc." I had seen Keyserling's power as inciter. And in his *Travel Diary*, I had found many pages that agreed perfectly with my way of thinking and feeling, something that always produces in the reader a sort of euphoria. For instance, "The more I see of art that is only art, the more conscious am I of my peculiar disposition which allows me to appreciate art only as the immediate expression of metaphysical reality. For that reason, truly great art means more to me than to the majority of its admirers, but I cannot do justice to small art, and many a masterpiece appears to me as such. Especially the purely decorative leaves me cold. The gracefulness, the charm of an arabesque has no profounder direct background than the choice taste of its inventor; and I do not know in what way it should concern me that a certain individual had taste. This, of course, only proves my limitations, not the lack of value of decorative art. Undoubtedly, its character is superficial, and it is ridiculous to compare Sansovino to Michelangelo. But it is not only profundity that has a right to exist."[22]

I had written to Keyserling commenting on the [preceding] passage:

> For X it is precisely the grace, the charm of the arabesque, the purely decorative, that counts in [the] first place. The most beautiful verses are those that don't exist except according to this aesthetic canon. The less sense they have, the more the fortunate choice of words and the unexpectedness of their order seems to delight. For him, Dante is a great poet because of certain minute verbal inventions or discoveries (as if it were possible to separate in this poet par excellence form from content). For X, art is a way of escaping thought; for me it is the only door to open to it.

22   I was in agreement with him in this matter regarding literature as a great art. On the other hand I am extremely sensitive to the grace and charm of an arabesque. And good taste in people concerns me directly for the pleasure it gives me.
Editor's note: Keyserling, *Travel Diary*, Vol. 1, p. 219.

Coincidences of this sort, his theory of "the fecundity of the insufficient" and his belief that great artists are great inciters were the cardinal points that had converted me to Keyserlingism. But after meeting him, I began to ask myself up to what point could I follow him. In this sense, I experienced the contrary of what Keyserling experienced regarding Houston Chamberlain, when he writes: "Involuntarily I stopped even asking myself the question ... if I could follow Chamberlain and up to where. Indeed, to begin with, I was indifferent to whether Chamberlain was *right* in any sense whatsoever." I, instead, began asking myself: "Up to where can I follow him without loss, without abdication, in a word, without betraying my own *dharma*?" And during the four weeks in which I went almost daily to visit him, I discovered with great consternation that I could not follow him fully under any pretext or for any cause, even that of the Spirit with capital S (at least as he understood it). This irredeemable divergence between him and myself, this impossibility to accept all his points of view, of accepting him except partially (as if I had said: You will never be for me a full moon, only a half moon) is to what he would refer later in his memoirs as medieval splitting.[23]

The fact of not sharing his opinions and not obeying his wishes, whatever they might be and in whatever realm, turned me in his eyes into one of the "most spiritual beings I have known" (see his *America Set Free*) in "the very incarnation of *gana*" (see *Travel through Time*). And he turned me into the incarnation of the slave of *gana*, precisely at the time in which I was showing irrefutable proof that I was overcoming it. Because when, finally, the misunderstanding between us went from a state of *drôle de guerre [the Phoney War]*[24] to that of Hiroshima, *gana* would have dictated to me a radical and brutal attitude, which was certainly not the one I adopted in order to "fulfil my promises" concerning Keyserling's tour in South America. He himself has had the kindness to mention and recognize this detail.

Of what precisely did this misunderstanding consist? Its essence can be defined, leaving aside the philosophical vocabulary (at least for the matter-of-fact woman that according to Keyserling I am). The extraordinary fervour of my enthusiasm for certain aspects of the Keyserlingian genius (I have thought and still think that this man had sparks of genius) had led him to believe that this enthusiasm was inseparable, unless medieval splitting occurred, from a great all-encompassing love that never inspired me. Noticing the absence of that feeling made me appear in his eyes as a monster and a traitor, when

---

23   If I were to put at the end of this essay a glossary of technical terms as they appear in books of popular psychoanalysis, in this case it would include: "Medieval splitting, (state of): according to Keyserling, diagnosed in the female subject who refuses to play the role of Francesca da Rimini at the same time as that of Beatrice Portinari, under the absurd pretext that Dante Alighieri doesn't have the face of Paolo Malatesta."

24   *Drôle de guerre* was the name given to the period from 3 September 1939 to 10 May 1940, after the German attack on Poland, when nothing appeared to happen.

I simply was a woman who was sorry to disappoint in this matter (which made me merit his response) and who obstinately in the beginning employed an endless regard trying to make him see his mistake. This regard coloured, at least in part, South America, in the chapter, *"Delicadeza"*, in the *Meditations*: "Thus, the South American sweetness and considerateness does not mean warmth" (p. 222);

> everybody will understand a man who draws his pistol because of a single unfriendly glance ... if wounded feeling leaves room for reflection, it is considered bad form to shoot a person from the front, since that might cause a disagreeable impression. To assassinate a man is considered nobler conduct than to fight a duel.
>
> (pp. 213–214)

I find this opinion somewhat exaggerated. And even pure-blooded Americans, those from the underground of the Third Day of Creation, know how to distinguish in their inner core a duel from a murder.[25]

In his feverish generalization, beginning with a certain fact, doubtful or false as the case might be, and in this case the starting point was extremely doubtful, Keyserling doesn't hold back: "Just so, South Americans cease to speak, wherever Europeans would raise their voices or scold. They would rather kill than use offensive language" (p. 218). I call to witness all the taxi drivers and all other drivers in Argentina as well as the ghost of my paternal grandfather who was sensitivity incarnate and incapable of killing a fly.

But what happened when, tired of a useless *delicadeza* that fell on deaf ears, I raised my voice (I do have a rather wide register)? I was called a vandal and an iconoclast. I was accused of delighting in my own destruction much as I had delighted in my "idolatry" (please note that the word idolatry was chosen by me to distinguish the love provoked by an idol of love, provoked by a god: adoration, then. Idolatry in the sense of the bull Apis, the Hebrews, Sinai. The term was employed, when it was, in a clearly pejorative sense: the cult of a false divinity). Therefore neither my South American *delicadeza* nor my North American frankness found favour in Keyserling's eyes when I tried to make him understand what he did not have the *gana* to understand. This would not have disconcerted me so much if I had not held him in such high regard; this ailment is a vulgar ailment, well known in men of every profession.

---

25 One is always surprised by the mocking and disdainful tone that Keyserling adopts to speak of *delicadeza*, when we read in *Travel through Time* lines such as these: "I could never forgive anyone who, under the sign of the coarse North American culture of sincerity that has unfortunately spread throughout the world, would tell me the truth ... A single affectionate word often granted me several days of a creative state of mind, a single expression of dry objectivity made me lose sympathy toward a person forever." So which is it?

Only when it appears in men whose profession is to express feelings, reactions, and thoughts, it is displayed as in a showcase.

Bernard Shaw and his Female Admirers

Bernard Shaw, in his *Sixteen Self Sketches*,[26] reserves a few pages for sex in biography. They are delightfully humorous, and they appear to be sincere, even though it's difficult to be sincere when dealing with the subject. Even those who want to be and make an effort to be truthful don't always attain the truth, even in our age of sexual nudity, as far as sexual behaviour is concerned. And today it's not even nudism – nudism needn't be obscene – but pure exhibitionism (See [Jean] Genet, Sachs, [Henry] Miller, etc.). It's difficult to conceive in our time that *Lady Chatterley's Lover* (a novel deemed obscene when it was published, which was in fact the cry of a puritan who discovers as in a rapture that physical love between a man and a woman who love one another can be beautiful) could have been forbidden by the censor in a country that today freely devours the truly obscene Hadley Chase. On the cover of one of his novels the reader is enticed with "a welcome puff of fetid air".[27]

In a word, neither the Kinsey Report[28] nor the fashion of erotic nudism in literature has saved us from the voluntary or involuntary lie. It's so natural for one's self-esteem to exaggerate in every direction! Men (and women) manage to be vain about everything, even about passing in the astonished reader's eyes as a more or less sacred monster ... Only saints cannot become vain about their fasts and flagellations because they would immediately stop behaving like saints. There is not a corner of human nature in which vanity, self-esteem, and pride don't seep in and make themselves at home, not to infest sneakily, cheekily. But this infection preys especially on the male as far as sex is concerned.

In his writings, Shaw seems quite free from this complex. He begins by explaining that if he maintained himself celibate until the age of twenty-nine (a quite rare case), neither did he establish a relationship between sexual activities and crime (a very unusual attitude in the masses even nowadays). From the moment he started to dress decently he began to be successful. Women sought him out. But his success as a well-dressed man coincided with his literary success, which allowed him that luxury. So his attire cannot be made responsible for the whole scope of his conquests. Here – a miracle! – is what he writes about the women who gathered around his new (or old) glory: "All my

26   Bernard Shaw, *Sixteen Self Sketches* (London: Constable and Company, 1949).
27   Editor's note: James Hadley Chase, pen name of René Lodge Brabazon Raymond (1906–1985), was a king of thriller writers.
28   Editor's note: Alfred Kinsey, Wardell Pomeray, Clyde Martin and Paul Gebhard, *Sexual Behavior in the Human Male* (1948), *Sexual Behavior in the Human Female* (1953), Philadelphia: W.B. Saunders.

pursuers did not want sexual intercourse" (p. 115). I say miracle because such a statement from a world-famous writer is rarer still than having remained continent until the age of twenty-nine. And the perspicacity that this statement implies, so contrary to the laws of masculine nature, is a miracle to the laws of nature itself. But his insight goes further (Oh, Montherlant![29]): "Some were prepared to buy friendship with pleasure, having learnt from a varied experience that men are made that way. Some were enchantresses, quite unbearable as housemates. No two cases were alike" (p. 115).

A woman can have different reasons to prostitute herself (if that term can be applied – as it must be applied – to giving oneself without love in exchange for some material and practical benefit). It's not only jewellery, furs, comfortable little flats, or daily bread. There are also ambitions of another sort: the screen, the stage, politics, marriage, even literary glory, and God knows what else! The male is made in such a way that he offers much to whoever is willing to pay him with the coin of pleasure, and even with the coin of satisfied self-esteem, with the coin of the flattering feeling of dominion. Woman is made in such a manner that if she finds herself in unfortunate circumstances she often gives in to the temptation (and those who have lived protected from such temptations and ignoring them, have no reason to boast). But in these not infrequent cases let me make it clear it's Adam who offers the apple, Adam who speaks first with the Serpent. We know full well that "the little plot hatched between the Woman and the Serpent destroyed the groundwork of the original plan" regarding the creation of the Primordial Author. But even if it's true that the undoing of that plan did not originate with man, he took his revenge later on, as far as tantrums are concerned. And a fair number of women sometimes feel like saying to him: Give me back the apple, take your rib, and there's an end to it.

I don't at all believe that Count Keyserling, whose ancestors had employed the Bachs, the Kants, and who were on first-name basis with emperors and chancellors, lent the slightest importance to these green grocer stories. I believe that, more similar to the Olympian gods than to the descendants of the couple in Eden, it merely irritated him that a simple mortal woman dared to contradict him and not ply herself to all his "poetic fantasies". I have a very nebulous idea of who my ancestors were and what they did at the time when the Keyserlings were lulled to sleep by the "Goldberg Variations", but I have a very clear idea of the role that I did not want to play in 1929, that of Leda. Swans, whether from Mantua or Combray, were never my favourite animals.[30]

In view of all these subterranean discords between reincarnated characters of Olympus and Genesis (discords that Keyserling would call, years later,

---

29 Editor's note: French writer and academician Henry de Montherlant (1895–1972) was well-known for his anti-feminist and misogynistic views.

30 Editor's note: The Roman poet Virgil is the Mantuan Swan. Combray is Marcel Proust's name for Swann's imaginary village in *À la recherche du temps perdu*.

"the most banal private events of my life"), the philosopher's sojourn at the Hôtel des Réservoirs was for me less an event of extraordinary interest, more a daily ordeal very hard to endure.

My *Delicadeza* is Put to the Test

He was always the man of genius, the brilliant conversationalist, unforesee-able, indefatigable, as all those who knew him well remember. But those who knew him as a guest will equally remember his demands and fits of violence. And in Versailles he was my guest. Consequently my duty was to remedy everything that in his view wasn't working at the Hôtel des Réservoirs. I've seen him grow pale with fury over a dish of mashed potatoes, and though violence occupies a preeminent place in my list of sins, I was frightened by the magnitude of his. He made use of the size of his giant's body. Even though he did not address me but the waiter, I suspected that I was the real recipient, and that the waiter and the mashed potatoes were pretexts to alleviate the tension. I begged him not to get in such a state because my nerves couldn't tolerate it, and I insisted once more when, for one reason or another, he did it again. This is how, in the *Meditations*, he translates the horror that his fits of anger produced in me. After establishing that South Americans are cold-blooded animals (of the batrachian order [frogs and toads]) and that they react to heat like no other being because they don't possess it, Keyserling adds: "He is permeable to warmth as well as to coldness …; this is why South American women have a horror unknown elsewhere of all hardness; anger to them is vice" (p. 30). If I remember correctly, the catechism of the Diocese of Bayona that I learned from A to Z at the age of nine, coincided with this prejudice against South American women: "in warm passionateness they sense fore-most the violence underlying it, and the violence they cannot bear. But on the other hand in their heart of hearts they desire to be violated; they want to be able to remain entirely passive, completely irresponsible; and the sexual success South American men so frequently have in Europe is due to the fact that, despite their delicacy [*delicadeza*], they violate as a matter of course" (p. 30).[31]

It's difficult to overlook certain contradictory and exaggerated elements in this interesting passage. Whoever hates violence and wrath cannot wish to suffer its effects unless it is a pathological case of masochism. This extreme masochism does not seem to be so widespread, as far as I know. And if South

---

31   In the French translation of the *Meditations* (Stock, 1932), it says: "*ils exercent le viol comme chose toute naturelle*"; in the Spanish of García Morente (Espasa-Calpe, 1933):"*ejercen la violencia con naturalidad primordial.*" I believe that the French version (from which I have translated all the passages in this book) is more faithful in regards to this word according to what I have heard Keyserling himself say about the matter.

Editor's note: (See Part One).

American men, for whom practising rape is something natural (I have lived my life with never having observed the alarming symptoms of such customs; why might that be?), have such success with European women, could it not be said of this phenomenon that the women of the Old World immediately learned to delight in rape and adopt the habits of our Cro-Magnons? No need, then, to be a cold-blooded animal from the world of the Third Day of Creation to behave in this manner.[32] And finally if we are to generalize, since we are in the right school to do so, we can conclude that this rape, universally though subterraneously longed for by women, can only be effected with any success by the Cro-Magnons (i.e., the South Americans). Something had to be left for these poor creatures.

As the weeks went by, my reserve of meekness and *delicadeza* was becoming depleted in my visits to Versailles. Keyserling remained deaf and blind to my hints and my wild colt-like bolting. Little by little, I began to be convinced that, sooner or later, I would have to end with kicking. But I considered with such lack of seriousness my *gana* to employ this method immediately that I did not want to disturb the gestation of our genius, and I treated the man with the precautions one might take with pregnant women. Keyserling later thought that he discovered in my attitude the tricks of an Indian. A Latin man or woman, from whatever Day of Creation, would not have made such a mistake. But he did not have even a pinch of the Latin, in spite of bragging of his Latin quickness and effervescence. Nothing in Keyserling sprang from that ethnic chaos so disparaged in *The Genesis of the Nineteenth Century* from his adored Houston Chamberlain. And I, instead, owed to this even the last drop of my reptilian blood, in spite of the fact that clarity was as necessary to me as to the great Baltic man.[33] The humblest of lizards also seeks the sun.

I could have invented a pretext after the experience of Versailles, regrettable from my personal point of view, to cancel the lecture tour. I had more than

32 Keyserling seems to have read distractedly (in the same way that he listened to me distractedly) the first book of the Pentateuch. The Third Day of Creation was dedicated to separating the water from the earth and to endow the dry parts of the world that was being born with plants. I know perfectly that facts did not matter to him. But when he writes (in *Travel through Time*) that he had seen (though he no longer saw) in me "the serpent of the Third Day of Creation" he speaks of an unborn ophidian that existed only in embryonic form, as a sketch in the mind of the Omnipotent and not on earth. The Divine Maker dedicated the fourth day to the sun, moon, and stars. No hint of serpents yet. Finally, on the fifth day, the birds and the fish appeared. I admit that a serpent-like animal might have slid in among them – an eel, for instance – but I admit this only to be agreeable. In fact, the serpent made its triumphant entrance into the world on the same day as man, on the sixth. Before the appearance of woman. If we were perversely inclined, we would say that the serpent and man had time to lay a trap for the woman before her appearance on earth.

33 Regarding certain South American modalities, I find these lines in the *Meditations*: "It is in its own way a world which shuns the light, insofar as every *sous-entendu* [innuendo] is instantly understood and rightly valued, whereas clarity is not misinterpreted, except in exceptional cases" (p. 214).

enough *ganas* to prolong my stay in Europe. But the thought did not cross my mind of sacrificing for the sake of my personal reactions a matter totally unrelated to them. The spectacle of Keyserling as a man of considerable size seemed to me always worthy of interest and admiration. I was certain of his success, and as long as people kept their distance and took the philosopher in reasonable doses there was no reason to fear a mishap.

My relationship with his daily person, with his reactions to the Spirit with capital S and with the mashed potatoes in lower case (I felt that at times he saw me as a recalcitrant potato that would not allow itself to be mashed), had taught me much about the limits of my endurance.

How the Plan Was Changed

I changed nothing as far as the lecture tour was concerned. But I decided: (1) not to return to Buenos Aires on the same ship as he; (2) to lodge Keyserling at the Plaza Hotel (the "little" hotel[34] near the port where, according to him, Tagore stayed) and not in my house; (3) not to employ with him, since he wasn't a primitive like we were,[35] those euphemisms, that *delicadeza*, that "female diplomacy", which I had thought myself obliged to use in Versailles, when he required a "creative spiritual state" that my coarseness might disturb.

That latter resolution gave rise to many trains of thought in his *Meditations*, the fruit of his South American trip. Because even though he considered himself incapable of reacting like a primitive and even though he loved clarity, Count Keyserling for all his Balticness reacted to every "disagreeable impression" like an ordinary Brazilian or Argentinian. I had proof of this when I went from the strategy of hinting (labelled in the *Meditations* as "female diplomacy") to that of brutal frankness, and from bolting to kicking. My new attitude made me not worthy of being classified amongst the animals of the sixth day of creation. No hope whatsoever. My frankness was treated as treason and my bucking as a poisoned arrow.

In a word, after the arrival of the philosopher in Buenos Aires, our relationship became more and more tense, until the moment in which I learned by chance Keyserling's opinion of my behaviour towards him. I felt as if splashed with acid by such injustice, and I wrote him a letter (he was on the point of departure) in which I explained to him with red-hot frankness what I thought and felt, what I had thought and felt since Versailles. Later, he told me that this was cruellest letter he had received in all his life. I kept a copy of the letter,

34   Editor's note: Ocampo insists correctly that the Plaza Hotel was actually one of the most luxurious hotels in the world. Juan Javier Negri, personal communication, 10 April 2022.

35   "Primitive man resents unpleasant impression only; accordingly, care is taken that he should never meet with such" (*Meditations*, p. 213).

though I'm not in the habit of doing so because I had made several drafts and I find, today after the tempest is passed, that it is cruel, but not exceedingly so.

I asked him then to return the tons of scribbles that I had sent him in exchange for his letters. Alexander Von Wuthenau, Secretary of the German Embassy, was charged with that mission. I had stopped being on "speaking terms" with Keyserling. I sent him a huge parcel of papers. I burned those he returned, except a few. It was also a "symbolic burial" that I performed as an auto-da-fé. The voice of Saint Rémi did not resound in my ears with the traditional words: "*Courbe la tête, fier Sicambre ... Brûle ce que tu as adore...*"[36] But it was all the same to me. I acknowledged being served notice.

The Need for Hero Worship

It is true that my inveterate need for "*hero worship*" was reborn from its ashes. Happily, neither a Gandhi nor a T. E. Lawrence could disappoint me. The one lived in the realm of near holiness, the other in that of death. And even if the latter had been alive, I don't believe the situation would have changed.

There are beings who find it impossible to live without admiring and for whom admiration means "*hero worship*". Though it is true that "*hero worship*" can be completed with another love, it is also perfectly possible to do without it, and this is one of its characteristics. In this latter form it is known as "*hero worship*" and not otherwise.

This kind of exultation is generally misunderstood by writers, in spite of the fact that they inspire it. So misunderstood that they often see in this an affront, a desertion, a crime of *lèse-genie*. This is the reason for there being in the history of literature and philosophy so many novels *à clef*, theories, systems of thought, philosophical vocabularies, etc. Where can one find a clearer image of thundering Jupiter than in the thinker, novelist or poet encountering a mortal woman who won't comply with his desires? Straightforward or devious revenge, conscious or unconscious, by means of the pen or the typewriter, we have a long and glorious tradition that will not be interrupted, *tant que vivront les plumes et le livre* [as long as the feathers and the books live (Ronsard)]. This said, in an unfortunate love affair, the most desperate songs are the most beautiful ones, as the poets say. But unfortunate self-esteem does not enjoy such fortunate inspirations.[37]

If someday a Montherlant in skirts is born, what a terrible *Pitié pour les hommes* [pity for men] she could write! But it's preferable that women's literature be not dishonoured by such an honour.

---

36 Editor's note: the speech of Saint Rémi (Remigius), Bishop of Reims, as he baptized Clovis is recorded as: "Bow your head, proud Sicambre!/ Love what you have burnt, burn what you have loved ..."

37 Editor's note: In "V.O.", *Travel through Time*, Vol. 2, Keyserling wrote, "I was not at all in love, not even of a burning passion" (Part Seven).

"Are you going to the women? Don't forget the whip!" Thus spoke Zarathustra.[38] Thus thought many others before and after him.

I heard the snap of Keyserling's whip symbolically in his farewell letter. It was too much for my Penthesilea complex. A deathly silence arose between us. Keyserling compares it to a cauldron, but for me it was the silence of the Bikini Atoll.[39]

Revolted for a time by the profession of secretary-hostess, I founded *Sur* a year after this settling of accounts. I saw in *Sur* better possibilities to establish relationships with writers and help them to make their works known.

Time and other projects and preoccupations had calmed me down as far as Keyserling was concerned, when his first letter arrived, an effort to reconstruct burnt bridges.

The *Meditations*

In 1932, *South American Meditations* appeared, bringing me with their pages a new wave of indignation. One feels a certain pleasure in reaching the pit of this feeling.[40]

I did not want to write any more about Keyserling; I only enjoy analysing what I can praise, and the *Meditations* didn't seem to me altogether worthy of praise. In that book of 350 pages, except for a few moments of wisdom, one felt repulsed by a frantic generalizing of capricious conclusions. I recognized opinions and observations with which I had entrusted the philosopher but distorted by I don't know what phenomenon of extraordinary inflation, an interpretative elephantiasis. Here and there, as was habitual, a spark of genius issued up from I don't know what Magma Mater and then fell back into it.

As far as these distortions are concerned, I will give a few examples (there are so many that one would have to go back through the whole book). On

38 Editor's note: "And thus spake the old woman: 'Thou goest to women. Do not forget thy whip!'" Friedrich Nietzsche, "Old and Young Women", *Thus Spake Zarathustra*, XVIII, trans. Thomas Common (New York: Modern Library, 1930).

39 Editor's note: In 1946, this remote chain of coral reefs was subjected to three nuclear detonations large enough to vaporize three of its islands.

40 Let us recall the passage in *Orlando* in which it is told what happened to the young lord, a lover of literature, after having hosted in the castle the writer Nick Greene. This writer composed an inspired satire. No one could doubt that the young lord mocked in it was Orlando. "... his private sayings and doings ... his enthusiasms..." were there fully present. Orlando read it, picked up the document with a pair of tongs and gave it to a servant to throw into the fire. Then he bought himself a couple of greyhounds because – "he murmured, scarcely above his breath as he turned to his books – 'I have done with men'" [Virginia Woolf, *Orlando*, p. 82]. Orlando's adventure has many similitudes with mine, but my particular occurrences and my enthusiasms had been collected and deformed in an improbable manner. Like him, I could not pick up the *Meditations* except with tongs. How far this book was from *Symbolic Figures* that had moved me so! The magnificent essay on Schopenhauer that is found there came to my mind in contrast.

pages 36–37, Keyserling quotes, without mentioning the author, as was his habit, one of the *Poemas Solitarios* of Ricardo Güiraldes that I had read to him in Versailles: "Here the contact which for man of the upper world is created through speech, is based on silence ... the faces are fixed and rigid... etc." (pp. 27–28). But he immediately sees nothing in this except a reptilian reflection. And the image of the queenly anaconda "throwing herself out – but immediately afterwards relapsing into brooding apathy" (p. 28), applied in general to the whole of the continent, is nothing more than the disagreeable impression caused by the transformation of my "splendid enthusiasm" into reasoned and reasonable admiration after Versailles.

Another example: according to Keyserling, Argentinian men attribute more importance than men of any other country to male sexual prowess. Their lives are oriented towards satisfying the senses and procreating. Up to a certain point he's right. But a few lines later he adds: "In South American brothels there is no shrill lewdness but *the silence of concentrated procreation*" (p. 29, italics mine). I don't know through personal experience the atmosphere of the brothels, and I am ignorant about what places chosen for their local colour the Argentinians belonging to "the world of official science and politics" took the wandering philosopher; but that "*sombre délire*" of procreation in an Argentinian brothel surprises me.

Another example: the exuberance of South American life never takes place under the sign of joy, Keyserling says. This is very true. But then he destroys the fairness of this assertion by adding: "Argentine life I called *una vida a la sordina* (a life with the mute [pedal/una corda] on). The streets are wrapped in semi-darkness by night; the faces are impassive, the voices subdued in speaking; externally the extreme of decorum is observed" (p. 31). It is difficult to agree with this vision of Argentina after having been to a soccer match or to a comedy at the cinema. The censorship of laughter that he thought he observed comes perhaps from an anecdote I told him: One night in Paris, I laughed so loudly in a vaudeville that the entire theatre began to laugh at my laughter, and my husband reprimanded me for causing a scandal.

Analysing in this way the *Meditations*, I discover the starting point of many errors, but others seem to be fashioned entirely by the unleashed fantasies of the author. Like people with a strong musical memory who are too lazy to read the score, he analysed the countries by ear. And the ear, however faithful it might be, cannot always reproduce in their integrity complicated counterpoints.

The reading of the *Meditations* renewed my sense of distance. I opened Keyserling's first letters, therefore, as if they contained nettles.

Kierkegaard Defines the Misunderstanding

Kierkegaard writes concerning misunderstanding: "What constitutes a misunderstanding is the fact that what one party regards as significant the other regards as insignificant, and this by reason of the fact that at bottom they are separated by a trifle, that the parties who are in disagreement through a misunderstanding have not taken the time to understand one another at the start. For at the bottom of all real disagreement there is an understanding. The groundlessness of 'misunderstanding' is due to the lack of preliminary understanding, without which both agreement and disagreement are alike a misunderstanding. Therefore it is possible for misunderstanding to be removed and to become agreement and understanding; but it is possible also for it to be removed and to become real disagreement. For there is no misunderstanding involved in the fact that two persons really disagree. They really disagree just because they understand each other."[41] And from the dialectical point of view, it is comical and tragic at the same time. It is evident that between us there had been a misunderstanding and an understanding at the same time. And the tragic had prevailed over the comical.

The new series of Keyserling's letters referred to business transactions, to his new books, to the publishing in *Sur* of certain chapters. Our disagreements were not mentioned. He would write to me: "The more creative one is, the more one perceives only one's own world. And ever since I gave birth to what is a personal Revelation, I can only see by means of it. The *Meditations* are not, of course, my last word, but I will certainly never deny them ... And it's better to be born at fifty than at the age that is normal worldwide." Having read in *Sur* my pages on D. H. Lawrence, he wrote: "Your article is of supreme interest. I don't know that your vision is just [he refers to Lawrence], but this is not important in the least: in any case it has evoked in you personal realizations that could have a general significance."

Statements of this kind made me tremble because by then I was aware that seeing me correctly or not had no importance for Keyserling. And if ever he used my person in his writings, it would be for a "personal realization", not taking into account the fairness or unfairness of the matter.

When the Spanish Civil War broke out, the letters spoke of the situation created by the events and of common friends. They were longer. I suppose, he would say, that you must be doing this or that, "because in the final account you are good." I came upon this "in the final account", and it almost made me lose my recovered balance. Need I make clear what it implied? I answered the business letters and those concerning third parties with the circumspection of which fiery temperaments are capable when they set their minds to it. A purely formal relationship between two cold correspondents was re-established.

---

41   Editor's note: Soren Kierkegaard, "No. 2: A Word about the Relation of my Literary Activity to 'The Individual', *The Point of View for My Work as an Author; A Report to History, and other Related Writings*, trans. Walter Lowrie, ed. Benjamin Nelson (New York: Harper, 1962), pp. 121–138.

Ten Years Later

Finally, in January 1939, ten years after our first meeting, I was in Paris when Keyserling's charming sister, the Baroness of Ungern-Sternberg, came to see me to speak of her brother. I had not seen him since his visit to Buenos Aires, and I had set up a meeting in the Valley of Josaphat, the only proper place, it seemed to me, to settle our accounts definitively. But Hitler brought his presence to bear even in this strictly personal matter. He had deprived Keyserling of his passport. The School of Wisdom had been forced to close. Its founder was not permitted to lecture in his own country or abroad. The sale of his books had been more or less forbidden. All this was explained to me with great eloquence by the Baroness. She begged me to forget the unfortunate occurrence that distanced me from her brother and to go visit him in Darmstadt where he was almost a prisoner in his own home. In the end, she pressed all the right buttons. She insisted once more in a letter: "You should go see him. Do it ... in the same way you have sent me these chocolates. He feels isolated. Life is hard for him. The very possibility of bringing happiness and interest to the life of a being so exceptional, as he is after all my brother, should mean something to a woman like you."

A woman like me (I don't really know what this might mean) is not easily soothed. And I would not have seen valid reasons to present myself at 4 Prinz Christiansweg, Darmstadt, with an olive branch in my hand, were it not for my horror of Hitler. But after my conversation with the Baroness, I no longer saw in Keyserling the philosopher for whom certain injustices lacked importance: I saw the victim of the Führer. I took the decision at once. I phoned Keyserling to let him know that I would come by car. He seemed happy with my decision and told me that his wife had left for Hamburg where the Bismarck family had assembled to witness the launch of a super-armoured ship that bore the name of their illustrious ancestor. I later learned when I saw him (at that time, nobody in Germany dared communicate over the phone the most innocent things) that the Countess was going to have lunch with Hitler and that she would profit from the occasion to ask him that her husband's passport be returned. The two children were also absent. To Keyserling, alone in Darmstadt as if punished, the hours seemed interminable, and the day I arrived, he was feeling that his freedom, if not his life, hung from a thread; the thread in the hands of the granddaughter of the Iron Chancellor on one side and the fearful Chancellor of the Third Reich on the other.

Darmstadt

I entered Darmstadt late at night. Keyserling wanted to see me immediately and in my room. Oblivious of any oratory precaution, he started shouting at the top of his voice that the hall of the hotel was full of spies. That night, we did not refer at all to our disagreement. We only spoke of Hitler and of nothing but Hitler. When I say we spoke, I mean this euphemistically: he spoke of Hitler, from ten at night until three in the morning. I listened to him, tongue-tied by the monstrosities he was describing (to which we have become so accustomed that we see them and sometimes suffer them like the rain or sunshine). All this narrated with cleverness and indignation and so brilliantly that I would end up laughing at the most sinister things, and he would laugh with me, happy to be able to speak his mind. At times I would ask him: can I repeat this? And he would answer: Yes but don't say it was I who told it to you. To which I would say: I won't repeat it then, because the observation carries your signature.

He would comment on the Führer with loud cries and thunderous laughter, furious and amused with the character: "Have you not noticed that he looks like a concierge from a first-rate hotel? That his uniform always has traces of livery? I'll show you photographs. Ridiculous. I cut them out from magazines and collect them." He told me that he had shown the handwriting of the Führer to a celebrated German graphologist without telling him who was the author. As he spoke, he tapped two fingers of his right hand into the large palm of his left. The graphologist had announced Hitler's suicide. "The suicide has begun", he said to me. "Hitler has murdered his best friend; that is a form of suicide. He is already committing suicide in the person of his friend." He was referring to the murder of Roehm. At the time of hearing these predictions, I did not take them seriously; but I remembered them when the events that are now public knowledge proved him right, years later.

Keyserling explained to me when and how the persecution of which he was victim had begun (and this though in the later years he never launched into an attack of the Nazi doctrines, as far as I know): "The boys [he was referring to his two sons, Manfred and Arnold] were in school, and we were vacationing in the mountains. I had already heard that I was not well-regarded. It suddenly occurred to me that the boys might be somehow harassed for this reason, and I sent a person whom I trusted to visit them and to find out how they were treated in school. My envoy reported that he had not observed anything out of the ordinary and that the boys made no complaints. But when we returned home, all of us, I myself questioned Manfred and Arnold, 'Have they spoken to you about me in a disagreeable way?' 'They told us they would hang you, Papa,' they answered, 'but we didn't want to ruin your holidays by telling you these trifles.' As you can see, they are extraordinary boys. Arnold has a very strong personality. I believe that we will soon find it difficult to live under the same roof. To conclude: the day on which the boys told me this, I picked up the phone and spoke with four or five of the most important people in Darmstadt. I told them: 'I'm returning from my holidays. I'm in top form. I have never felt better physically. My height is 1', 89". If, when we go for a walk, my family and I, someone dares look at us in a way that might subjectively disgust me, I will twist his neck with my left hand because he is unworthy of my right.'" He spoke with heat, but it was difficult to tell where reality ended and fantasy began.

On the day following my arrival, I went to lunch at Keyserling's house. I could tell that the rise of National Socialism had curtailed neither his appetite nor his thirst. His house with a garden at the front was very agreeable and very German. The maid who served us lunch spoke only German, and so we could speak freely. After lunch he had me climb up to his study by a staircase next to a wall full of portraits (including, if I remember correctly, a portrait of myself). The first thing that I saw upon entering was, hanging over his desk, an oil painting depicting Orpheus with his lyre, surrounded by the beasts, including the serpent in the foreground. I approached the canvas and, pointing to the reptile, asked, "Is that my portrait?" He started to laugh and said, "That is not an anaconda." The conversation then drifted into the personal realm for the first time, and I spoke to him very frankly but trying not to hurt him in the least. After our conversation the atmosphere cleared; at least that is what I thought. In the afternoon we went for a car ride through the outskirts of the city. It was a radiant cold day. I did not know that in Germany in winter, light could be so crystal clear. We crossed groups of the Hitler Youth who were marching down the road singing. "The cult of Mithra[42]", Keyserling said when he saw them.

He wanted me to wait in Darmstadt for his wife and children to return, but I considered my mission accomplished: to find out if there was anything I could do. The Nazi atmosphere was too repulsive to me to endure it voluntarily more than was indispensable.

When It Rains, It Pours

On my return journey, a few kilometres outside Sarrebrück, I had a car accident that almost cost me my life. I was therefore in bed and in quite bad shape when a very long letter arrived from Keyserling who did not yet know about the accident. It completed the effect of the blow I had received to the neck. He said he was moved by my visit. Nothing would prevent us from now on being friends "in a perpetual constellation from one hemisphere to another". However, he wanted to warn me that he saw with different eyes the reasons why the spiritual fervour that he or his oeuvre inspired in me, had been (according to my vocabulary) poisoned in Versailles. "It is the worst injustice, a million times worse in my eyes than that which you suffered by my fault, to idealize someone as you have idealized me; because no man could be as you conceived me, and such an idealization amounts in practice to a denigration and a defilement of the true man. Unconsciously you demanded that

---

42   In the Roman Empire, the worship of Mithra, the pre-Zorastrian Iranian god of the sun, justice and war, was associated with the Roman army's devotion or loyalty to the emperor.

I had to be as I could not be, and everything that happened since is due to a psychological process, by means of which – unconsciously, of course – you made me pay for the fact of reality".[43]

Is it idealizing a man of great intelligence, whom one does not know personally, an author of many pages that have dazzled us, to imagine that he might recognize when the moment comes (as Shaw did) that his admirers are not obliged to admire him beyond the field of his creative genius? And that this devotion certainly doesn't imply that they feel for him a different kind of passion?

Keyserling's mental attitude in this regard is illogical and contradictory. In his chapter on Houston Chamberlain he writes: "I don't like to be idealized and therefore involuntarily I myself destroy the idol that others adore in me …"; while in the chapter on V.O., he declares: "And yet such idealizing and being idealized has never harmed a worthy man; it has always been a strong stimulus, even if most often it later led to disillusionment. As a matter of fact, this idealizing and being idealized is the correlate of the birth of one becoming conscious of one's uniqueness, and thus of the superhuman in man". If my idealization of his person was, in Keyserling's eyes, a denigration and a stain, one cannot then understand why he says that the idealization cannot harm any being of value (such as himself).

If the *coup de foudre* [being struck by love at first sight] can fall on simple-minded women who feel for an author a certain degree of *hero worship* (to a less intense degree than what in North American film jargon is called to be a *fan* of a star, or on the soccer fields of Argentina, a *hincha*), it can just as appropriately not fall.

This said, it is true that I expected – but did not demand – that Keyserling be what he could not be, given his nature. I had not assimilated from his thinking more than what could serve my own development, how to be very different from him. The rest, which was as alien and involuntarily noxious as could possibly be, as in blood transfusions (the blood type of Subject X as regards to Subject Z), I did not grasp until I saw it in Versailles. That is to say, I did not grasp Keyserling's total personality until after our clash.

Books don't give us anything except what we seek in them. Part of Keyserling had been revealed to me through reading him. But Keyserling was not only that part. His books were not only that part. They were a totality that enclosed many parts. And I could not be in agreement with all of them. I learned to read the books better through the person of the author. That is to say, I learned to read them with discrimination and lucidity. And only in this sense could Keyserling have accused me of having idealized him before getting to know him.

43   Editor's note: See Part Six.

"You clearly separate the spirit from the man, which is always false, and in my case so false that no one I have ever met has understood me so badly as you at the beginning of our meeting," he wrote to me. Of course it's a mistake. But as soon as the man's presence shed light on his work, I regulated my conduct with and my opinion of the man and the work according to the sum total, because in the case of Keyserling it was impossible, in practice, to separate the spirit from the man. The man occupied a lot of space and would not be ignored.

This brings to mind a dialogue related by Madame de Sévigné:

'Very well', she said, 'I don't share Saint Paul's opinion'.
'Take heed, Madame: it is the Holy Spirit that speaks through his mouth.'
'That may be so, but in that case, I don't agree with the Holy Spirit'.[44]

Not being in agreement with Keyserling's opinion placed me beyond the pale. It was as scandalous as what was expressed by the lady in the anecdote. I therefore exposed myself to disagreeable things happening to me; for instance, to being taken off the pedestal where I had been placed when I seemed to share the same opinion.

Praise that Offends

Keyserling spoke in his letter about the schizophrenic splitting (he didn't mince words) between the made-up ideal and reality that had skewed my vision of his personality in Versailles: "You have since seen in a completely false light or falsely viewed the relationship of my spirit with my flesh, of the man and the work, you misunderstood me to the point of speaking of my talent ... this complete ignorance on the part of a woman as intelligent as you (and who had understood for a while) can only be explained by the pathology that I have diagnosed" (that is to say, the medieval splitting).

My disagreement with the Holy Spirit brought as a consequence this diagnosis. Now it brings a smile, but after my Darmstadt visit and the Sarrebrück accident it was really too much.

The letter continued: "Here I come to an injustice that I really did to you: from the beginning of our meeting, I saw in you a *ganic* being who aspired desperately, exclusively, to spirit, like the plumed serpent. But why did I get to see only a boa, only an anaconda? It was due to the same schizophrenic split from which you suffered and which had repercussions in me." A first-rate example of the mote in the brother's eye.[45]

44   Marie de Rabutin-Chantal, Marquise de Sévigné (1626–1696).
45   Matthew 7:3. Christ advises the hypocrite to remove the massive mote that prevents him from seeing clearly before admonishing others to remove much smaller motes affecting their sight.

The blow that I had received to my neck made breathing difficult. The reading of this letter added to the feeling of a physical stifling that of a moral stifling. "Your worthwhile life – apart from your contribution to the *Meditations* – has only just begun. You must wait for your peak, if you truly yearn for spirit, after your sixties, probably much later … This letter does not require an answer: there is never anything to discuss (when it comes to interior and subjective things), it is completely indifferent whether one is right or wrong in everything. I know what I wrote to you is the ultimate truth to me and if you stay with the contrary conviction, that is your business. The [bad] past is [amortized] objectively by your visit, whether you understand it or not. If you seriously meditate on this letter, you will quickly come to consider yourself from a point of view and at a higher level than you [seem] yet to do. But I hasten to add: if you feel the inner need, discuss with me in the name of God! Do answer, do not 'show' nothing, this letter constitutes an attempt at a psychoanalysis, it will necessarily evoke counter-movements that should not be repressed. I am so happy now that the ugliness of 1929 has been wiped out of our lives that I am ready for all intellectual sacrifices to satisfy the needs of your soul, as far as I can."

The recommendation was superfluous. I wasn't in the mood to repress anything. Everything that stuck in my throat was said and sent without delay. As from that letter of mine, Keyserling renounced his project to convince me of my schizophrenic splitting, and put his resolution in these words: "*Let's agree to differ*". He seemed to accept that the lady was not of the Holy Spirit's opinion. As far as the lady was concerned (who could no longer hear the word "telluric" without pulling out her gun), after having written her final truth to the philosopher, she felt a great relief. She attributed much value, no doubt because of her feeble imagination, to intellectual honesty. It seemed to her that in that regard it is never indifferent to be or not to be in the right.

I have often asked myself if my "ill chance" with Keyserling is not the way of an expiation for "the almost monstrous and almost continuous superabundance of religious emotion wasted on a profane object"[46] which has been my lot in life.

Does It Matter to Be or Not to Be in the Right?

I persist in not admitting that it is indifferent to be or not in the right about everything. This might be a truth for shopkeepers, as Wilde might say; but I stick to it. On the other hand, I understand perfectly (and this is one of the spiritual attitudes that attracted me to Keyserling) that a book, a person, an event are of value to us to the degree that they enrich us with our own riches, that they allow us to live on our zenith, and that their intrinsic value is of

---

46   Charles du Bos (1883–1939), a French critic and essayist.

scant importance. In that sense, it matters little that the objective value not correspond to the subjective value. What matters is the maieutic phenomenon.[47] I had discovered this before reading Keyserling but I found in his writings profound and beautiful pages on this subject. The *raison d'être* of this maieutics can only be understood by those who had the courage to be themselves and to live according to their particular law of life. Their *dharma*, I would say. "Whoever does not unwaveringly keep to his personal line and give a purely personal meaning to everything that happens to him, that can happen to anyone in fact, will not experience anything significant, even if he is to witness the creation of the world or the end of civilization" [Keyserling, "V.O." See Part Seven.] Here is, in my opinion, the genius aspect of Keyserling.

The letters that I received from him after having sent him mine, in which I delighted in not holding back on anything, did not mention again the medieval splitting: they were interesting and full of witty remarks. I keep them still. Anxious in giving me news that the Censor would not allow to pass and sceptical about Teutonic perspicacity, he made use of subterfuges and metaphors that would not have deceived a Latin American in diapers.

Let's Agree to Differ [English]

After having received my roar of a letter (the only way not to repress myself) and having found out about my car accident, he would write to me with unusual angelic docility:

> I regret that my psychoanalytic letter will have found you in such a bad state. If it hurts you in any way, please forgive me. For me everything is fine now, but I know that happy new relationships can only be established [on] the basis of full knowledge and acceptance of each other's views and feelings.
>
> [Yet] there is no need to agree; I believe, on the contrary, that our motto [should] be forever and ever: let's agree [to differ ...], our reactions and our intimate needs are completely different. But [can] we not be friends, celestial body to celestial body, through empty space?
>
> Each sun has its system of planets. You certainly do not belong to mine, and I know that I must fight against my natural inclination to attract everyone and everything into my orbit, in order to be able to maintain and cultivate friendly relations [with] a being like you. In fact on the telluric level, our meeting looked a lot like that of a Boa with a Tiger. Fortunately, neither managed to defeat the other.

---

47 Editor's note: Maieutics is the pedagogical method associated with Socrates, akin to midwifery, in which latent truth in the individual human mind must be birthed with questions.

You know that the [Greek] term *Paradeisos* (Paradise) originally means Garden (Zoological). It is within the framework of such a symbolic Paradise, managed perhaps by a discreetly invisible Orpheus, that I best understand future relationships between you and me.

You did very well to write me this long letter. It helped me get the point right. If there is [friendship] between the Tiger and the Serpent, whose instincts [cannot] match, the two must see very clearly, I mean, they must [know] what they would never guess.

And he added this P.S.: "I am framing your three portraits together, and I will hang them in my study under the canvas depicting Orpheus with his lyre moving the animals, including the Tiger and the Serpent."

No doubt, Keyserling expected to move, with the plucking of this symbolic lyre, the photographic portraits and through them the person depicted.

In March 1939, he wrote to me,

"I reflected again on your reflection that I too must participate in the 3rd day of creation, that is to say I reflected on the reason for your question: in fact, despite a fundamental incompatibility between our two ways of life, there is a kinship, the same effusive vitality due to a rooting in elementary life much deeper than that of most, and the same tension between this life and spiritual aspiration, but as for the rest, there is no affinity. But that doesn't matter anymore."

And because I wrote to him that I did not understand why he identified with an animal that resembled him so little, the tiger, when he evidently belonged among the northern animals, he answered me with a long letter that I could only half-decipher: "I was seized by an immense nostalgia for the vast, the infinite, the *all-encompassing* [English] of the Russian soul, with legends in which I participate more than any other collective soul. And I clearly understand how your vitality and your violence are incompatible with mine. All our European traditions – Greek, Slav, Germanic, and especially Caucasian – embody vitality in the form of the Dionysian ... You, on the other hand, vital and more realistic than me, have nothing of the Dionysian ... You detest wine, orgies, violence, clamour, writing. The two forms of vitality relate well ... [here, a few unintelligible words] cold-blooded to warm-blooded. You don't understand any of these metaphors [more unintelligible words] *So, if I see myself as Tiger,* it's to such a point that I recognize myself in every tiger – it is infinitely more true [unintelligible words] fixed in materiality, you cannot perceive this from the outside, you believe me to be a Nordic animal ... But it is not that superficial aspect that matters. And the same can be said, *mutatis mundi*, of the vision that I have of you. I have to resign myself to the fact that where I start to get serious, you start to laugh, and that where the European begins to see the beginning of a Revelation of the spirit, the *macana* appears to the South American, putting an end to any attempt at profundity. Your continent is indeed the anti-metaphysical continent. That is precisely why it means so much to me. You belong to the world of my Antipodes. I think above all of this when I *visualize* you in the company of Gabriela Mistral. However her soul might be (I'm ignorant of her work, and if I did know it, it would probably tell me little), as type Gabrielle Mistral is essentially Serrana Indian, from alma de bronce. A magnificent creature ... [unintelligible words].

"Greek ecstasy being the exiting of one's self into drunkenness, the desire for communion with the entire world in a rapture, while the Indian accepts everything, except coming out from behind the mask of his impassable flesh."

At Christmas 1939 he wrote to me from Schönhausen: "I send you this letter thinking of the fatal *development* which will no doubt take place during the next Christmas dinner. I have finished another chapter of my memoirs in which I speak of several women, each different the one from the others, who have contributed to my formation (don't worry: I don't include you in the lot). Would you be interested in this for *Sur*?

"I'm sure that the consequences of this war, that from certain points of view is not a war, will be more profound than those of World War [I] ... the ancient regime will certainly disappear, whatever the outcome of the fighting. But it's impossible to foresee the actual contents of the New Order."

"Greetings *De Profundis*"

Communication became more and more difficult for him. The letters were staggered and soon ceased altogether. In regards to the world conflict, he wrote: "One can only place oneself in favour (within certain reasonable limits) of that which in its essence turns out to be less destructive (whatever that might be in the present moment) as opposed to that which proves itself to be more destructive. And now Soviet Russia has placed itself definitively on the side of what is destructive."

In one of the last letters (March 1940) that he managed to send me because a friend had posted it outside Germany: "I cannot even foresee when I'll be able to publish anything again. Perhaps never in my life. But it is necessary that I have known all the heights and all the depths in order to acquire all the experience whose accumulation seems to me the only, truly the only, excuse for our exile on this filthiest of planets – *in spite of the climate of Mar del Plata*." This last phrase was written in Spanish and refers to a letter of mine in which I praised the incomparable climate of our seaside resort because I did not feel up to praising anything else in a country that, in my view, was going downhill.

In that same Mar del Plata, that preserves its bracing climate in spite of being part as well of the filthiest of planets, I pull out opened envelopes, stamped by the censor, these memories withered by time. I iron them out one by one because to write memoirs is to adopt the ironing skills of a washer woman. Keyserling's letters were full of the starch of his interpretative delirium. Various elements can act as starch in this sort of work. Starch is indispensable for men's shirts (the starched shirt-fronts that are beginning to fall from use), but then I don't iron men's clothes, I iron women's handkerchiefs that are opposed to starch. They don't even require an iron. I dry them by sticking them on a mirror.

I have spent all my life peering out of books, peering out of those magical windows:

> ... magic casements, opening on the foam
> of perilous seas, in faery lands forlorn ...[48]

I don't regret it, in spite of the disappointments that the "cult of authors" provoked in me. I also got to know, through it, great joys. I owe one of these joys to reading Keyserling, and I will not abjure it. Neither will I abjure my meeting (or my clash) with him. It was a learning experience, and I no longer regret having been through it.

Drieu and Keyserling

Drieu, who had fought and been wounded in Charleroi, wrote: "I will not deny Charleroi." It is in that sense that I say it. Not only combat on a battlefield gives us stern lessons. The adventures of the spirit, or rather the adventurers of the spirit expose themselves to equivalent dangers. They run serious risks for their souls, and through their souls for their bodies; the conflicts of the soul resound always on the antennae of the flesh, on the body. Nietzsche is the clearest case of what I'm saying. He went mad in the same way that others die on the battlefield: in order not to retreat a single inch, to arrive at the bottom of himself. A T. E. Lawrence could have died mad, for the same reasons.

> I got to prove my soul!
> I see my way as birds their trackless way.
> I shall arrive! What time, what circuit first,
> I ask not ...[49]

When I arrived in Europe after the war (in May of 1946) I learned of Keyserling's death. I had the intention of visiting him, if possible, imagining the hard times he had been through. From Drieu, I learned that his eldest son, Manfred, seriously wounded during the Russia campaign, had had a leg amputated. Only a year earlier, Drieu himself, before committing suicide, had written to me: "The last letter I received is from Keyserling. He has felt

---

48   John Keats, "Ode to a Nightingale", ll. 69–70.
49   Robert Browning, "1, Paracelsus Aspires", *Paracelsus* (London: Effingham Wilson, 1835), 28.

the use of placing before my eyes, at the last moment, something intelligent." I had met these two men, so different, the same winter in the same city. At the time, Drieu would joke about Keyserling, and jokingly he would say to me, speaking of him, "your Prophet." As Mauriac[50] saw so well with his great sense of justice, that man, who was so cynical in his words and liked to play at being indolent, was underneath the mask, an inflexible spirit. Only, this adjective does not satisfy me. I would say, for want of something more precise, implacable. Oddly implacable with his friends and with himself. I believe he was only indulgent, very indulgent, with his enemies.

Petit Jean,[51] in a recent article, points out that Drieu's curses ended up being always against himself, but I say that they did not "end up", rather he directed them relentlessly against himself. His most terrible curses, were they not directed at his heart's core? At France? And I must say that what contributed to the sympathy that he inspired in me when I met him, was the contrast that his mental attitude presented, compared to that of Keyserling. It was refreshing after the Versailles sessions, to hear him denigrate himself and puncture all the balloons, including the hot air balloon in the basket in which he was riding.

Keyserling considered Drieu one of the most intelligent and open-minded Frenchmen of his generation. Barely a year between them, they were both entering the mysterious realm of metempsychosis. Drieu, "like an exhausted stag pursued by the pack"; Keyserling, weakened by privations imposed on him (according to his sons); the one, the cynic, the curser, would leave a tenderly bitter letter for me written in the moment of his suicide; the other, the imaginative one, the Creator of Meaning and the Enemy of Facts, left a chapter of his memoirs for thousands of his readers; a chapter in which he transformed me into a myth, into a symbol fashioned by his giant's hand, drunk in an interpretative delirium; a chapter in which the truth of my person, as human being, was not respected and which counts, more or less, like a brick to the mason who applies to it the mortar without asking its permission. But the fact is that this brick, like Pascal's reed,[52] is a thinking brick.

V.O. Used as Symbol

Countess Keyserling, entirely dedicated to the memory of her husband and to the publication of his posthumous works, wrote an answer to a letter in which I pointed out to her that Keyserling distorted certain facts in the chapter on V.O.: "I understand the impression that reading something in which one is

---

50 François Mauriac (1885–1970), French writer, académicien, and winner of the Nobel Prize in Literature.
51 Armand-Marcel Petitjean (1913–2003), French writer, friend of Drieu de la Rochelle.
52 "Man is but a reed, weakest in nature, but a reed which thinks." Blaise Pascal, *The Thoughts of Blaise Pascal*, trans. C. Kegan Paul (London: George Bell, 1901), p. 47.

treated as a myth must produce. I suppose one would require a superhuman indifference to bear seeing oneself used as symbol, as myth, and not as a simple human being. It seems to me that you have not entered completely into the spirit in which the book and especially that chapter were written, if you insist on facts. But, of course, I understand very well that it must be disconcerting to read one's name and to be in life and in mythology at one and the same time ... I can assure you that all those here who have read the chapter and know nothing about you think it's one of the best." There she put her finger into the wound. That can only be thought by leaving me completely aside. Countess Keyserling, whom I have never met, is an intelligent woman skilled in the art of diplomacy. She knows how to defend her husband's cause, and she defends it nobly. She elicits great sympathy in me, and I'm sorry not to be able to agree with her in this particular. The facts on which I insist are important, and if they are undervalued the meaning is distorted.

Of course, it matters little that the hovel in the port where Tagore was lodged (as Keyserling says in the chapter on V.O.) was in fact the Plaza Hotel; and that my house in Palermo Chico (placed at his entire disposal when I ignored his volcanic personality) had not been built *especially* for him as he says; and that Fanny and José[53] did not get me out of trouble, in spite of their good intentions, etc. If Keyserling was amused in seeing a luxurious palazzo as a hovel, that was his business. But that he catalogued me as the prototype of the *ganic* for the simple reason that *I found my terrestrial being incompatible with his* and that he diagnosed in me a *medieval splitting*, a case of schizophrenic cleaving, because I did not accept and admire him totally, is carrying "poetic fantasy" too far.

In Questions of Love ...

In questions of Love with a capital "L", I refer to a great amorous passion, the rarest of emotions:

> I have said that the soul is not more than the body,
> And I have said that the body is not more than the soul ...[54]

Impossible to separate one from the other. Of course, there's a series of shades of love that goes from the almost purely physical attraction in which the body is more than the soul[55] to a spiritual attraction (a kind of religious

---

53   Ancient servants of a now extinct race that with time became friends and family members.

54   Editor's note: Walt Whitman, *Leaves of Grass*, ed. David S. Reynolds (New York: Oxford University Press, 2005), p. 41.

55   To this kind of attraction, Shaw's definition applies: "The sexual relationship is not a personal relationship. It can be irresistibly desired and rapturously consummated between two people who could not endure one another for a day in any other relationship". *Sixteen Self Sketches*, 113.

fervour) that someone like Gandhi inspired, in which only the soul seems to exist (call it sublimation or whatever else). There also exists, but this cannot be classified as love, the animal attraction of anonymous sex, not towards an incarnated being, not of a particular body towards another particular body. In this case, the partner doesn't exist in a differentiated manner, he or she is an object: an object of lust. That is equivalent to the solitary vice.

When one is prey to an intellectual enthusiasm, a spiritual devotion for a certain thinker, writer, wise man or hero, there is no reason for this to end inevitably in an amorous passion. But it is true that most thinkers, writers, heroes, and even wise men, whether they own up to it or not, often wager their self-esteem (in most cases it is not love) on conquering that terrain. Even if it's for no other reason than to prove to themselves their power, and to satisfy a very natural instinct of domination, certainly not worthy of respect. It must be agreeable to feel oneself adored as a thinker, writer, hero, or wise man; it must be more flattering to be desired as a man. Thinkers, writers, heroes, and men of genius detest, in most cases, that a woman assimilates them to the saints of the calendar. They won't admit that an ordinary woman might do this without being somewhat unbalanced, and they attribute so unusual a phenomenon to any pathological state that they are pleased to diagnose. Blind and deaf to any reality that they themselves don't create, they see then in that imperfect and untamed creature "the incarnation of the clearest divorce between Nature and Spirit".

Conceit

If I had any doubt about this question, the chapter "V.O." in *Travel through Time* would have convinced me up to what point Keyserling barely listened and understood me. He didn't listen to anyone except himself. He listened to me so poorly (because of his conceit) that he did not understand, for instance, what I said at Versailles about Christ, which he quotes distortedly in his memoirs. "She [I] contended that Christ's greatness would have consisted in the fact that he did not want to change man but felt mercy towards him just as he was, and comforted him and forgave him. This alone was what was meant by Christian love." Well, no. That was not what I meant. I believe that Christ took pity on man as he was, but also wanted to transform him. And in this regard it is enough to read a few pages of my essays. What I had tried to tell Keyserling was a commentary on the following passage of *De Profundis* that I quoted to him in the conversation to which he alludes: "Christ had no patience with the dull lifeless mechanical systems that treat people as if they were things, and so treat everybody alike: for him there were no laws: there were exceptions merely, as if anybody, or anything, for that matter, was like aught else in the world!"[56] I repeated to him then that we never should forget nor throw away that essential truth key to our relationships to our fellow

---

56   Oscar Wilde, *De Profundis* (Mineola, NY: Dover Publications, 1996), p. 65.

men[57] but he probably had his mind elsewhere or was pursuing his line of thought and his interpretation of my person and my problem without taking into account either my real person or my real problem, so that he misheard what I was saying. He only heard what he thought I was going to say. We all do this to a larger or lesser degree, but unconsciously. He did it with a frenzy.

Keyserling had the right to think about the universe and about that grain of sand, that part of the universe, V.O., whatever he wanted; agreed. Since the question of justice was not his concern, it didn't disturb him, because that is what he seems to mean when in the chapter on V.O. he sides with Wagner. This musician, Keyserling says, stumbling in a text of a Brahms *Lied* with the word "justice", muttered: "I have never been able to find sounds capable of expressing that word; it is not possible to put it into music."

Puna, Llama, and Telluric Woman

Therefore the chapter "V.O." (that is to say, the chapter that depicts Keyserling suffering from the effects of the *puna* or studying the habits of marsupials on the continent on the Third Day of Creation) appears in *Travel through Time* to serve the requirements of a thesis. A thesis that has its starting point something in the style of a sentence that occurred to Keyserling long before knowing South America: "The most interesting thing in South America is *puna*".

Prepared beforehand to suffer the effects of this sickness, even if it were only under the rule of a reinforced auto-suggestion, he endured them. His impression then was analogous to "what those reptiles must have felt when telluric influences put before them the alternative either to become mammals, or to die" (*Meditations,* p. 9). The *puna* must have given him a fair shock. But had he not decided beforehand that he would be shocked? Let's go from his ideas about the *puna* to his ideas about the llama. "It was not man who tamed the llama, as it is man who created the dog; the llama bred man in order to give a meaning to its own existence .... The llama is all things, can do all things, and requires nothing. It need not be fed, nor otherwise cared for. But on the other hand it clothes, it carries, heats, and after death nourishes ... Upon these heights in the beginning was the llama, not man" (*Meditations,* pp. 13–14).

As a worthy companion of the *puna* and the llama, as the worthy product of the Third Day of Creation, the one hundred per cent telluric woman could not be absent from the cast. That woman had to be the intermediary element between the *puna* and the llama: "the llama is all things, can do all things, and requires nothing." Circumstances made it so that Keyserling included me in

---

57   Keyserling knew and said it admirably that Christ did not ask man to love mankind, an abstraction that the religions of reason commit, but our fellow man, something very concrete and often difficult.

his vision of South America, together with *puna* and the llama. But the truth is, if I didn't disappoint him as *puna*, I rather disappointed him as llama. It is known that these animals refuse to walk if they are loaded with more weight than they can carry. That was my only resemblance to them, poor me. And so I became deserving of punishment for my Andean splitting.

An Explanation of the Chapter "V.O."

After a careful reading of the first volume of *Travel through Time* (of the second, I know only of the chapter that concerns me), I have come to the conclusion that the true explanation of the chapter "V.O." was found in the last chapter of the first volume, entitled "Mothers", much more than in "V.O." itself.

There, Keyserling relates the conflict with his mother that he associates with the Orestes-Clytamnestra conflict and with that of Hamlet.[58]

After the death of her husband, whom she adored and who had spoiled her excessively, Johanna Pilar von Pilchau, Keyserling's mother, suddenly went from the state of inconsolable widow to that of a woman in love, and then to that of legitimate wife of her son's Russian tutor. Hermann, who was fifteen at the time, wept in pain and rage on the night he knew that his father was going to be replaced, and replaced by a man of "lowly standing", a "child-sitter": "My mother, like every woman enslaved by an emotion, gave herself up at that time to her *gana*." It is evident that for Johanna, as for many women who have been happy in their home, loneliness became an unbearable load. It is also evident, as can be read between the lines, that she was madly in love with the tutor of her children, however plebian he might have been. She cared nothing for her family prejudices, and she gave herself joyfully to the misalliance. But to the young and violent Hermann whose *gana* blew in a very different direction, that attitude seemed monstrous.[59] To the point that Georg Groddeck later said that the inferiority complex that tormented Keyserling "stemmed from not having shot on the following day ... the successor who had usurped my father's place, something that I planned, among many other things, that first terrible night" (*Travel through Time*).[60] The situation must have been truly painful for the fifteen-year-old, both from an affective point of view and from that of the traditional ideas in which he had been raised. He

58   "Today I know that the relationship between mother and son is so deep that every Orestes-Clytamnestra situation, or at least its analogue to Hamlet, not only creates guilt that afterwards calls into action the Erinyes but also constellates and evokes true evil in the mother and son" (*Travel through Time*).

59   "I never totally recovered from that emotional shock" (*Travel through Time*).

60   Regarding his father, Keyserling said, "My father was so gentle in his ways that he had never been in a duel at a time when not to have done so constituted a feat. And yet when I was just thirteen, he said to me: 'If ever you have a teacher who dares raise a hand to you, shoot him; consequences are always a matter of indifference'" (*Travel through Time*).

never got over that trauma. "As my mother was a renegade, if ever there was one, to ease her conscience, she inverted the roles, pretending that the renegade was I" (*Travel through Time*). At that point, young Hermann became hard and even malicious towards her. And as a consequence of this state of things, of this conflict without an apparent solution (this statement seems to me very important), "I instinctively felt as maternal everything belonging to the earth and, a priori, it deserved my mistrust ... because I felt the whole of the telluric world as maternal, what I experienced towards my mother transmitted itself to the telluric world." It was thus that the image of his mother and the telluric were mingled in him indissolubly. Johanna-Rhea-Cybeles were three persons and a single living monster. What happened next? "My interior-spiritual world and the world beyond my door in which I had to fight for my existence were drifting further and further apart, consolidating itself more and more on different planes, irreconcilably; as in my spirit and my soul, I became more and more ethereal and an outsider to the world; as a practical man, on the contrary, in stark contrast, I became a feet-on-the-ground positivist to the uttermost extreme." I believe that this doubling (and with this doubling, he carried the victor's palm) did not ever cease. Those who had to deal with Keyserling know how little of the ethereal was in him when he was conducting business. He had every right to defend his interests, and I will not be the one to criticize him.

But this is where the "V.O." chapter begins to become clear in a new light. "When in Argentina I suddenly came into complete contact with the earth ... it is not surprising that the pristine image of the mother as Magna Mater or Kali is more familiar or plausible to me than that of the Mother of God." Let us leave now the posthumous book and go back to the *Meditations*. There, we will find that sentiment projected onto an entire continent. "There [in South America], involuntarily man sees the Magna Mater face to face" (p. 21).

Here things become complicated, because if it's true that the Sibyl and the Muse cannot belong to the type of woman that is brutally terrestrial, they must however be "terrestrial from head to foot", and every creation has its origin in the earth. For Keyserling this was a dead end. Everything that is the earth evokes for him the demonic through his Orestes-Clytamnestra complex. However like Antaeus, Keyserling feels that he cannot forego the earth to receive from her his strength and inspiration. A dead end, because the fundamental disagreement with his mother, found in him an exact correspondence in his disagreement between nature and spirit. A disagreement that he projected onto my person.

For him, his mother had fallen to an inferior level from the moment she married a man who incarnated an inferior level. In his maturity that same phenomenon would repeat itself. I would descend a grade and would go from being eminently spiritual to being eminently *ganic*, for not having bowed to the demands of his poetic fantasy.

And yet these two experiences, Mother – South America (South America equals V.O.), one in his adolescence, the other in adulthood, were, as he confessed himself, the richest of his life.[61]

The Johanna-Rhea-Cybeles trinity became, with the inclusion of my name, the Johanna-Rhea-Cybeles-Victoria quartet. A quartet of demonic divinities because he saw his mother in the guise of a demon,[62] in the same way that he later saw me in the guise of a serpent or an Indian who shot poisoned arrows at him.

As he says himself, Keyserling always felt himself obsessed with demons. From his earliest childhood, before his father's death, at nightfall he felt himself assaulted by rebel angels to the point that he could not fall asleep without a light burning. Towards the age of fifty the hellish denizens became even more demanding, and Keyserling had to expend even more energy each day keeping them at bay (p. 379 *Travel through Time*). Therefore, when in the "V.O." chapter he says, "In this way, out of the feeling of being betrayed, I transfigured Victoria Ocampo into a she-devil or an Indian who shot poisoned arrows at me at close range", it is best to explain that this "feeling" was provoked by the same demons that obsessed Keyserling since his childhood, and not by the Indian she-devil *puna*-llama who lived in Palermo Chico and who "faithfully fulfilled her promises from a material point of view". Not having made any other promises, it is difficult for me to accept being accused of treason.

I believe that only one person was capable of playing the necessary role of Orpheus in the tumultuous life of Keyserling: his wife. I take my hat off to her because it requires heroism to live next to the crater of a volcano. Whether the Baltic count's explosions of temper came from the tension in his blood of the lords of Raykül and of Johanna-Rhea-Cybeles (a matter of chromosomes), or from an education that, instead of *"mettre un frein à la fureur des flots* [reining in the fury of the waves]", spurred it on (had not his father advised him to shoot his teacher if he lifted a hand?), matters little. The volcano inside him required periodical eruptions. Very candidly Keyserling assures us that his greatest luck consisted in the fact that these eruptions were outward: "My organism would have hardly resisted a discharge directed inwards." But what about the organisms of others? What of the organism of the inhabitants of the symbolic Pompeiis and Herculaneums,[63] and the very concrete and

---

61 "In that way, surely, I have to thank for my most profound visions of the concatenation of the world my maternal experience that with its constant presence prevented me from petrifying and falling into lethargy ... This is what can be said in the most notable way about the *Meditations* in regards to my other books."

62 "My mother would present herself to me over and over to me as a demon" (*Travel through Time*).

63 Editor's note: That is to say, those living in close proximity to Etna's eruptions.

contemporary Hôtel des Réservoirs, where such excellent mashed potatoes were served?

The Truth about the Dead

Another question: Is it proper to speak about a dead person as if he were alive, that is to say, evoking stories about mashed potatoes? Again, let's hear Keyserling's voice on the subject: "To attack the living can be a vile deed, and it is almost always done with the intent to cause harm. The dead cannot be harmed at all; in regards to them, the only thing possible is truth, because only the truth about the dead can be of help to the living" (*Travel through Time*).

Furthermore, the above pages are not an attack but a necessary clarification. Dead or alive, Keyserling could not have made me alter it. Neither have I ever shared the odd superstition that makes us think of a dead person attributing to him qualities and virtues that he did not possess when alive. One loves whomever one loves in spite of his defects and vices (as long as the types of defects and vices are not particularly intolerable to us). And when we evoke the dead we evoke them in their entirety as they live in us, without conventional lies, without transforming them into the celestial spirits they never were.

Let us leave aside now these disagreements, these passionate disagreements that because they were the clash of two violent natures were crowned with a great crest of smoke and sparks. What had impressed me in Keyserling at the beginning and that flows from his work, continues to attract me after having been through years of disgust during which I was not able to open one of his books without feeling my stomach churn. The last fit of nausea seems to have taken place after reading the "V.O." chapter. The toxic purgation ended when these pages were written. Now I separate *ce qu'il y a à prendre et à laisser*[64] in Keyserling's work from my point of view. His leading idea, which he took from Goethe: the fecundity of the insufficient, always seemed to me marvellous.

Christian religion teaches the sinner that his sin, however serious that sin might be that bans him from society, might be redeemed by the Redeemer if the sinner is conscious of his sin. *Mutatis mutandis*, for Keyserling insufficiency is not necessarily a negative sign, and on the happiest occasions it becomes the strongest incentive to overcome one's faults. We know to what degree hearing and touch develop and become keener in the blind person as if to compensate the terrible handicap that the organism has to bear. The fecundity of the insufficient acts somewhat in the same way. Certain deficiencies, certain disappointments, certain misfortunes, even catastrophes in our life, can be "blessings in disguise".[65] They end up enriching us, in a spiritual

64   Editor's note: what to take from what to leave, the wheat from the chaff.
65   Editor's note: Ocampo uses the English phrase.

sense, more than a series of successes and strokes of luck, if we are capable of morally digesting them. In this, I am completely in agreement with Keyserling. But it is difficult to regard as a celestial envoy, from the very start, the being whose appearance in our life takes on the form of a catastrophe. Unless, of course, one is a saint. Needless to say, neither Keyserling nor I belonged to the heavenly hosts. He, in spite of the School of Wisdom, was not even wise; I, in spite of being South American, was not even a one-hundred percent telluric woman.

Only the truth about the dead can help the living, he affirmed. The truth is that Keyserling was a great man not only because of his stature. There was in him something like the exuberance of the tropical forest in a northern man. In spite of having seriously offended him by attributing talent to him, I continue to believe that he had it. It was in him, a question of natural aptitudes, not of acquired faculties. I never saw such a gift for languages; but this was nothing but a minor aspect, though very symptomatic, of his extravagant multifaceted personality.

As stimulants, his books have had for me undeniable virtues, like those of certain vegetables. His faults belong to the realm of character. He himself declared: "Whoever applies in an egotistical way his superior faculties that spirituality breeds, becomes satanic." As far as we can judge our fellow human beings without fear, I would say that his greatest sin was in that direction. But I am not entitled to throw the first stone.

Keyserling and Valéry

I said a moment ago that Keyserling acted as a stimulant. To clarify this, I will use the example of Valéry.[66] Nothing is more different than the pleasure reading these two writers elicits, whose personalities are on opposite poles. In Valéry, a certain perfection, which is his own, *jette le froid* [which has a chilling effect]. We cannot go back or forward even an inch in his thoughts except to walk in his stride. He writes what he wants to say with perfect voluntary lucidity and with that exquisite science of words that he handles with a goldsmith's hand. We read what he writes with great pleasure; we agree or not (if one cannot be in agreement, on the surface at least, with something that presents itself under the guise of reason and intelligence) but it is difficult to add anything of our own harvest, and this is one of the pleasures in reading Keyserling, to whom we are always adding things. Valéry has led us down a well-tended path whose curves and limits he knows. He points out those curves and limits to us. When he arrives at the limits, he stops and he stops us with him. Then, instead of continuing forward, we retrace our steps, thinking, "What a beautiful stroll. How exquisite!" None of this takes place

66   Paul Valéry (1871–1945), French poet, essayist and philosopher.

with Keyserling. He leads us down a bad earthen road, often full of swamps, full of stars, of which he himself does not seem very sure, in spite of his ostentatious declaration to the contrary. But we always feel the desire to know what will come "next". We leave him behind. We leap forward, we run back. We stroll around at will, in whatever direction we like. It's a game of skipping school and running off to discover new horizons.

There are, of course, semi-gods like Shakespeare or Dante who seem to have it all and in whose works we swim freely as in the sea that envelops us and holds us up at the same time. And titans such as Dostoevsky and Tolstoy, whose translations we are told are for the most part bad but whose genius and powerful personalities forego the habitual interpreters to reach the intelligence and heart of the reader. But how many miracles of this kind can there be?

Getting back to Keyserling and Valéry, whom I have known not only in their writings but in the flesh, there is nothing more representative of two mentalities, two sensibilities, two physiologies. Valéry said that the sixth, seventh, and eighth stanzas of *"Le Cimetière Marin"*[67] were autobiographical. As an autobiography, it does not go very far. Valéry only knew to speak about himself in an indirect manner; a manner that in the end was as subjective (without seeming to be so) as that of a Proust. It is nothing more than a different modality.

Conclusion

Keyserling, on the contrary, only knew to speak about himself. He did not believe, and he was right, that the objective manner is more interesting than the subjective. If that were true, he would say, no one would enjoy novels: "Of all the dominant prejudices, I believe that one of the silliest and ugliest, and above all more an enemy of progress, is the one that pretends that only in the case of imaginary destinies and characters it is licit to put the accent on the personal ... From an authentic and sincere self-avowal one can learn more than from thousands of theoretical considerations ... It is never exaggerated to lament how few have written unguardedly about themselves; every confession that a man of worth does not make public, means (I am convinced) a theft from the spiritual patrimony of humanity." If we find it legitimate that exceptional brains be bequeathed by their owners to be weighed and studied, how much more thrilling might be the living product of that brain in the form of an autobiography.

Saint Augustine's *Confessions* were a revelation for Keyserling in his youth. Like Montaigne, he could have said that the principal subject of his future

---

67   Paul Valéry, "Le Cimitière Marin"/"The Graveyard by the Sea", *Poems* (bilingual edition) Bollingen Series XLV-I, trans. David Paul (Princeton: Princeton University Press, 1972), pp. 212–221.

books would be himself. One can speak of oneself by means of philosophical systems, cosmogonies, novels, anything at all, as insistently as in confessions. Chestov and Ortega have stressed how the novel lends itself to autobiographical confession. But Keyserling could not create through the medium of the novel a creation that might have unburdened his self of its multiple facets. There was only one myth: himself. And in order to accompany that central myth, he imposed mythical transformations onto those who entered into opposition with him.

I share his taste, his preference for subjective works (frankly subjective, it is understood, because they are all subjective). Thus, when T. E. Lawrence suppressed from his *Seven Pillars of Wisdom* every subjective element and published *Revolt in the Desert*, he killed the magic of the book.[68] The most astounding pages in *Seven Pillars* are the ones that concern him directly.

Travel through Time is a sort of general confession: that is its main attraction. But it is not enough to render a confession public in order to guarantee its authenticity. Frequently the contrary happens. This is the problem. Keyserling expects that the myth of his life lived will be felt by many as a vicarious auto-revelation. Yes. There might be much to learn in it, but much to unlearn as well.

I have always had difficulty admitting that prudence might be a virtue. However if imprudence is a vice, then prudence must be a virtue. It is thanks to Keyserling that I have thought about this. Had I not been imprudent with him (and my imprudence consisted in having deified him a lot but not having turned him into a god, I see a difference in this), he would not have had the pretext to behave towards me like an Olympian god; he would not have had occasion to place me on a pedestal and then take me off it because I wouldn't meekly play the part of the mortal woman submitting to his "poetic fantasy". So be it. I think I will never learn prudence.

These are details that will not interest in the least Keyserling's readers. His wife let me know that everyone who had read the "V.O." chapter and didn't know me found it admirable. I've already said this. But because V.O. is not a character in a novel whom an author can shape at will, because she is a determined human being, these pages of clarification became necessary. As well, they might perhaps help clarify Keyserling's psychology through one of his polarizations.

68   Editor's note: In her biography of T. E Lawrence, Ocampo writes: "It is a curious experiment to compare *The Revolt in the Desert* with *Seven Pillars*, of which it is an abridgement ... *The Revolt* was a dish prepared for what Lawrence called 'general consumption', and he has cut out everything to do with himself and his emotions ... For readers who are not particularly interested in military exploits and war histories, *The Revolt in the Desert* is – one must admit it – a dull book. While *Seven Pillars* may become one of the books from which one never wishes to be parted." Ocampo, *338171,* pp. 54–55.

When *South American Meditations* appeared, I resolved to remain silent, in spite of the continuous, transparent, and distorting allusions I saw there. My name was not mentioned. It is no doubt healthy that the "V.O." chapter has forced me to break my silence. The inventory I have just made demanded it.

> How strange, that all
> The terrors, pains, and early miseries,
> Regrets, vexations, lassitudes interfused
> Within my mind, should e'er have borne a part,
> And that a needful part, in making up
> The calm existence that is mine when I
> Am worthy of myself![69]

How strange! Writing about Keyserling reconciles me with his shade as in a dialogue beyond the grave. Great Baltic man, let's agree to differ. And forgive this indomitable mortal woman, as she forgives you. You had struggled through the incidents of a stormy life to maintain your myth, your poetic fantasies in open spaces, like Tiepolo[70] setting up pyramids on clouds. You were "a fever of thyself".[71]

I place at the end of these pages, that contain nothing I haven't told you, nothing that I would not have told you when you were living, and that you would have read half-amused and half-furious (because you had an exceeding wealth of humour), Saint Augustine's thought that appears at the beginning of *Travel through Time*: "For all the acts of your servants were done either to indicate something which needed showing in their own times, or else to foretell what was to come in the future."[72]

---

69   William Wordsworth, "The Prelude", Book One, ll. 344–350, in *The Prelude with a Selection from the Shorter Poems, the Sonnets, The Recluse, and The Excursion*, ed. Carlos Baker (New York: Holt, Rinehart, and Winston, 1954), p. 212.

70   Giovanni Battista (Giambattista) Tiepolo (1696–1770), Italian painter and printmaker.

71   "Thou art a dreaming thing,/ A fever of thyself ...", John Keats, "Hyperion: A Vision", ll. 168–169, in *The Complete Poetical Works and Letters of John Keats*, ed. Horace E. Scudder (New York: Houghton Mifflin, 1899), p. 235.

72   Saint Augustine, *The Confessions of Saint Augustine*, Book 3:9, trans. Rex Warner (New York: Mentor/New American Library, 1963), p. 65.

Bibliography

Beccacece, Hugo. "Victoria Ocampo, Escritora." *Academia Argentina de Letras* 90 (2021): 29–43.

Beebe, John. *Energies and Patterns in Psychological Type: The Reservoir of Consciousness*. London: Routledge, 2017.

Bordelois, Ivonne. *Victoria: Paredón y Después*. Buenos Aires: Zorzal, 2021.

Borges, Jorge Luis. "VO." *La Nación*, 25 February 1979. In *Páginas de Jorge Luis Borges seleccionadas por el autor*. Buenos Aires: Celtia, 1982.

Caillois, Roger and Victoria Ocampo. *Correspondence (1939–1978)*. Edited by Odile Felgine with Laura Ayerza de Castilho. Paris: Stock, 1997.

Casares, Adolfo Bioy, *Borges*. Edición al cuiudado de Daniel Martino. Barcelona: Destino, 2006.

Castilho, Laura Ayerza de, and Odile Felgine. *Victoria Ocampo*. Translated by Roser Berdagué. Barcelona: Circe, 1991.

Columbus, Christopher. *The Four Voyages: Being His Own Log-book …* Translated by J. M. Cohen. New York: Penguin Classics, 1992.

Dourado, Leonardo. *Keyserling, the Philosopher Who Envisioned Paradise*. www.yout ube.com/watch?v=RSZkUVeu4eI. Downloaded 30 April 2018.

Drieu la Rochelle, Pierre and Victoria Ocampo. *Drieu: Suivi de lettres inédites de Pierre Drieu la Rochelle à Victoria Ocampo*. Translated by André Gabastou. Paris: Bartillat, 2007. Published in Spanish as *Amarte no fue un error: Correspondencia, 1929–1944*, edited by Julien Hervier and translated by Juan Javier Negri. Buenos Aires: Sur, 2022.

Fleischmann, Raoul, Harold Ross, and James Thurber. "Count Keyserling Again." *The New Yorker*. 31 March 1928, 8.

Fuechtner, Veronika. *Berlin Psychoanalytic: Psychoanalysis and Culture in Weimar Republic Germany and Beyond*. Berkeley: University of California Press, 2011.

Garcia, Edgar. *Signs of the Americas: A Poetics of Pictography, Hieroglyphs, and Khipu*. Chicago: University of Chicago Press, 2020.

Grimm, Jacob and Wilhelm Grimm. *Complete Fairy Tales*. London: Routledge Classics, 2002.

Güiraldes, Ricardo. *Don Segundo Sombra: Shadows on the Pampas*. Translated by Harriet de Onís. New York: Signet Classic, 1935/1966.

Jung, Carl Gustav. *Aion: Researches into the Phenomenology of the Self*. Collected *Works, Volume 9.ii*. Translated by R. F. C. Hull. Princeton NJ: Princeton University Press, 1959.

———. *C. G. Jung Speaking: Interviews and Encounters.* Edited by W. McGuire and R. F. C. Hull. Princeton, NJ: Princeton University Press, 1977.

———. "Commentary on *The Secret of the Golden Flower.*" *Collected Works of C. G. Jung, Volume 13: Alchemical Studies.* Princeton, NJ: Princeton University Press, 1968, 1–56.

———. *Letters, Volume 1.* Princeton, NJ: Princeton University Press, 1973.

———. "Marriage as a Psychological Relationship." *The Development of Personality, Collected Works of C. G. Jung, Volume 17.* Princeton, NJ: Princeton University Press, 1954, 187–201.

———. "A Psychological Approach to the Dogma of the Trinity." *Psychology and Religion: West and East. Collected Works of C. G. Jung, Volume 13.* Princeton, NJ: Princeton University Press, 1958, 107–200.

———. *Psychological Types, Collected Works of C. G. Jung, Volume 6.* Translated by R. F. C. Hull. Princeton, NJ: Princeton University Press, 1971.

———. "The Psychology of the Transference." *The Practice of Psychotherapy. Collected Works of C. G. Jung, Volume 16.* Princeton, NJ: Princeton University Press, 1954, 163–323.

———. "Religion and Psychology: A Reply to Martin Buber." *The Symbolic Life: Miscellaneous Writings. Collected Works of C. G. Jung, Volume 18.* Princeton, NJ: Princeton University Press, 1976, 663–670.

———. "La Révolution Mondiale." *Civilization in Transition. Collected Works of C. G. Jung, Volume 10.* Princeton, NJ: Princeton University Press, 1964, 496–501.

———. "The Rise of a New World." *Civilization in Transition. Collected Works of C. G. Jung, Volume 10.* Princeton, NJ: Princeton University Press, 1964, 489–495.

———. "The Swiss Line in the European Spectrum." *Civilization in Transition. Collected Works of C. G. Jung, Volume 10.* Princeton, NJ: Princeton University Press, 1964, 479–488.

———. *Visions: Notes of the Seminar Given in 1930–1934.* Edited by Claire Douglas. Princeton, NJ: Princeton University Press, 1997.

———. "Woman in Europe." *Civilization in Transition. Collected Works of C. G. Jung, Volume 10.* Princeton, NJ: Princeton University Press, 1964, 113–133.

———. "Yoga and the West." *Psychology and Religion: West and East. Collected Works of C. G. Jung, Volume 11.* Princeton, NJ: Princeton University Press, 1958, 529–537.

Jung, Emma. "Letters to Oskar Schmitz, 1921–1931." *Psychological Perspectives* 6:1 (1975) 79–95. DOI: 10.1080/00332927508409439

Kaminsky, Amy. *Argentina: Stories for a Nation.* Minneapolis: University of Minnesota Press, 2008.

Keyserling, Count Hermann, ed. *The Book of Marriage: A New Interpretation by Twenty-Five Leaders of Contemporary Thought.* New York: Harcourt, Brace, 1926.

Keyserling, Count Hermann. "Begegnungen mit der Psychoanalyse", *Merkur*, 4:2, November 1950, 1151–1168.

———. *Das Buch vom persönlichen Leben.* Berlin: Deutsche Verlagsanstalt, 1936.

———. "Carta del Conde Keyserling sobr el Coloquio, 22-VII-36." *Un coloquio sobre Victoria Ocampo.* Buenos Aires: Luis Fariña, 1963.

———. *Creative Understanding.* Translated by Teresa Duerr. London: Jonathan Cape, 1929.

———. *Das Gefüge der Welt: Versuch einer kritischen Philosophie.* München: Bruckmann, 1906.

———. "Gemeinsamkeit." *Betrachtungen der Stille und Besinnlichkeit.* Jena: Diederichs, 1941.

———. *Reise durch die Zeit* (1948/1958/1963) http://schuledesrades.org/palme/schule/reise/

———. *South American Meditations: On Hell and Heaven in the Soul of Man.* Translated by Teresa Duerr. New York: Harper and Brothers, 1932.

———. *The Travel Diary of a Philosopher.* Volumes 1 & 2. Translated by J. H. Reece. New York: Harcourt, Brace, 1925.

———. *Unsterblichkeit.* München: Lehmann, 1907.

———. *Der Weg zur Vollendung.* 1920.

———. *The World in the Making.* Translated by Maurice Samuel. London: Jonathan Cape, 1927.

Kushari Dyson, Ketaki. *In Your Blossoming Flower-Garden: Rabindranath Tagore and Victoria Ocampo.* New Delhi: Sahitya Akademi, 1988.

Landau, Ron. *God Is My Adventure.* London: Faber and Faber, 1935.

Lojo, Maria Rosa. *Free Women in the Pampas: A Novel about Victoria Ocampo.* Edited and translated by Norman Cheadle. Montreal: McGill-Queen's University Press, 2021.

———. *Las libres del Sur.* Buenos Aires: Debolsillo, 2004.

Matamoro, Blas. *Genio y Figura de Victoria Ocampo.* Buenos Aires: Editorial Universitaria de Buenos Aires, 1986.

Meyer, Doris. *Victoria Ocampo: Against the Wind and the Tide.* New York: George Braziller, 1979.

Mistral, Gabriela and Victoria Ocampo. *This America of Ours: The Letters of Gabriela Mistral and Victoria Ocampo.* Edited and translated by Elizabeth Horan and Doris Meyer. Austin: University of Texas Press, 2003.

Ocampo, Victoria. *338171 TE: Lawrence of Arabia.* Translated by D. Garnett. London: Victor Gollancz, 1963.

———. *Autobiografía,* Vols. 4, 5, 6. Buenos Aires: Sur 1982/1984.

———. *De Francesca a Beatrice.* Madrid: Revista de Occidente, 1924.

———. *Domingos en Hyde Park.* Buenos Aires: Sur, 1936.

———. "La historia viva." *Domingos en Hyde Park.* Buenos Aires: Sur, 1936, 8–25. "Living History", *Victoria Ocampo: Against the Wind and the Tide.* Translated by Doris Meyer, 217–222.

———. *El viajero y una de sus sombras: Keyserling en mis memorias.* Buenos Aires: Editorial Sudamericana, 1951.

———. "Victoria Ocampo Pays Jung a Visit." Translated by Martin Nozik. In Carl Gustav Jung, *C. G. Jung Speaking: Interviews and Encounters.* Edited by W. McGuire and R. F. C. Hull. Princeton, NJ: Princeton University Press, 1977.

———. *Victoria Ocampo: Writer, Feminist, Woman of the* World. Translated and edited by Patricia Owen Steiner. Albuquerque: University of New Mexico Press, 1999.

Papadopoulos, Renos K., ed. *The Handbook of Analytical Psychology: Theory, Practice and Applications.* Hove: Routledge, 2006.

Rowland, Susan. *Jung: A Feminist Revision.* Cambridge: Polity, 2002.

Saban, Mark. *'Two Souls Alas': Jung's Two Personalities and the Making of Analytical Psychology*. Asheville, NC: Chiron Publications, 2019.

Segal, Robert. Review of Richard Noll, *The Jung Cult*. *Journal of Analytical Psychology* 40 (1995): 597–608.

Singer, Thomas and Samuel L. Kimbles, eds. *The Cultural Complex*. London: Routledge, 2004.

Struve, Walter. *Elites against Democracy: Leadership Ideals in Bourgeois Political Thought in Germany, 1890–1933*. Princeton, N.J.: Princeton University Press, 2015.

Vázquez, María Celia. *Victoria Ocampo, cronista outsider*. Buenos Aires: Sur, 2019.

Vázquez, Rolando. *Vistas of Modernity: Decolonial Aesthetics and the End of the Contemporary*. Amsterdam: Mondriaan Fund, 2020.

Victoria, Marco. *A Colloquium on Victoria Ocampo*. Buenos Aires: Luis Fariña, 1936 (2nd edition 1963).

Zweig, Stefan. *Brazil: A Land of the Future*. Riverside, CA: Ariadne Press, 2007.

Index

For Product Safety Concerns and Information please contact our EU
representative GPSR@taylorandfrancis.com
Taylor & Francis Verlag GmbH, Kaufingerstraße 24, 80331 München, Germany

www.ingramcontent.com/pod-product-compliance
Lightning Source LLC
Chambersburg PA
CBHW050637280326
41932CB00015B/2680